D0610636

COLLINS
BUSINESS
FRENCH

HarperCollins*Publishers*

First published 1992

© HarperCollins Publishers 1992

First reprint 1993

ISBN 0 00 433625 9

*A catalogue record for this book is
available from the British Library*

*Printed in Great Britain by
HarperCollins Manufacturing, Glasgow*

Editorial Director
Lorna Sinclair

Editorial Management
Vivian Marr

Editors
Stephen Clarke

Diana Feri
Manuelle Prunier

Assisted by
Elspeth Anderson   Lucy Dawes   Susan Dunsmore
Joyce Littlejohn   Carol MacLeod   Val McNulty
Megan Maxwell   Christine Penman

We are indebted to the following for their
specialist contributions:
Sandy Anderson   Ray Carrick   Marion R Chalmers,
Pieda plc   Colette Clenaghan   Kate M Crooks
Jack Denny   Alec Dickie   Catherine Girvan
Jim Irvine   Hugh McGhee   Charles Ranstead
Stewart Reid-Foster   Janet Richardson
Lesley Robertson   Peter Stafford
David Swarbrick   Brian Turtle   Gary Weir

CONTENTS

🔊 BUSINESS FRENCH *is available with an accompanying cassette featuring selected material from these topics.*

INTRODUCTION

Your Collins Business French dictionary is a handy quick-reference guide that will be an invaluable aid when doing business with the French-speaking world. It has been designed to provide you with the French vocabulary necessary to communicate clearly and efficiently in a wide range of business situations, whether you are working from your own office or in a French-speaking country. The information it contains will enable you to translate both out of and into English and is arranged as follows:

ENGLISH INTO FRENCH

TOPICS
These cover areas of general business interest (e.g. **IN THE OFFICE, COMPANY STRUC-TURES**), specific business fields (e.g. **ACCOUNTS AND PAYMENTS, INSURANCE**), and subjects which have an impact on business (e.g. **THE EUROPEAN COMMUNITY, THE ENVIRON-MENT**). Each topic consists of an alphabetical list of the most widely used items for that topic, along with a selection of useful phrases arranged alphabetically by the key word they contain, and their translations.

Some terms could be assigned to several different topics but to avoid duplicating information we have listed them in only one place. However, topics are cross-referred to related topics, so if a term that you might expect to find under one topic is not there, you should look for it under the other topics referred to at the top of the page.

For appropriate topics, such as **ENTERTAINING, MAKING CONTACT** and **TRAVEL**, where cultural information is as important as the vocabulary itself, we have supplied useful background information and tips.

ABBREVIATIONS
This is a list of the most widely-used abbreviations and acronyms in general and business English. For acronyms of the names of national and international organizations, you should consult either **INSTITUTIONS AND ORGANIZATIONS** or **THE EUROPEAN COMMUNITY**.

FRENCH INTO ENGLISH

GLOSSARY
The glossary at the end of the book contains over 4,000 words and is an alphabetical list of the French translations from the topics. The plural forms of French hyphenated compounds (e.g. *carte-réponse, procès-verbal*) are shown in this list. For the most commonly used words, basic meanings as well as business-specific meanings are translated.

ABBREVIATIONS AND INSTITUTIONS
This is a list of essential French abbreviations and acronyms of the kind that you are likely to come across in a range of business material, from articles in magazines and newspapers to shipping documents and forms.

ABBREVIATIONS USED IN THE TEXT

adj	*adjective*	**m/f**	*masculine or feminine*
adv	*adverb*	**n**	*noun*
f	*feminine*	**pl**	*plural*
inv	*invariable*	**prep**	*preposition*
m	*masculine*	**vb**	*verb*

THE FRENCH ALPHABET

	Phonetically	*Pronounced approximately as*
A	[a]	**ah**
B	[be]	**bay**
C	[se]	**say**
D	[de]	**day**
E	[ə]	**uh**
F	[ɛf]	**ef**
G	[ʒe]	**zhay**
H	[aʃ]	**ash**
I	[i]	**ee**
J	[ʒi]	**zhee**
K	[ka]	**kah**
L	[ɛl]	**el**
M	[ɛm]	**em**
N	[ɛn]	**en**
O	[o]	**oh**
P	[pe]	**pay**
Q	[ky]	**koo**
R	[ɛr]	**air**
S	[ɛs]	**ess**
T	[te]	**tay**
U	[y]	**oo**
V	[ve]	**vay**
W	[dublə ve]	**dooble-vay**
X	[iks]	**eeks**
Y	[i grek]	**ee grek**
Z	[zɛd]	**zed**

NUMBERS

CARDINAL NUMBERS

0	zéro	60	soixante
1	un(e)	70	soixante-dix
2	deux	71	soixante-et-onze
3	trois	80	quatre-vingts
4	quatre	81	quatre-vingt-un
5	cinq	90	quatre-vingt-dix
6	six	91	quatre-vingt-onze
7	sept	99	quatre-vingt-dix-neuf
8	huit	100	cent
9	neuf	101	cent un
10	dix	102	cent deux
11	onze	110	cent dix
12	douze	150	cent cinquante
13	treize	182	cent quatre-vingt-deux
14	quatorze	200	deux cent(s)
15	quinze	300	trois cent(s)
16	seize	400	quatre cent(s)
17	dix-sept	500	cinq cent(s)
18	dix-huit	600	six cent(s)
19	dix-neuf	700	sept cent(s)
20	vingt	800	huit cent(s)
21	vingt et un	900	neuf cent(s)
22	vingt-deux	1,000	mille
23	vingt-trois	1,001	mille un
30	trente	1,500	mille cinq cents
31	trente et un	2,000	deux mille
32	trente-deux	10,000	dix mille
40	quarante	100,000	cent mille
50	cinquante	200,000	deux cent mille

a million	un million
two million	deux millions
a billion (1,000 million)	un milliard
two billion	deux milliards
a million units	un million d'unités
2 billion francs	2 milliards de francs

In Belgium and Switzerland, *septante* is commonly used instead of *soixante-dix* and *nonante* instead of *quatre-vingt-dix*. You may also hear *octante* for *quatre-vingts*.

deux cents, trois cents etc lose the *s* when followed by another number, e.g. *deux cent cinquante*

NB To divide the larger numbers clearly, a space or a point is often used in French where English places a comma: e.g. English 1,000 = French 1 000 or 1.000; English 2,304,770 = French 2 304 770 or 2.304.770. (This does not apply to dates, e.g. 1992)

ORDINAL NUMBERS

1st	*premier(-ière)*	**1er, 1ère**
2nd	*deuxième*	**2e**
3rd	*troisième*	**3e**
4th	*quatrième*	**4e**
5th	*cinquième*	**5e**
6th	*sixième*	**6e**
7th	*septième*	**7e**
8th	*huitième*	**8e**
9th	*neuvième*	**9e**
10th	*dixième*	**10e**
11th	*onzième*	**11e**
12th	*douzième*	**12e**
13th	*treizième*	**13e**
14th	*quatorzième*	**14e**
15th	*quinzième*	**15e**
16th	*seizième*	**16e**
17th	*dix-septième*	**17e**
18th	*dix-huitième*	**18e**
19th	*dix-neuvième*	**19e**
20th	*vingtième*	**20e**

NB Ordinal numbers are not used in dates, with the exception of *premier*. See **THE TIME AND DATE**.

DECIMALS

In French, a comma is used where English uses a point: e.g. English 3.56 = French 3,56 (*trois virgule cinquante-six*); English .07 = French ,07 (*virgule zéro sept*)

FRACTIONS

$\frac{1}{2}$	un(e) demi(e)
$\frac{1}{3}$	un tiers
$\frac{2}{3}$	deux tiers
$\frac{1}{4}$	un quart
$\frac{3}{4}$	trois quarts
$\frac{1}{2}$l	un demi-litre
$\frac{1}{2}$lb	une demi-livre
1$\frac{1}{2}$l	un litre et demi
1$\frac{1}{2}$lb	une livre et demie
2$\frac{1}{2}$kg	deux kilos et demi

PERCENTAGES

2$\frac{1}{2}$% two and a half per cent *2,5% deux et demi pour cent*

18% of the people here are over 65 *18% (dix-huit pour cent) des gens ici ont plus de soixante-cinq ans*

Production has risen/fallen by 8% *la production a augmenté/ diminué de 8% (huit pour cent)*

THE TIME AND DATE

SAYING THE TIME

The 24-hour clock is used extensively in mainland Europe so if you use the 12-hour clock to arrange a meeting, it is wise to specify *du matin, de l'après-midi* or *du soir*. If a French speaker simply says *sept/huit/neuf/dix/onze heures* he or she usually means the morning. If you are telling someone what time it actually is, it is quite alright to use the 12-hour clock.

WRITING THE TIME

When writing the time, French speakers use the letter "h" (small or capital) instead of a full stop, e.g. 9.00 = 9h, 10.30 = 10h30. Remember that French speakers do not use *am* and *pm*. Again, you can specify *du matin* etc, but it is probably easier to use the 24-hour clock.

13h	13.00	*treize heures*	1pm
14h	14.00	*quatorze heures*	2pm
15h	15.00	*quinze heures*	3pm
16h	16.00	*seize heures*	4pm
17h	17.00	*dix-sept heures*	5pm
18h	18.00	*dix-huit heures*	6pm
19h	19.00	*dix-neuf heures*	7pm
20h	20.00	*vingt heures*	8pm
21h	21.00	*vingt-et-une heures*	9pm
22h	22.00	*vingt-deux heures*	10pm
23h	23.00	*vingt-trois heures*	11pm

at 10am	*à 10h*	*à dix heures du matin*
at 4pm	*à 16h*	*à quatre heures de l'après-midi*
at 11pm	*à 23h*	*à onze heures du soir*

QUESTIONS AND ANSWERS

what's the time? *quelle heure est-il?*
what time do you make it? *quelle heure avez-vous?*
have you the right time? *avez-vous l'heure exacte?*

it's 1 o'clock *il est une heure*
it's 2 o'clock *il est deux heures*
it's 5 past 4 *il est quatre heures cinq*
it's 10 to 6 *il est six heures moins dix*
it's a quarter past 9 *il est neuf heures et quart*

it's a quarter to 2 *il est deux heures moins le quart*
it's half past 8 *il est huit heures et demie*
I make it 2.20 *d'après ma montre il est 2h20*
my watch says 3.37 *il est 3h37 à ma montre*
it's just after 3 *il est trois heures passées*
it's nearly 9 *il est presque neuf heures*
about 8 o'clock *aux environs de huit heures*

what time does it start/end? *à quelle heure est-ce que cela commence/se termine?*
when do you open/close? *à quelle heure ouvrez-vous/fermez-vous?*

at exactly 3 o'clock, at 3 sharp, at 3 on the dot *à trois heures exactement, à trois heures précises*
at midday *à midi*   **at midnight** *à minuit*
until 8 o'clock *jusqu'à huit heures*
closed from 1.30 to 4.30 *fermé de une heure et demie à quatre heures et demie*

how long will it take? *combien de temps est-ce que cela va prendre?*
how long will the meeting last? *combien de temps est-ce que la réunion va durer?*

half an hour *une demi-heure*
a quarter of an hour *un quart d'heure*
three quarters of an hour *trois quarts d'heure*

when do you need it? *quand en avez-vous besoin?*
I need it for 9am tomorrow *j'en ai besoin pour neuf heures de-main matin*
by Wednesday at 4pm *mercredi à seize heures*
at/by 6 o'clock at the latest *à six heures au plus tard*

THE DATE

The full date may be written exactly as in English, e.g. 11.7.91. If mentioning only the day and month, French style is very simple:
May 31 *31 mai*   **December 25** *25 décembre*

When saying the date, remember to add the article *le*, e.g. **the first of May** will be *le premier mai*. The French usually say the year as if it was a simple number, e.g. 1992 is said *mille neuf cent quatre-vingt-douze*. But they will often refer to the year simply as *91, 92* (*quatre-vingt-onze, quatre-vingt-douze*).

Note that the article *le* is used in front of the days of the week only when regular occurrence is implied, e.g. *le mardi* = every

Tuesday or on Tuesdays. If you want to say **on Tuesday**, you simply say *mardi*.

in April *en avril*   **on Monday** *lundi*
in 1992 *en 1992*   **on Sundays** *le dimanche*
on June 26 *le 26 juin*

The days of the week and the months are written with small letters in French:

lundi	*janvier*	*juillet*
mardi	*février*	*août*
mercredi	*mars*	*septembre*
jeudi	*avril*	*octobre*
vendredi	*mai*	*novembre*
samedi	*juin*	*décembre*
dimanche		

QUESTIONS AND ANSWERS

what's today's date? *quelle est la date aujourd'hui?*
today's the 12th *aujourd'hui nous sommes le 12*
the first/second of July *le premier/deux juillet*
about the 4th of July *aux environs du 4 juillet*
from the 14th to the 18th *du 14 au 18*
in the 1980s/90s *dans les années quatre-vingt/quatre-vingt-dix*

when? *quand?*   **until/since when?** *jusqu'à/depuis quand?*
how long have you worked here? *depuis combien de temps travaillez-vous ici?*

yesterday *hier*   **today** *aujourd'hui*   **tomorrow** *demain*
the day after tomorrow *après-demain*
last/next week *la semaine dernière/prochaine*
last/next month/year *le mois/l'an dernier/prochain*
every day/Friday *tous les jours/tous les vendredis*
one Thursday in October *un jeudi en octobre*
in 2 days *dans 2 jours*
they finished it in 2 days/weeks/months *ils l'ont terminé en 2 jours/semaines/mois*
I've worked here for 2 years *je travaille ici depuis 2 ans*
I'm in Switzerland for 2 days *je suis en Suisse pour 2 jours*
it will take 3 days *cela va prendre 3 jours*

1   ACCOUNTS AND PAYMENTS

See also **BUYING AND SELLING**

absorption costing	*coûts mpl complets*
account	*compte m*
on account	*en compte, à valoir*
accountancy	*comptabilité f*
accountant	*comptable m/f*
accounting	*comptabilité f*
accounting period	*exercice m financier*
accounting procedures	*procédures fpl comptables*
accounting standards	*normes fpl comptables*
accounting system	*système m comptable*
accounts *(accountancy)*	*comptabilité f*
accounts payable	*comptes mpl fournisseurs*
accounts receivable	*comptes mpl clients*
accrued charges	*frais mpl non-échus*
accrued interest	*intérêts mpl courus*
administrative expenses	*frais mpl d'administration*
all-in rate	*tarif m tout compris*
allocation of overheads	*ventilation f des frais généraux*
allow	*accorder*
allowance *(discount)*	*remise f, rabais m*
allowance *(tax)*	*abattement m*
allowance *(on balance sheet)*	*provisions fpl*
amortization	*amortissement m*
annual report	*rapport m annuel*
anticipated profit	*bénéfice m escompté*
appreciate	*prendre de la valeur*
appreciation	*valorisation f, plus-value f*
appropriation	*affectation f*
appropriation account	*compte m d'affectation*
arrears	*arriéré m*
assets	*actif m*
audit *n*	*vérification f des comptes,*
	apurement m
audit *vb*	*vérifier*
auditor	*commissaire m aux comptes*
average cost	*coût m moyen*
average fixed cost	*coût m fixe moyen*

to keep the accounts *tenir la comptabilité*
the total amount payable is ... *le montant total (à payer) est de ...*
to fall into arrears *être en retard pour les paiements*
to carry out a complete audit *procéder à une vérification approfondie des comptes*

average variable cost	*coût m variable moyen*
backdate	*antidater*
bad debt	*créance f douteuse or irrécouvrable*
balance *n*	*solde m*
balance *vb*	*équilibrer*
balance in hand	*solde m disponible*
balance sheet	*bilan m*
bank(er's) draft	*traite f bancaire*
bill *n*	*facture f*
bill *vb*	*facturer*
bill of exchange	*lettre f de change*
bills payable	*effets mpl à payer*
bills receivable	*effets mpl à recevoir*
book-keeping	*comptabilité f*
break-even point	*seuil m de rentabilité*
budget *n*	*budget m*
budget *vb*	*établir un budget*
budgetary control	*contrôle m budgétaire*
budget period	*période f budgétaire*
capital account	*compte m de capital*
capital budget	*budget m d'investissement*
capital charges	*intérêt m des capitaux*
capital employed	*capital m investi*
capital expenditure	*dépenses fpl d'équipement*
capital formation	*formation f de capital*
capital gains	*plus-value f*
capital goods	*biens mpl d'équipement*
capital-intensive	*à forte proportion de capitaux*
capital investment	*dépenses fpl d'investissement*
cash account	*compte m de caisse*
cash book	*livre m de caisse*
cash flow	*cash-flow m*
cash-flow statement	*état m de trésorerie*
cash reserves	*liquidités fpl*

your salary increase will be backdated to May *votre augmentation de salaire est rétroactive à mai*
to balance the books *faire la balance des comptes*
the books *or* **accounts don't balance** *les comptes ne sont pas équilibrés*
to be £1 million in the black *avoir un compte créditeur d'un million de livres sterling*
to keep to budget *se tenir au budget*
to go over budget *dépasser le budget*
we are budgeting for sales/losses of ... *des ventes/pertes de ... sont prévues dans le budget*

certified accountant	*expert-comptable m*
chartered accountant (CA)	*expert-comptable m*
circulating capital	*capitaux mpl circulants*
collateral	*nantissement m*
consolidated accounts	*comptes mpl consolidés*
consolidated balance sheet	*bilan m consolidé*
consolidation	*consolidation f*
cost *n*	*coût m*
cost *vb (have a price)*	*coûter*
cost *vb (calculate cost of)*	*établir le coût de*
cost accountant	*analyste m/f de coûts*
cost accounting	*comptabilité f analytique*
cost-benefit analysis	*étude f du rapport coûts-bénéfices*
cost control	*contrôle m des coûts*
cost-effective	*rentable*
cost-effectiveness	*rentabilité f*
costing	*calcul m du prix de revient*
cost-plus pricing	*prix m à régie intéressée*
credit *n*	*crédit m*
credit *vb*	*créditer*
credit balance	*solde m créditeur*
credit control	*contrôle m du crédit*
credit limit	*limite f de crédit*
credit note	*avoir m*
creditor	*créancier(-ière) m(f)*
credit transfer	*virement m bancaire*
current assets	*actif m circulant*
current cost accounting	*comptabilité f en coûts réels*
current liabilities	*passif m exigible*
daybook	*brouillard m*
debenture	*obligation f*
debit	*débit m*
debit balance	*solde m débiteur*
debit note	*note f de débit*
debtor	*débiteur(-trice) m(f)*
deferred	*différé(e)*
deposit *n (advance payment)*	*arrhes fpl, acompte m*

---

in duplicate/in triplicate/in 5 copies *en deux/trois/cinq exemplaires*
to do something as a cost-cutting exercise *faire quelque chose pour réduire les frais*
to agree to defer payment for 60 days/until the end of next month *accepter de différer le règlement de 60 jours/jusqu'à la fin du mois prochain*

deposit *n (in bank account)*	*dépôt m*
depreciate	*déprécier, se déprécier*
depreciation	*dépréciation f, amortissement m*
direct cost	*coût m variable*
distribution cost	*coût m de la distribution*
draft accounts	*comptes mpl préliminaires*
drawer	*tireur(-euse) m(f)*
due date	*date f d'échéance*
earned income	*revenu m du travail*
earnest money	*acompte m, arrhes fpl*
economize	*économiser*
entry	*passation f d'écriture*
equity capital	*capitaux mpl propres*
estimate *n*	*estimation f, prévision f*
estimate *vb*	*estimer*
estimator	*expert m (évaluateur)*
ex gratia payment	*versement m à titre gracieux*
expenditure	*dépense f*
external auditor	*vérificateur(-trice) m(f) externe*
fees	*frais mpl, honoraires mpl*
final demand	*dernier rappel m*
financial statement	*état m financier*
financial year	*exercice m*
fixed assets	*immobilisations fpl*
fixed charge	*frais mpl fixes*
forecast *n*	*prévision f*
forecast *vb*	*prévoir*
forward contract	*contrat m à terme*
frozen assets	*actifs mpl gelés*
general audit	*vérification f annuelle*
gross profit	*bénéfice m brut*
gross sales	*ventes fpl brutes*
half-yearly	*semestriel(le)*
idle money	*argent m improductif or qui dort*
incidental expenses	*faux frais mpl*
income	*revenu m*
income and expenditure account	*compte m de recettes et de dépenses*

we have noted an error and would be grateful if you would amend your invoice *nous avons remarqué une erreur et nous vous serions obligés d'amender votre facture*

we are sorry for this error and enclose a credit note for the sum involved *nous regrettons cette erreur et vous trouverez ci-joint une note de crédit pour ce montant*

instalment	*acompte m, versement m partiel*
integrated accounting package	*logiciel m intégré de comptabilité*
interim accounts	*comptes mpl semestriels or trimestriels*
internal audit	*vérification f interne*
internal auditor	*vérificateur(-trice) m(f) interne*
investment income	*revenu m de placement*
invisible assets	*actif m incorporel*
invoice *n*	*facture f*
invoice *vb*	*facturer*
labour costs	*coût m de la main-d'œuvre*
ledger	*grand livre m*
letter of credit	*lettre f de crédit*
liabilities	*passif m*
liquidity	*liquidité f*
management accountant	*responsable m/f de la comptabilité de gestion*
management accounting	*comptabilité f de gestion*
marginal cost	*coût m marginal*
materials	*matériaux mpl*
monies due	*somme f exigible*
monthly instalment	*mensualité f*
national insurance contributions	*cotisations f(pl) à la sécurité sociale*
negative cash flow	*trésorerie f négative*
net assets	*actif m net*
net loss	*perte f nette*
net profit	*bénéfice m net*
non-payment	*non-paiement m*
non-profit-making	*à but non-lucratif*
operating costs	*charges fpl d'exploitation*
operating profit	*bénéfice m d'exploitation*
outgoings	*sorties fpl*
output, outturn	*rendement m net*
overhead absorption	*ventilation f des frais généraux*
overheads	*frais mpl généraux*
overspend	*trop dépenser*
paper profit	*profit m fictif*
part payment	*acompte m*

to invoice a customer *facturer un client*
to invoice goods *établir une facture pour les marchandises*
on your invoice dated 15 October *dans votre facture en date du 15 octobre*
please find enclosed our invoice no. 151058 *veuillez trouver ci-joint notre facture n⁰ 151058*
to go into liquidation *déposer son bilan*

pay *n*	*salaire(s) m (pl)*
pay *vb*	*payer*
payable at sight	*payable à vue*
payable in advance	*payable à l'avance*
payable on demand	*payable sur présentation*
payee	*bénéficiaire m/f*
payment in full	*paiement m intégral*
payment on invoice	*paiement m sur réception de facture*
pay out	*verser*
petty cash book	*livre m de petite caisse*
plant cost	*frais mpl d'équipement*
pledge *n*	*gage m*
positive cash flow	*trésorerie f positive*
profit	*bénéfice m*
profitable	*rentable*
profit and loss account	*compte m de pertes et profits*
profit centre	*centre m de profit*
profit-making	*à but lucratif*
pro-forma invoice	*facture f pro forma*
pro rata *adj, adv*	*au prorata*
provision	*provision f*
quotation	*devis m*
quote *n*	*devis m*
quote *vb*	*indiquer un prix*
rate of return	*taux m de rendement*
rationalization	*rationalisation f*
rationalize	*rationaliser*
reallocation of resources	*réaffectation f des ressources*
receivable	*à recevoir*
replacement cost	*coût m de remplacement*
reserves	*réserves fpl*
return on capital	*rendement m du capital*
revenue	*recettes fpl*
revenue account	*compte m de produits*
revenue expenditure	*dépenses fpl de fonctionnement*

payable at 90 days/within 90 days of invoice *réglable à 90 jours/dans les 90 jours à compter de la date de facturation*
they are slow payers *ils paient toujours avec du retard*
payment to be made by *payable avant le*
we would appreciate immediate/prompt payment *votre règlement immédiat/votre prompt règlement sera apprécié*
the department is showing an increased/a reduced profit *les bénéfices du service ont augmenté/baissé*
to be £1 million in the red *avoir un million de livres sterling de découvert*

revolving credit	crédit m à renouvellement automatique
running costs	frais mpl de fonctionnement
salary	salaire m
settle	régler
share capital	capital m social
single-entry bookkeeping	comptabilité f en partie simple
sinking fund	fonds m d'amortissement
solvency	solvabilité f
solvent	solvable
standard cost	prix m de revient standard
statement of account	relevé m de compte
stock n	stock m
taxable	imposable
tax year	année f fiscale
terms of payment	conditions fpl de paiement
trade reference	référence f commerciale
trading account	compte m d'exploitation
treasury bill	bon m du Trésor
turnover	chiffre m d'affaires
undischarged debt	dette f non-acquittée
unearned income	revenu m financier
unit cost	coût m unitaire
unit price	prix m unitaire
unpaid	impayé(e)
update n	mise f à jour
update vb	mettre à jour
variance	écart m
venture capital	capital-risque m sing
voucher	bon m
wage	salaire m
waste of resources	gaspillage m des ressources
working capital	fonds m de roulement
work in progress	travaux mpl en cours
write-off n	perte f sèche
write off vb	passer aux profits et pertes, amortir

in round figures en chiffres ronds
what state are the company's finances in? quelle est la position financière de la société?

See also **MARKETING AND PR**

above-the-line advertising expenditure	*dépense f en publicité-média*
account	*budget m*
account executive	*responsable m/f de clientèle*
actor	*acteur(-trice) m(f)*
ad	*pub f*
adult audience	*public m d'adultes*
adult publishing	*publications fpl pour adultes*
advertise	*faire de la publicité (pour)*
advertisement	*réclame f, publicité f*
advertiser	*annonceur m*
advertising	*publicité f*
advertising agency	*agence f de publicité*
advertising allowance	*participation f publicitaire*
advertising brief	*résumé m des objectifs publicitaires*
advertising budget	*budget m publicitaire*
advertising campaign	*campagne f de publicité*
advertising manager	*directeur(-trice) m(f) de la publicité*
advertising media	*supports mpl publicitaires*
advertising rates	*tarifs mpl publicitaires*
advertising space	*espace m publicitaire*
advertising standards	*normes fpl publicitaires*
advertising strategy	*stratégie f publicitaire, politique f de commercialisation*
agent *(literary)*	*agent m littéraire*
agent *(theatrical)*	*agent m d'art*
article	*article m*
artwork	*maquette f*
audience figures	*taille f de l'audience*
audience research	*étude f d'opinion*
Audit Bureau of Circulation	*bureau m de contrôle du tirage des journaux*
author	*auteur m*
bestseller	*best-seller m, succès m de librairie*

to advertise on TV/on the radio/in the press *faire de la publicité à la télévision/à la radio/dans la presse*
what are your advertising rates? *quels sont vos tarifs publicitaires?*
to increase the public's awareness of the product *augmenter la notoriété du produit auprès du public*

bestselling author	*auteur m à succès*
bi-annual	*semestriel(le)*
billboard	*panneau m d'affichage*
billing	*affichage m*
bi-monthly *adj (twice a month)*	*bimensuel(le)*
bi-monthly *adj (every two months)*	*bimestriel(le)*
bi-monthly *adv (twice a month)*	*bimensuellement*
bi-monthly *adv (every two months)*	*tous les deux mois*
blanket coverage	*couverture f intensive*
body copy	*texte m*
bold type	*caractères mpl gras*
book rights	*droits mpl de publication*
brand awareness	*notoriété f de la marque*
brand image	*image f de marque*
broadcast *n*	*émission f*
broadcast *vb*	*diffuser*
broadcasting *(television)*	*télévision f*
broadcasting *(radio)*	*radiodiffusion f*
broadsheet	*journal m plein format*
business section *(in newspaper)*	*rubrique f affaires*
cable TV	*télévision f par câble*
camera *(cinema, TV)*	*caméra f*
camera *(for photos)*	*appareil-photo m*
cameraman	*caméraman m*
capital (letter)	*majuscule f*
caption	*légende f*
cassette	*cassette f*
CD (compact disc)	*CD m (disque m compact)*
centre spread	*publicité f en double page*
children's publishing	*publications fpl enfantines*
cinema	*cinéma m*
circulation	*tirage m*
classified advertisements	*petites annonces fpl*
comedy	*comédie f*
commercial *adj*	*commercial(e)*
commercial *n*	*message m publicitaire*
commercial break	*spot m (publicitaire)*
copy *n (of book, magazine)*	*exemplaire m*
copy *n (text)*	*texte m*
copywriter	*rédacteur(-trice) m(f) publicitaire*
corporate advertising	*publicité f institutionnelle*
cover price	*prix m de l'exemplaire*
creative department	*service m de création*

customer profile	*profil m de la clientèle*
daily *adj*	*quotidien(ne)*
daily (newspaper)	*quotidien m*
designer	*créatif(-ive) m(f)*
desktop publishing (DTP)	*publication f assistée par ordinateur (PAO f)*
direct-mail advertising	*publicité f par courrier individuel*
display advertising	*publicité f rédactionnelle*
docudrama	*docudrame m*
documentary *n*	*documentaire m*
double-page spread	*publicité f en double page*
down-market *adj*	*bas de gamme*
draft *n*	*brouillon m*
drama series	*série f dramatique*
edit *(newspaper, magazine)*	*diriger*
edit *(text)*	*éditer*
edit *(film)*	*monter*
endorsement	*recommandation f*
euro-ad	*pub f paneuropéenne*
exclusive (story)	*reportage m exclusif*
feature film	*long métrage m*
feature-length	*long métrage inv*
film *n*	*film m*
film *vb*	*filmer*
film crew	*équipe f de tournage*
film industry	*industrie f du film*
film rights	*droits mpl d'adaptation (cinématographique)*
freesheet	*journal m gratuit*
glossy magazine	*revue f de luxe*
hard-hitting	*frappant(e)*
hoarding	*panneau m d'affichage*
independent TV company	*chaîne f de télévision indépendante*
insert *n*	*insertion f*
insert *vb*	*insérer*
ISBN (International Standard Book Number)	*ISBN m*
italics	*italique m*
jingle	*sonal m*
journalist	*journaliste m/f*

to endorse a product *approuver un produit*
she is handling the Cowan account *elle est responsable du budget Cowan*
to launch a new publication *lancer une nouvelle publication*

leaflet	*prospectus m, brochure f*
logo	*logo m*
magazine	*revue f*
mass-market *adj*	*grand public inv*
mass media	*mass media mpl*
media	*médias mpl*
media analysis	*analyse f des médias*
media buyer	*acheteur(-euse) m(f) d'espace média*
media coverage	*reportage(s) m(pl) des médias*
media interest	*intérêt m des médias*
media planner	*média-planneur m*
media research	*étude f des médias*
microphone	*microphone m*
mid-market	*de niveau moyen*
monthly (magazine)	*revue f mensuelle*
music industry	*industrie f de la musique*
national press	*presse f nationale*
newspaper	*journal m*
niche publishing	*édition f de créneau*
packaging	*conditionnement m*
paste-up *n*	*collage m*
periodical	*périodique m*
photo call	*photo-call m*
photograph *n*	*photo(graphie) f*
photograph *vb*	*photographier*
photographer	*photographe m/f*
photo opportunity	*occasion f pour une photo*
point-of-sale advertising	*publicité f au point de vente*
poster	*affiche f*
postproduction	*postproduction f*
(the) press	*(la) presse f*

to get the media interested in something *susciter l'intérêt des médias pour quelque chose*

to increase media awareness of something *faire mieux connaître quelque chose aux médias*

to get good media coverage *obtenir une bonne couverture médiatique*

to attract media interest (in a product) *attirer l'intérêt des médias (sur un produit)*

to have a strong media presence *être présent partout dans les médias*

to get a mention in a publication *être mentionné dans une publication*

please listen to/look at this and give me your opinion *pouvez-vous écouter ceci/jeter un coup d'œil à ceci et me donner votre avis?*

to place an advert in a publication *mettre une annonce dans une publication*

press agent	*agent m de publicité*
press call	*appel m de presse*
press conference	*conférence f de presse*
press officer	*attaché(e) m(f) de presse*
press release	*communiqué m de presse*
preview *n*	*avant-première f*
prime time	*heure(s) f(pl) de grande écoute*
produce *vb (play)*	*mettre en scène*
produce *vb (TV, radio)*	*réaliser*
produce *vb (film)*	*produire*
producer *(theatre)*	*metteur m en scène*
producer *(TV, radio)*	*réalisateur(-trice) m(f)*
producer *(film)*	*producteur(-trice) m(f)*
production company	*producteur m*
programme *(TV, radio)*	*émission f*
prospectus	*prospectus m*
public *n*	*public m*
publication *(act, title)*	*publication f*
publication date	*date f de parution*
publicity	*publicité f*
publicize	*faire connaître*
publish	*publier*
publisher	*éditeur(-trice) m(f)*
publishing *(industry)*	*édition f*
publishing house	*maison f d'édition*
pulp fiction	*romans mpl à sensation*
quality fiction	*romans mpl de qualité*
quarterly	*trimestriel(le)*
radio	*radio f*
ratings	*indice(s) m(pl) d'écoute*
reach *n*	*audience f cumulée*
reach *vb*	*atteindre*
record *n*	*disque m*
record *vb*	*enregistrer*
recording studio	*studio m d'enregistrement*
reference publishing	*publication f d'ouvrages de référence*
review *n*	*critique f*
review *vb*	*faire la critique de*

the ad is going out during prime time *la publicité passera aux heures de grande écoute*
the general public *le grand public*
the public response was very promising *la réaction du public a été très encourageante*

review copy	*exemplaire m de service de presse*
rights	*droits mpl*
roman	*romain m*
royalties	*droits mpl d'auteur*
satellite	*satellite m*
satellite TV	*télévision f par satellite*
sequel	*suite f*
serial *(TV)*	*feuilleton m*
serialize	*publier en feuilleton*
series	*série f*
short film	*court métrage m*
single-column spread	*colonne f entière*
slogan	*slogan m*
sloped roman	*romain m incliné*
sneak preview	*avant-première f exclusive*
solus	*annonce f isolée*
sound engineer	*ingénieur m du son*
sponsor *n*	*commanditaire m*
sponsor *vb*	*commanditer*
spot	*spot m (publicitaire)*
subliminal advertising	*publicité f subliminale*
Sunday newspaper	*journal m du dimanche*
Sunday supplement	*supplément m au journal du dimanche*
synopsis	*synopsis m*
tabloid	*quotidien m populaire*
target *vb*	*cibler*
target audience	*public m cible*
targeting	*choix m de cible*
target market	*marché-cible m*
teaser	*annonce f mystère*
teenage publishing	*publications fpl pour les jeunes*
teletext	*télétexte m*
television	*télévision f*
television company	*société f de télévision*
television rights	*droits mpl de télévision*
television film	*téléfilm m*
testimonial	*recommandation f*
time slot	*plage f*

they want the UK rights for ... *ils veulent les droits britanniques pour ...*
they are running the ad all this week *ils feront passer l'annonce toute cette semaine*
to sponsor a sporting event *parrainer une rencontre sportive*
we are targeting young people *nous visons les jeunes*

title *(of book, film etc)*	*titre m*
trade press	*presse f professionnelle*
TV company	*société f de télévision*
typeface	*police f (de caractères)*
up-market *adj*	*haut de gamme, de luxe*
video *(film)*	*vidéo f*
video *(cassette)*	*vidéocassette f*
video camera	*caméscope ® m*
viewing figures	*taux m d'écoute*
weekly *adj*	*hebdomadaire*
young audience	*public m de jeunes*

the central theme of a campaign *le thème central d'une campagne*

Banks in mainland Europe usually close for lunch but may well open early (8am or 8.30am) and close later in the evening (4.30pm–5.30pm). Some French banks open all day on Saturday and close on Monday. Swiss banks, which usually close at 4.30pm, may have extended opening until 6pm or 6.30pm on Friday.

If you simply want to cash traveller's cheques or change money, then a bureau de change or your hotel will probably be more convenient and the commission may not be much higher. Major credit cards are widely accepted in the larger towns and cities but before using your credit card in a hotel or restaurant it is wise to check that it will be accepted. Most major credit cards are known by the same name in French but Access may be better known as Mastercard.

It is advisable to carry your passport as well as your Eurocheque card for all banking operations as you may be asked to show it as proof of identity.

For a vocabulary list of banking terms, see **BANKING AND FINANCE**

PHRASES USED BY THE CUSTOMER

Where's the nearest bank/cash dispenser? *où se trouve la banque la plus proche/le distributeur de billets le plus proche?*

The account is in the name of Penman *le compte est au nom de Penman*

I have an account with ... *j'ai un compte au/à la ...*

Do you have an agreement with ...? *avez-vous un accord avec ...?*

What is the charge for that service? *quels sont les agios pour ce service?*

Do you cash traveller's cheques? *est-ce que vous encaissez les chèques de voyage?*

Do you change money? *est-ce que vous changez de l'argent?*

Can I cash a cheque/make a deposit here? *puis-je toucher un chèque/faire un dépôt ici?*

To withdraw money from an account *retirer de l'argent d'un compte*

To deposit money in/pay money into an account *déposer de l'argent/verser de l'argent dans un compte*

Can I withdraw cash on my credit card? *est-il possible de retirer de l'argent sur ma carte de crédit?*

How much can I withdraw per day? *combien peut-on retirer par jour?*

How long will the cheque take to clear? *combien de temps faudra-t-il pour compenser le chèque?*

Who should I make the cheque out to? *à l'ordre de qui faut-il libeller le chèque?*

I'd like to open an account *je voudrais ouvrir un compte*

I'd like to close my account *je voudrais fermer mon compte*

What is the interest rate on that account? *quel est le taux d'intérêt sur ce compte?*

Your cash dispenser isn't working *votre distributeur de billets ne marche pas*

Your cash dispenser has swallowed my card *votre distributeur de billets a avalé ma carte*

PHRASES USED BY THE BANK

We have an agreement with ... *nous avons un accord avec ...*

Their customers can use our services free of charge/for a charge of ... *leurs clients peuvent utiliser nos services gratuitement/ pour ...*

There is a charge for that service *ce service n'est pas gratuit*

I'm sorry, we can't cash this cheque *je regrette, mais nous ne pouvons pas encaisser ce chèque*

I'm sorry, we don't accept those cards *je regrette, mais nous n'acceptons pas ces cartes*

The cheque will take five working days to clear *il faudra cinq jours ouvrables pour compenser le chèque*

Allow five days for the cheque to clear *comptez cinq jours pour que l'argent soit versé sur votre/son/leur compte*

Your account will be credited next Monday/on 1 July *votre compte sera crédité lundi prochain/le premier juillet*

I'm sorry, but the cheque bounced *je regrette, mais le chèque était sans provision*

Make the cheque out to ... *libellez le chèque à l'ordre de ...*

Do you have any other form of identity? *avez-vous d'autres pièces d'identité sur vous?*

The interest rate on that account is 11.5% net/gross *le taux d'intérêt sur ce compte est de 11,5% net/brut*

See also **ACCOUNTS AND PAYMENTS, AT THE BANK, ECONOMICS** *and* **INVESTMENTS**

acceptance	*acceptation f*
accommodate	*consentir une aide financière*
accommodation	*aide f financière*
accommodation bill	*billet m de complaisance*
accommodation party	*avaliseur m*
account	*compte m*
account number	*numéro m de compte*
accrual	*accumulation f*
accrued interest	*intérêts mpl courus*
act of bankruptcy	*manifeste m d'insolvabilité*
allocation of overheads	*ventilation f des frais généraux*
amortization	*amortissement m*
annual percentage rate (APR)	*taux m effectif global (TEG m)*
annual return	*rapport m annuel*
anticipated profit	*bénéfice m escompté*
appreciate	*prendre de la valeur*
appreciation	*valorisation f, plus-value f*
arrears	*arriéré m*
arrestment	*blocage m*
assets	*capital m, actif m*
asset-stripping	*réalisation f de l'actif de l'entreprise (en difficulté)*
authorized capital	*capital m social*
automatic telling machine (ATM)	*guichet m automatique de banque (GAB m)*
backer	*bailleur m de fonds*
backing	*soutien m (financier)*
back-to-back loan	*crédit m adossé*
backward integration	*intégration f en amont*
bad debt	*créance f douteuse*
balance *n*	*solde m*
balance *vb (budget)*	*équilibrer*
balance *vb (account)*	*balancer*
bank *n*	*banque f*
bank *vb (money)*	*mettre en banque*
bank with	*avoir un compte à*
bank account	*compte m en banque*
bankbook	*livret m de banque*
bank charges	*frais mpl de banque*

to look for/obtain backing for something *rechercher/obtenir un appui financier pour quelque chose*

bank deposit	dépôt m bancaire
bank(er's) draft	traite f bancaire
banker	banquier m
banker's card	carte f d'identité bancaire
banker's reference	références fpl bancaires
Bank for International Settlements (BIS)	Banque f des règlements internationaux (BRI f)
bank giro credit	virement m bancaire
bank holiday	jour m férié
banking (profession)	banque f
banking facilities	services mpl bancaires
banking services	services mpl bancaires
bank loan	prêt m bancaire
bank manager	directeur(-trice) m(f) d'agence bancaire
banknote	billet m de banque
Bank of England	Banque f d'Angleterre
bank rate	taux m d'escompte
bankrupt adj	en faillite, failli(e)
go bankrupt vb	faire faillite
bankruptcy	faillite f
bank statement	relevé m de compte
base rate	taux m de base
basket of currencies	corbeille f de devises
bearer	porteur(-euse) m(f)
bearer bill	effet m au porteur
benchmark	repère m
bid n	offre f
bid vb	faire une offre
bill-broker	courtier m d'escompte
bill of exchange	lettre f de change
blacklist n	liste f noire
blue-chip investment	investissement m de premier ordre
book value	valeur f comptable
borrow	emprunter
borrower	emprunteur(-euse) m(f)
borrowing	emprunt m
branch	agence f
branch manager	directeur(-trice) m(f) d'agence
break even	équilibrer le budget
break-even point	seuil m de rentabilité

to go bankrupt faire faillite
to put in a bid for something faire une offre pour quelque chose

break-up value	*valeur f de liquidation*
bridging loan	*prêt m relais*
building society	*caisse f d'épargne et de financement immobilier*
buoyant	*actif(-ive)*
buy out	*racheter*
capital	*capital m*
capital account	*compte m de capital*
capital allowance	*déduction f (fiscale) pour investissement*
capital assets	*immobilisations fpl*
capital expenditure	*dépenses fpl d'investissement*
capital gains	*plus-value f*
capital goods	*biens mpl d'équipement*
capital-intensive	*à forte proportion de capitaux*
capital investment	*dépenses fpl d'investissement*
cartel	*cartel m*
cash *n*	*espèces fpl*
cash *vb (cheque)*	*encaisser, toucher*
cash account	*compte m de caisse*
cash card	*carte f de retrait*
cash dispenser	*distributeur m (automatique) de billets*
cash flow	*cash-flow m*
cashier	*caissier(-ière) m(f)*
cash-in-hand	*encaisse f*
cash reserves	*liquidités fpl*
central bank	*banque f d'émission*
cheap money	*argent m bon marché*
cheque	*chèque m*
cheque (guarantee) card	*carte f d'identité bancaire*
circulating capital	*capitaux mpl circulants*
clearing bank	*banque f de dépôt*
clearing house	*chambre f de compensation*
collateral	*nantissement m*
collecting bank	*banque f présentatrice*
commercial bank	*banque f de dépôt*
compound interest	*intérêts mpl composés*
contingent liabilities	*dettes fpl éventuelles*
convertible currency	*monnaie f convertible*
convertible loan stock	*titres mpl convertibles*

to go out of business *fermer*
this company has capital of £20 million *cette société a un capital de 20 millions de livres sterling*
to pay in cash *payer en argent liquide* or *en espèces*

corporate planning	*planification f de l'entreprise*
cost control	*contrôle m des coûts*
costing	*calcul m du prix de revient*
countersign	*contresigner*
counter staff	*guichetiers(-ières) mpl (fpl)*
credit *n*	*crédit m*
credit *vb*	*créditer*
credit agency	*agence f de notation de solvabilité*
credit balance	*solde m créditeur*
credit card	*carte f de crédit*
credit facilities	*facilités fpl de paiement*
credit limit	*limite f de crédit*
creditor	*créancier(-ière) m(f)*
credit rating	*notation f de solvabilité*
credit transfer	*virement m bancaire*
crossed cheque	*chèque m barré*
current account	*compte m courant*
current liabilities	*passif m exigible*
cut back *vb*	*réduire*
cutback *n*	*réduction f*
dear money	*argent m cher*
debenture	*obligation f*
debenture capital	*capital-obligations m*
debit	*débit m*
debit balance	*solde m débiteur*
debit note	*note f de débit*
debt	*dette f*
debt collection agency	*agence f de recouvrement*
debtor	*débiteur(-trice) m(f)*
deferred annuity	*rente f différée*
deferred creditor	*créancier(-ière) m(f) différé(e)*
deficit	*déficit m*
denomination	*valeur f, coupure f*
deposit *n*	*dépôt m*
deposit *vb*	*déposer*
deposit account	*compte m sur livret*
deposit receipt	*récépissé m de dépôt*
deposit slip	*bordereau m de versement*
devaluation	*dévaluation f*
direct debit	*prélèvement m automatique*
discounted cash flow	*cash-flow m actualisé*
downward trend	*tendance f à la baisse*

to be in debt *être endetté(e)*

drawee	*tiré m*
drawer	*tireur(-euse) m(f)*
earnings	*revenu m*
earnings per share	*bénéfice m par action*
easy money	*argent m facile, crédit m à bon marché*
electronic funds transfer (EFT)	*transfert m électronique de fonds*
encash	*toucher*
endorse	*endosser*
endorsee	*endossataire m/f*
endorser	*endosseur m*
Eurocheque	*eurochèque m*
Eurocheque card	*carte f eurochèque*
exchange control	*contrôle m des changes*
exchange rate	*taux m de change*
Exchange Rate Mechanism (ERM)	*mécanisme m de change*
expenditure	*dépense f*
factoring	*affacturage m*
finance *(world of)*	*finances fpl*
finance *(backing)*	*financement m*
finance company	*société f de financement*
financial management	*gestion f financière*
financial risk	*risque m financier*
financial statement	*état m financier*
financial year	*exercice m*
financier	*financier m*
financing	*financement m*
fiscal year	*année f fiscale*
fixed assets	*immobilisations fpl*
fixed charge	*frais mpl fixes*
floating capital	*fonds m de roulement*
floating charge	*frais mpl flottants*
flotation	*lancement m (en Bourse)*
foreclose	*saisir*
foreclosure	*saisie f (du bien hypothéqué)*
foreign exchange *(system)*	*change m*
foreign exchange *(currency)*	*devises fpl*

to expand into new markets *s'étendre à d'autres marchés*
to finance a project *financer un projet*
to get the necessary finance for a project *obtenir les fonds requis pour un projet*
to seek/obtain/provide financial assistance *rechercher/obtenir/offrir une aide financière*
financially sound/unsound *financièrement sain(e)/peu solide*

foreign exchange broker	*cambiste m/f*
foreign exchange dealer	*courtier(-ière) m(f) en devises*
foreign exchange market	*marché m des devises*
forward exchange	*opération f de change à terme*
forward integration	*intégration f en aval*
forward rate	*taux m de change à terme*
franchise	*franchise f*
frozen account	*compte m bloqué*
frozen assets	*actifs mpl gelés*
going concern	*affaire f prospère*
handling charge	*agios mpl*
hard currency	*devise f forte*
high-interest account	*compte m à intérêts élevés*
holding company	*holding m*
horizontal integration	*intégration f horizontale*
idle money	*argent m qui dort or improductif*
indemnity	*cautionnement m*
insolvency	*insolvabilité f*
insolvent	*insolvable*
interest	*intérêts mpl*
interest-earning account	*compte m rémunéré*
interest-free credit	*crédit m gratuit*
interest-free loan	*crédit m gratuit*
interest rate	*taux m d'intérêt*
international division	*service m international*
investment bank	*banque f de placement*
investment income	*revenu m de placement*
investment portfolio	*portefeuille m d'investissements*
invisible assets	*actif m incorporel*
issued capital	*capital m émis*
joint account	*compte m joint*
joint-stock bank	*société f bancaire anonyme par actions*
joint venture	*entreprise f en participation*
labour-intensive	*intensif(-ive) en main-d'œuvre*
lend	*prêter*
lending rate	*taux m d'escompte*
letter of credit	*lettre f de crédit*
letter of guarantee	*lettre f de garantie*
letter of indemnity	*avis m d'indemnisation*
limited liability	*responsabilité f limitée*

to get one's money back from a project *recouvrer les dépenses occasionnées par un projet*
a solid *or* **safe investment** *un placement sûr*

liquidate	*liquider*
liquidation	*liquidation f*
liquidator	*liquidateur(-trice) m(f)*
liquidity ratio	*indice m de liquidité*
loan *n*	*prêt m*
loan *vb*	*prêter*
loan account	*compte m de prêt*
loan capital	*capital-obligations m*
loss leader	*article m sacrifié*
management buyout	*rachat m de l'entreprise par ses salariés (RES m)*
merchant bank	*banque m d'affaires*
merchant banker	*banquier m*
merger	*fusion f*
money	*argent m*
moneymaking *n*	*acquisition f d'argent*
moneymaking *adj*	*lucratif(-ive)*
money market	*marché m monétaire*
moratorium	*moratoire m*
mortgage *n (home-buyer's loan)*	*emprunt-logement m*
mortgage *n (second mortgage)*	*hypothèque f*
mortgage *vb*	*hypothéquer*
mortgagee	*créancier(-ière) m(f) hypothécaire*
mortgagor	*débiteur(-trice) m(f) hypothécaire*
near-money	*quasi-monnaie f*
negative cash flow	*marge f brute négative*
night safe	*coffre m de nuit*
non-convertible currency	*devise f non-convertible*
non-profit-making	*à but non-lucratif*
non-taxable	*non-imposable*
numbered account	*compte m numéroté*
offer document	*document m d'offre*
official receiver	*administrateur m judiciaire, mandataire-liquidateur m*
open cheque	*chèque m non-barré*
operation	*opération f*
overdraft	*découvert m*
overdraft limit	*limite f de découvert*
overheads	*frais mpl généraux*
paper profit	*profit m fictif*

to go into liquidation *déposer son bilan*
to grant/refuse somebody a loan *accorder/refuser un prêt à quelqu'un*
to lose/make money *perdre de l'argent/faire du bénéfice*
to offset losses against tax *déduire les pertes des impôts*

payable on demand	payable sur présentation
payable to	à l'ordre de
payee	bénéficiaire m/f
pay in	verser
pension fund	caisse f de retraite
personal loan	prêt m personnel
petrodollar	pétrodollar m
pledge n	gage m
positive cash flow	trésorerie f positive
post-dated cheque	chèque m postdaté
pre-tax	avant impôt(s)
privatize	privatiser
profitability	rentabilité f
profit-making	à but lucratif
profit margin	marge f bénéficiaire
rate of return	taux m de rendement
rationalization	rationalisation f
rationalize	rationaliser
receivership	see phrases below
regulator	régulateur(-trice) m(f)
reschedule (debt)	rééchelonner
rescheduling (debt)	rééchelonnement m
reserve currency	monnaie f de réserve
reserves	réserves fpl
restricted currency	devise f à convertibilité limitée
return on investments (ROI)	rentabilité f des investissements
revaluation	réévaluation f
revolving credit	crédit m à renouvellement automatique
risk capital	capital-risque m sing
savings	économies fpl
savings account	compte m d'épargne
savings bank	caisse f d'épargne
secure vb	assurer
secure adj	sûr(e)
secured creditor	créancier(-ière) m(f) garanti(e)
security (for loan)	garantie f

to plough back the profits into the business réinjecter les bénéfices dans l'entreprise
to go public être admis(e) à la cote
to put money into a venture mettre de l'argent dans une affaire
to put up 20% of the capital for ... fournir 20% du capital pour ...
to go into receivership être en règlement judiciaire
a good/bad risk un placement or un client sûr/un placement or un client à risque

self-financing *n*	*autofinancement m*
share capital	*capital m social*
silent partner	*commanditaire m*
solvency	*solvabilité f*
solvent	*solvable*
sort code	*numéro m d'agence*
special drawing rights (SDR)	*droits mpl de tirage spéciaux (DTS mpl)*
specimen signature	*spécimen m de signature*
standing order	*virement m automatique*
statement (of account)	*relevé m de compte*
stop payment	*faire opposition (à)*
takeover bid	*offre f publique d'achat (OPA f)*
taxable	*imposable*
tax-free	*exempt(e) d'impôts*
tax haven	*paradis m fiscal*
tax year	*année f fiscale*
teller	*caissier(-ière) m(f)*
trade reference	*référence f commerciale*
transaction	*opération f*
transfer *n*	*virement m*
transfer *vb*	*virer*
traveller's cheque	*traveller m, chèque m de voyage*
treasury bill	*bon m du Trésor*
trend	*tendance f*
uncrossed cheque	*chèque m non-barré*
undercapitalized	*sous-capitalisé(e)*
undischarged bankrupt	*failli(e) m(f) non-réhabilité(e)*
undischarged debt	*dette f non-acquittée*
unissued capital	*capital m non-émis*
unsecured creditor	*créancier(-ière) m(f) sans garantie*
unsecured loan	*prêt m non-garanti*
upward trend	*tendance f à la hausse*
venture	*opération f spéculative*
venture capital	*capital-risque m sing*
vertical integration	*intégration f verticale*
voluntary liquidation	*liquidation f volontaire*
wind up	*liquider*
winding up	*liquidation f*

we have a 10% stake in the company *nous avons 10% des parts de l'entreprise*
what state are the company's finances in? *quelle est la position financière de la société?*

withdraw	*retirer*
withdrawal	*retrait m*
World Bank	*Banque f mondiale*

See also **ACCOUNTS AND PAYMENTS, ADVERTISING AND MEDIA** *and* **MARKETING AND PR**

all-in price	*prix m tout compris*
allow	*accorder*
asking price	*prix m demandé*
banded pack	*vente f groupée*
bar code	*code m barres*
bar-code reader	*lecteur m de code barres*
bargain *n*	*affaire f*
bargain price	*prix m sacrifié*
bonus	*prime f*
bonus pack	*offre f promotionnelle*
break-even chart	*graphique m de rentabilité*
break-even point	*seuil m de rentabilité*
broken lot	*articles mpl dépareillés*
brown goods	*produits mpl audio-visuels*
bulk buying	*achat m en gros*
business trip	*voyage m d'affaires*
buy	*acheter*
buyer	*acheteur(-euse) m(f)*
buyer's market	*marché m à la baisse*
call frequency	*fréquence f des visites*
calling cycle	*cycle m des visites*
call report	*compte-rendu m de visite*
canvass	*prospecter, démarcher*
canvasser	*démarcheur(-euse) m(f)*
canvassing	*démarchage m, prospection f*
cash discount	*escompte m de caisse, remise f au comptant*
cash on delivery (COD)	*livraison f contre remboursement*
cash price	*prix m au comptant*
cash with order (CWO)	*paiement m à la commande*
catalogue	*catalogue m*
chain store	*magasin m à succursales multiples*

to accept/send goods on approval *accepter/envoyer des marchandises à l'essai*
to sell at pre-Budget prices *vendre aux prix d'avant le budget d'État*
I will call again tomorrow *(visit)* je reviendrai vous voir demain; *(phone)* je rappellerai demain
I regret that we must cancel our order *nous sommes au regret de devoir annuler notre commande*
we reserve the right to cancel this order *nous nous réservons le droit d'annuler cette commande*

check-out (desk)	*caisse f*
circular	*circulaire f*
classified advertisements	*petites annonces fpl*
clearance sale	*liquidation f*
client	*client(e) m(f)*
cold call *n (visit)*	*visite f impromptue*
cold call *n (phone call)*	*appel m impromptu*
commando selling	*vente f agressive*
commission	*commission f*
commodity	*produit m, marchandise f*
competition	*concurrence f*
competitive advantage	*avantage m concurrentiel*
competitive edge	*léger avantage m concurrentiel*
competitive price	*prix m concurrentiel*
concessionaire	*concessionnaire m/f*
conditions of sale	*conditions fpl de vente*
consumer	*consommateur(-trice) m(f)*
consumer credit	*crédit m à la consommation*
consumer goods	*biens mpl de consommation*
consumerism	*défense f du consommateur*
consumer market	*marché m des consommateurs*
convenience goods	*produits mpl de consommation courante*
cooling-off period	*délai m de réflexion*
credit	*crédit m*
credit account	*compte m du client*
credit note	*note f d'avoir*
customer	*client(e) m(f)*
customer credit	*crédit m à la consommation*
cut-price	*au rabais, à prix réduit*
cut-throat competition	*concurrence f acharnée*
dead account	*compte m inactif*
deadline	*date f or heure f limite*
deal	*affaire f, marché m*
dealer	*marchand(e) m(f)*
deal in	*faire le commerce de*
deal with	*traiter avec*

to close or **conclude a sale** *conclure une vente*
to do cold calls *(visit) faire des visites impromptues; (phone) faire des appels impromptus*
"no cold calling" *"pas de démarchage"*
we are regrettably unable to accept your conditions of payment/delivery *nous regrettons de ne pas pouvoir accepter vos conditions de paiement/de livraison*
to do a deal *conclure un accord*

demonstration	*démonstration f*
demonstration model	*modèle m de démonstration*
deposit *n*	*arrhes fpl, acompte m*
direct-mail advertising	*publicité f directe par correspondance*
discount *n*	*remise f, rabais m*
discount *vb*	*vendre au rabais*
discount house	*magasin m de demi-gros*
discount store	*magasin m de demi-gros*
dispenser	*distributeur m*
display *n*	*étalage m, présentation f*
display *vb*	*mettre à l'étalage, exposer*
distributor	*distributeur(-trice) m(f)*
distributor network	*réseau m de distribution*
domestic sales	*ventes fpl sur le marché intérieur*
door-to-door salesman/woman	*démarcheur(-euse) m(f)*
door-to-door selling	*vente f porte-à-porte*
down-market *adj*	*bas de gamme*
down payment	*acompte m*
drop shipment	*livraison f directe*
dump bin	*présentoir m en vrac*
Dutch auction	*enchères fpl à la baisse*
end user	*utilisateur(-trice) m(f) final(e), consommateur(-trice) m(f)*
estimate *n (quotation)*	*devis m*
exclusive agency agreement	*accord m d'agence exclusive*
exhibit *vb*	*exposer*
exhibitor	*exposant(e) m(f)*
expense account	*note f de frais*
expenses	*frais mpl*
face-to-face selling	*vente f face à face*
fair wear and tear	*usure f normale*
fast-moving consumer goods (FMCG)	*biens mpl de consommation à débit rapide*
feature	*caractéristique f*
firm price	*prix m ferme*

please confirm that you can deliver within 30 days *veuillez nous confirmer que vous pouvez livrer dans les 30 jours*

we require delivery of the goods within 30 days *nous voulons la livraison des marchandises dans les 30 jours*

to go down-market *viser le grand public*

to make an estimate *effectuer une estimation*

we estimate *or* **forecast sales of ... units in the first year** *nous prévoyons des ventes de ... unités pour la première année*

in good faith *de bonne foi*

flash pack	*emballage m portant une réduction de prix*
fluctuate	*fluctuer, varier*
fluctuation	*fluctuation f, variation f*
follow-up *n*	*relance f*
follow up *vb*	*relancer*
follow-up call *(visit)*	*visite f de relance*
follow-up call *(phone)*	*appel m de relance*
foreign sales	*ventes fpl à l'étranger*
forward sales	*ventes fpl à terme*
franchise *n*	*franchise f*
franchise *vb*	*franchiser*
franchisee	*franchisé m*
franchiser	*franchiseur m*
freebie	*cadeau m*
gift voucher	*chèque m cadeau*
gimmick	*astuce f promotionnelle*
give-away	*cadeau m publicitaire*
goods	*marchandises fpl*
goods on approval	*marchandises fpl à l'essai*
goods on consignment	*marchandises fpl en consignation*
gross sales	*ventes fpl brutes*
guarantee *n*	*garantie f*
under guarantee	*sous garantie*
hard sell	*vente f agressive*
hire purchase	*achat m à crédit*
home sales	*ventes fpl intérieures*
hype *n*	*matraquage m publicitaire*
hype *vb*	*faire du matraquage publicitaire (pour)*
incentive	*prime f, stimulant m*
indirect demand	*demande f indirecte*
instalment	*acompte m, versement m partiel*
introductory offer	*offre f de lancement*
lead time *(for delivery)*	*délai m de livraison*
lease back *vb*	*vendre en cession-bail*
leaseback *n*	*cession-bail f*
line	*gamme f*
list price	*prix m de catalogue*
market *n*	*marché m*

to pay in instalments *payer par versements échelonnés*
an introductory offer will attract more buyers *une offre de lancement attirera davantage d'acheteurs*
the lead time for delivery is ... *le délai de livraison est de ...*

market *vb*	*commercialiser*
market leader *(company)*	*leader m du marché*
(product)	*produit m en tête du marché*
market price	*prix m marchand*
market value	*valeur f marchande*
mark-up *(increase)*	*majoration f de prix*
mark-up *(profit margin)*	*marge f bénéficiaire*
merchandise *n*	*marchandise f*
merchandise *vb*	*commercialiser*
merchandiser	*marchandiseur m*
model	*modèle m*
new *(brand new)*	*neuf (neuve)*
new *(different)*	*nouveau (nouvelle)*
offer *n*	*offre f*
offer *vb*	*offrir*
order *vb*	*commander*
order book	*carnet m de commandes*
order form	*bon m de commande*
order number	*numéro m de commande*
order processing	*traitement m de commandes*
outlet *(retail)*	*point m de vente*
outlet *(gap in the market)*	*débouché m*
out of print	*épuisé(e)*
own brand	*marque f du distributeur*
pack *n*	*paquet m*
packaging	*conditionnement m*
point of sale (POS)	*lieu m de vente*
point-of-sale material	*matériel m de publicité sur le lieu de vente, matériel m PLV*
potential customer	*client(e) m(f) potentiel(le)*
premium offer	*prime f*
price *n*	*prix m*
price *vb (goods)*	*fixer le prix de*
price-cutting	*réductions fpl de prix*
price list	*tarif m*

we would like to place a regular order for ... *nous voudrions passer une commande à titre régulier pour ...*

we confirm receipt of your order of 25 November *nous accusons réception de votre commande en date du 25 novembre*

with reference to your order of 26 June *comme suite à votre commande du 26 juin*

please find enclosed our order no. 2511 for ... *veuillez trouver ci-joint notre commande n° 2511 pour ...*

to perform well against the competition *être performant(e) par rapport à la concurrence*

price range	*gamme f de prix*
price tag	*étiquette f porte-prix*
price war	*guerre f des prix*
pricing policy	*politique f des prix*
product	*produit m*
product range	*gamme f de produits*
profit	*bénéfice m*
profitable	*rentable*
profit margin	*marge f bénéficiaire*
promote	*promouvoir*
promotion	*promotion f*
proprietary brand	*marque f déposée*
pro rata *adj, adv*	*au prorata*
publicize	*faire connaître*
purchase order	*ordre m d'achat*
purchase price	*prix m d'achat*
quote *n*	*devis m*
range	*gamme f*
recommended retail price (RRP)	*prix m conseillé*
repeat order	*commande f de réapprovisionnement*
resale price maintenance (RPM)	*vente f au détail à prix imposé*
retail outlet	*magasin m de détail*
retail price	*prix m de détail*
returns	*marchandises fpl renvoyées*
sale	*see phrases below*
sales	*ventes fpl*
sales analysis	*analyse f des ventes*
sales campaign	*campagne f de ventes*

we are currently having problems with our supplier *nous avons des problèmes avec notre fournisseur actuellement*

please find enclosed our quotation for the supply of ... *veuillez trouver ci-joint notre devis pour la fourniture de ...*

to quote for a job *faire un devis pour des travaux*

these retail at £75 *ceux-ci se vendent à 75 livres sterling au détail*

to pay a retainer *verser une provision*

to make a sale *faire une vente*

the product will be on sale to the public next month *le produit sera en vente pour le public le mois prochain*

they have a sale on *ils font des soldes*

to accept/supply goods on a sale or return basis *accepter/livrer des marchandises en commission*

sales of ... are rising/falling/stable *les ventes de ... sont en hausse/en baisse/stables*

sales are up/down on last quarter *les ventes sont plus élevées/moins élevées que le trimestre dernier*

sales conference	*réunion f du service commercial*
sales drive	*campagne f de promotion des ventes*
sales figures	*chiffres mpl de ventes*
sales force	*force f de vente, équipe f de vente*
sales forecast	*prévision f de ventes*
sales literature	*documentation f publicitaire*
salesman *(sales rep)*	*représentant m de commerce*
salesman *(in shop, showroom)*	*vendeur m*
sales manager	*directeur(-trice) m(f) commercial(e)*
salesmanship	*art m de la vente, sens m commercial*
sales meeting	*réunion f de vente*
sales planning	*planification f des ventes*
sales report	*rapport m de ventes*
sales representative	*représentant m de commerce*
saleswoman *(sales rep)*	*représentante f de commerce*
saleswoman *(in shop, showroom)*	*vendeuse f*
sample	*échantillon m*
second-hand	*d'occasion*
sell-by date	*date f limite de vente*
seller's market	*marché m à la hausse*
service charge	*service m*
showcard	*affiche f cartonnée*
showroom	*magasin m or salle f d'exposition*
slack period	*période f creuse*
soft sell	*promotion f de vente discrète*
sole agent	*agent m exclusif*
sole trader	*commerçant(e) m(f) indépendant(e)*
special offer	*réclame f*
spot price	*prix m sur place*
stock *n*	*stock m*
stock *vb*	*stocker*
in stock	*en stock, en réserve*
out of stock	*en rupture de stock*
subcontract	*contrat m de sous-traitance*
supplier	*fournisseur(-euse) m(f)*
telesales	*ventes fpl par téléphone*

I will be speaking about this at the sales conference *j'en parlerai à la réunion du service commercial*
this item is out of stock *cet article est épuisé or en rupture de stock*

tender *n*	*soumission f*
tender for *vb*	*faire une soumission pour*
testimonial	*recommandation f*
trade discount	*remise f professionnelle*
trade fair	*foire(-exposition) f commerciale*
trade-in price	*prix m à la reprise*
trade mission	*mission f commerciale*
trade price	*prix m de gros*
travelling salesman	*voyageur m de commerce*
undersell	*vendre moins cher que*
unique selling point (USP)	*proposition f exclusive de vente*
unit cost	*coût m unitaire*
unit price	*prix m unitaire*
up-market *adj*	*haut de gamme, de luxe*
vending machine	*distributeur m automatique*
volume discount	*remise f sur la quantité*
warranty	*garantie f*
under warranty	*sous garantie*
white goods	*électroménager m*

to put something out to tender *faire un appel d'offres pour quelque chose*
we regret that the following items are unavailable at the moment *malheureusement, les articles suivants ne sont pas disponibles pour le moment*
to go up-market *viser un public haut de gamme*

See also **CONFERENCES AND PUBLIC SPEAKING, PERSONNEL** *and* **PROJECT MANAGEMENT**

accountant	*comptable m/f*
accounts (department)	*(service m de) comptabilité f*
acting manager	*directeur(-trice) m(f) intérimaire*
administrator	*administrateur(-trice) m(f)*
affiliated company	*filiale f*
apprentice	*apprenti(e) m(f)*
apprenticeship	*apprentissage m*
area manager	*directeur(-trice) m(f) régional(e)*
assistant	*assistant(e) m(f)*
assistant manager	*sous-directeur(-trice) m(f)*
associate director	*directeur(-trice) m(f) adjoint(e)*
board of directors	*conseil m d'administration*
boss	*patron(ne) m(f)*
branch *(of company)*	*succursale f*
branch *(of bank)*	*agence f*
branch manager	*directeur(-trice) m(f) de succursale or d'agence*
businessman	*homme m d'affaires*
business people	*hommes mpl et femmes fpl d'affaires*
businesswoman	*femme f d'affaires*
cashier	*caissier(-ière) m(f)*
certified accountant	*expert-comptable m*
chairman	*président m*
chair(person)	*président(e) m(f)*
chairwoman	*présidente f*
channels of communication	*canaux mpl de communication*
chargehand	*chef m d'équipe*
chartered accountant (CA)	*expert-comptable m*
chief executive	*directeur(-trice) m(f) général(e) (DG m/f)*
clerk	*employé(e) m(f) de bureau*
company	*société f*
company director	*administrateur(-trice) m(f)*

I am Sales Manager with Contax in London *je suis directeur(-trice) commercial(e) chez Contax à Londres*
that department is based in London *ce service est basé à Londres*
I have been with the company for 3 years *je suis dans la société depuis 3 ans*
to be on the board of a company *faire partie du conseil d'administration d'une société*
he is chairman of ... *il est président de ...*

company secretary	*secrétaire m/f général(e)*
complaints department	*service m des réclamations*
computer programmer	*programmeur(-euse) m(f)*
computing department	*service m d'informatique*
conglomerate	*conglomérat m*
consultant	*conseiller(-ère) m(f)*
co-ownership	*copropriété f*
copy typist	*dactylo m/f*
corporate identity	*image f de l'entreprise*
corporate image	*image f de marque de l'entreprise*
corporation	*société f*
cost accountant	*analyste m/f de coûts*
customer services department	*service m clientèle*
delegate *vb*	*déléguer*
department	*service m*
departmental	*du service*
department manager	*chef m de service*
deputy chief executive	*directeur(-trice) m(f) général(e) adjoint(e)*
design department	*service m de création*
designer	*concepteur(-trice) m(f)*
direct labour	*main-d'œuvre f directe*
director	*directeur(-trice) m(f), administrateur(-trice) m(f)*
dispatch department	*service m des expéditions*
estimator	*expert m (évaluateur)*
executive director	*directeur(-trice) m(f)*
export department	*service m d'exportations*
export manager	*directeur(-trice) m(f) du service d'exportations*
factory worker	*ouvrier(-ière) m(f)*
field sales manager	*responsable m/f de l'équipe de représentants*
finance director	*directeur(-trice) m(f) financier(-ière)*
financial accountant	*responsable m/f de la comptabilité générale*
financial controller	*contrôleur(-euse) m(f) financier(-ière)*
foreman	*contremaître m*
forewoman	*contremaîtresse f*

that is dealt with by our ... department *c'est notre service de/du/des/de la ... qui s'en occupe*

freelance (worker)	*travailleur(-euse) m(f) indépendant(e)*
general manager	*directeur(-trice) m(f) général(e) (DG m/f)*
head of department	*chef m de service*
head office	*siège m social*
homeworker	*travailleur(-euse) m(f) à domicile*
job evaluation	*évaluation f des tâches*
job title	*titre m*
keyboarder	*opérateur(-trice) m(f) de saisie*
lawyer *(company lawyer)*	*juriste m/f*
lawyer *(barrister)*	*avocat(e) m(f)*
legal department	*service m du contentieux*
line manager	*chef m hiérarchique*
machinist	*machiniste m/f*
mailroom	*salle f du courrier*
(the) management	*(la) direction f*
management consultant	*conseiller(-ère) m(f) de direction*
manager(ess) *(of department)*	*chef m, directeur(-trice) m(f)*
manager(ess) *(of shop, restaurant)*	*gérant(e) m(f)*
manager(ess) *(of company, business)*	*directeur(-trice) m(f)*
managing director (MD)	*directeur(-trice) m(f) général(e) (DG m/f)*
market development manager	*chef m du développement des marchés*
marketing (department)	*(service m du) marketing m*
marketing director	*directeur(-trice) m(f) du marketing*
marketing manager	*chef m du marketing*
MD (managing director)	*DG m/f (directeur(-trice) m(f) général(e))*
merger	*fusion f*
middle management	*cadres mpl moyens*
non-executive director	*administrateur(-trice) m(f)*
office junior	*commis m de bureau*
office manager	*responsable m/f administratif(-ive), chef m de bureau*
office worker	*employé(e) m(f) de bureau*
organization chart	*organigramme m*
parent company	*société f mère*

I would like to meet your ... *je voudrais voir votre ...*
I work in our Glasgow office *je travaille au bureau de Glasgow*

part-timer	*employé(e) m(f) à temps partiel*
personal assistant (PA)	*secrétaire m/f particulier(-ière)*
personnel department	*service m du personnel*
personnel management	*direction f du personnel*
personnel manager	*chef m du personnel*
plant engineer	*mécanicien(-ienne) m(f)*
president	*président(e) m(f)*
press officer	*attaché(e) m(f) de presse*
production control	*contrôle m de (la) production*
production manager	*directeur(-trice) m(f) de la production*
product manager	*chef m or directeur(-trice) m(f) de produit*
profit centre	*centre m de profit*
project manager	*chef m de projet*
public relations (department)	*(service m des) relations fpl publiques*
public relations officer	*responsable m/f des relations publiques*
quality controller	*contrôleur(-euse) m(f) de la qualité*
R & D (research and development)	*R-D f (recherche-développement f)*
rationalization	*rationalisation f*
receptionist	*réceptionniste m/f*
records department	*service m des archives*
registered office	*siège m social*
research and development (R & D)	*recherche-développement f (R-D f)*
safety officer	*responsable m/f de la sûreté*
sales department	*service m des ventes*
sales force	*force f de vente, équipe f de vente*
sales manager	*directeur(-trice) m(f) commercial(e)*
sales representative	*représentant(e) m(f) de commerce*
secretary	*secrétaire m/f*
security guard	*vigile m*
service department	*service m d'entretien*
shipping department	*service m des expéditions*
sole agent	*agent m exclusif*

he/she is their representative in Geneva *il/elle est leur représentant(e) à Genève*

subsidiary (company)	*filiale f*
switchboard operator	*standardiste m/f*
temporary staff	*personnel m temporaire*
think tank	*groupe m de réflexion*
trainee	*stagiaire m/f*
typing pool	*équipe f de dactylos*
typist	*dactylo m/f*
undermanning	*manque m de main-d'œuvre, manque m de personnel*
vice-chairman	*vice-président m*
vice-chair(person)	*vice-président(e) m(f)*
vice-chairwoman	*vice-présidente f*
vice-president	*vice-président(e) m(f)*
works council	*comité m d'entreprise*

we are a subsidiary of ... *nous sommes une filiale de ...*
the company has 3 subsidiaries, with 10,000 employees worldwide *la société a 3 filiales et 10.000 employés dans le monde entier*

See also **MAKING CONTACT**

MAKING THEM

ON BEHALF OF YOUR COMPANY

We ordered it/them three weeks ago *cela fait trois semaines que nous avons passé cette commande*

Our order still hasn't arrived *notre commande n'est toujours pas arrivée*

There must be some mistake *il doit s'agir d'une erreur*

This is not what we ordered *ce n'est pas ce que nous avons commandé*

Your service isn't fast enough *votre service est trop lent*

It's too expensive *c'est trop cher*

We need it/them sooner *il nous le/la/les faut plus tôt (que cela)*

The samples you sent us were damaged/faulty *les échantillons que vous nous avez envoyés étaient endommagés/défectueux*

Your service department has let us down again *votre service d'entretien nous a de nouveau fait faux bond*

If the parts don't arrive by Friday we'll have to cancel the order *si les pièces n'arrivent pas d'ici vendredi, nous serons obligés d'annuler la commande*

Part of the order is missing from the consignment *il manque une partie de la commande dans l'envoi*

This is the third time this has happened *c'est la troisième fois que cela se produit*

What are you going to do about it? *quelles mesures allez-vous prendre?*

You have not kept to the terms of our contract *vous n'avez pas respecté les modalités de notre contrat*

Could you do something about it right away/as soon as possible/by tomorrow morning? *pourriez-vous faire quelque chose tout de suite/dès que possible/d'ici demain matin?*

I'm afraid this is not good enough *je regrette mais cela ne suffit pas*

I need it by tomorrow at the latest *il me le/la faut demain au plus tard*

We were expecting it last Tuesday *nous devions le/la recevoir mardi dernier*

Your service engineer didn't turn up *votre technicien d'entretien n'est pas venu*

We are dissatisfied with your after-sales service *nous sommes mécontents de votre service après-vente*

We may be forced to take legal action *nous pourrions nous voir dans l'obligation d'engager des poursuites judiciaires*

IN A SHOP

I bought this here yesterday/last week *j'ai acheté ceci ici hier/la semaine dernière*

This razor/lighter/calculator doesn't work *ce rasoir/ce briquet/ cette calculatrice ne marche pas*

It doesn't work properly *cela ne fonctionne pas bien*

It's broken/faulty *c'est cassé/défectueux*

It has a hole/tear in it *il y a un trou/une déchirure*

It doesn't do what it's supposed to *cela ne marche pas comme il faut*

It's shop-soiled *c'est abîmé*

It's the wrong model *ce n'est pas le bon modèle*

It's not what I asked for *ce n'est pas ce que j'ai demandé*

Here's my receipt *voici le reçu*

I've lost my receipt *j'ai perdu le reçu*

I'd like a refund *je voudrais être remboursé(e)*

I'd like to exchange it for something else *je voudrais l'échanger contre quelque chose d'autre*

I'd like a replacement *je voudrais qu'on me le/la/les remplace*

I've been overcharged *on m'a fait payer trop cher*

You've short-changed me *vous ne m'avez pas rendu assez (de monnaie)*

HANDLING THEM

BY TELEPHONE

Can you tell me what the problem is? *pouvez-vous me décrire le problème?*

When did you place your order? *quand avez-vous passé votre commande?*

When did this happen? *quand cela s'est-il produit?*

Has this happened before? *est-ce que cela s'est déjà produit?*

Is the item still under guarantee? *est-ce que l'article est encore sous garantie?*

I see *je comprends*

I'm sorry (about that) *je suis désolé(e)*

Please accept our apologies *je vous prie de nous excuser*

I'll see what I can do *je vais voir ce que je peux faire*

Just leave it with me *je vais m'en occuper*

I'll speak to the manager right away *je vais en parler immédiate-ment au directeur/à la directrice*

I'm sure we'll be able to sort it out for you *je suis sûr(e) que nous pourrons arranger cela*

I'll keep you informed *je vous tiendrai au courant*

I'll get back to you as soon as possible *je vous rappellerai dès que possible*

BY LETTER

Provided the article is still under guarantee, we will replace/repair it free of charge *si l'article est encore sous garantie nous le remplacerons/réparerons gratuitement*

We will send you a replacement immediately/by return of post *nous vous le/la/les remplacerons immédiatement/par retour de courrier*

You will not be charged for delivery/your order *nous ne vous ferons pas payer la livraison/votre commande*

This was due to a clerical error *ceci est dû à une erreur d'administration*

I shall arrange for one of our service engineers to call on you *je vais vous envoyer un de nos techniciens d'entretien*

We shall be glad to give you a discount on your next order *nous vous accorderons avec plaisir une réduction sur votre prochaine commande*

I am afraid we cannot help you with this particular problem *malheureusement, nous ne pouvons rien faire pour vous à l'égard de ce problème*

Our customer services department will be happy to help you *notre service clientèle se fera un plaisir de vous aider*

Please contact your distributor *veuillez vous adresser à votre distributeur*

This is not really our responsibility *ceci ne relève pas vraiment de notre responsabilité*

Please send us details of your complaint in writing *veuillez nous envoyer les détails de votre réclamation par écrit*

IN PERSON

I doubt very much whether we shall be able to repair this *je ne pense vraiment pas que nous soyons en mesure de le réparer*

If you could just bear with me for a moment, I'll fetch the manager *si vous voulez bien patienter un instant, je vais chercher le directeur*

I can see why this problem has caused you great distress *je comprends que ce problème vous ait contrarié(e)*

I suspect the cause of the fault is purely mechanical *je pense que ce problème est purement mécanique*

Would you mind leaving the item with us so that we can take a closer look at it? *cela vous ennuierait-t-il de nous confier l'article pour que nous puissions l'examiner de plus près?*

I think I see where the problem lies *je crois savoir d'où vient le problème*

Marie-Jacqueline Vannier
16 rue de la pierre plastique
17028 La Rochelle

Équipements Dufour
14 rue Montpensier
91300 Paris

Monsieur/Madame,

La Rochelle, le 18 mai 1991

L'appareil que j'ai acheté dans votre établissement le 8 mai 1991, numéro de commande 1963, présente les défauts suivants qui en empêchent la bonne marche:

le moteur ne fonctionne pas bien
le bouton de mise en marche est coincé
le couvercle est fêlé

Je désire que le contrat de vente soit annulé et que vous me fassiez parvenir le remboursement intégral du prix que j'ai versé, soit 1.500FF.

Veuillez agréer, Monsieur/Madame, l'expression de mes sentiments distingués.

MJVannier

Marie-Jacqueline Vannier

Dear Sir/Madam,

The machine I bought in your shop on 8 May 1991, order number 1963, has the following faults:

the motor does not work properly
the start button is jammed
the lid is cracked

I wish to cancel the sale and be reimbursed in full for the price I paid, namely 1,500FF.

Yours faithfully,

MJVannier

Marie-Jacqueline Vannier

abort	*abandonner*
access *n*	*accès m*
access *vb*	*accéder à*
access time	*temps m d'accès*
A/D converter	*convertisseur m analogique-numérique*
AI (artificial intelligence)	*IA f (intelligence f artificielle)*
alphanumeric	*alphanumérique*
analog(ue)	*analogique*
application	*application f*
application package	*progiciel m d'application*
application software	*logiciel m d'application*
archive	*archives fpl*
ASCII	*ASCII*
azerty keyboard	*clavier m AZERTY*
back-up (copy)	*copie f de sauvegarde*
back-up disk	*disque m de sauvegarde*
bandwidth	*largeur f de bande*
baud rate	*vitesse f en bauds*
benchmark tests	*tests mpl d'évaluation de performance*
bespoke software	*logiciel m sur mesure*
binary code	*code m binaire*
binary compatible	*compatible binaire*
boot (up)	*initialiser, amorcer*
bpi (bits per inch)	*bits mpl par pouce*
bps (bits per second)	*bits mpl par seconde*
bubble memory	*mémoire f à bulles*
buffer	*mémoire f tampon*
bug	*erreur f*
bulletin board	*tableau m d'affichage*
bundle	*lot m*
byte	*octet m, multiplet m*
CAD (computer-assisted design)	*CAO f (conception f assistée par ordinateur)*
CAD/CAM (computer-assisted design/manufacture)	*CFAO f (conception f et fabrication f assistées par ordinateur)*
CAL (computer-assisted learning)	*EAO m (enseignement m assisté par ordinateur)*
CAM (computer-assisted manufacture)	*FAO f (fabrication f assistée par ordinateur)*
cartridge	*chargeur m, cartouche f*

to do a back-up *faire une copie de sauvegarde*

CD ROM	*disque m compact-ROM*
centre *n*	*centre m*
centre *vb*	*centrer*
CGA (colour graphics adaptor)	*adaptateur m de graphique couleur*
character	*caractère m*
character set	*répertoire m de caractères*
chip	*puce f*
CIM (computer input from microfilm)	*entrée f en ordinateur par microfilm*
CIM (computer-integrated manufacturing)	*FIO f (fabrication f intégrée par ordinateur)*
clipboard	*bloc-notes m*
code	*code m*
command	*commande f*
compatible	*compatible*
computer	*ordinateur m*
computer agency	*bureau m d'informatique*
computer game	*jeu m électronique*
computer language	*langage m machine*
computer literate	*initié(e) à l'informatique*
computer science	*informatique f*
computer scientist	*informaticien(ne) m(f)*
computing	*informatique f*
computing department	*service m d'informatique*
console	*console f*
control key	*touche f de commande*
control unit	*unité f de commande*
copy *n*	*copie f*
copy *vb*	*copier*
corrupt *adj*	*altéré(e)*
corrupt *vb*	*altérer*
corruption	*altération f*
cpi (characters per inch)	*CCPP mpl (caractères mpl par pouce)*
CPM (critical path method)	*méthode f du chemin critique*
cps (characters per second)	*caractères/seconde*
cps (cycles per second)	*cycles mpl par seconde*
CPU (central processing unit)	*unité f centrale de traitement*
crash *vb*	*tomber en panne*
create *(file)*	*créer*

to do something by computer *faire quelque chose avec l'ordinateur*
the computer can handle the whole operation *l'ordinateur peut effectuer toute l'opération*

cursor	*curseur m*
cut and paste *n*	*coupe f et insertion f*
cut and paste *vb*	*couper-coller*
cybernetics	*cybernétique f*
D/A converter	*convertisseur m numérique-analogique*
data	*données fpl*
databank	*banque f de données*
database	*base f de données*
database management	*gestion f de bases de données*
(data) capture	*saisie f (de données)*
data collection	*collecte f de données*
data processing (DP)	*traitement m de données, informatique f*
data protection law	*législation f de la protection des données*
data security	*sécurité f des informations*
debug	*mettre au point*
default *adj*	*implicite*
default *n*	*valeur f par défaut*
delete	*effacer*
delivery time	*délai m de livraison*
deskside computer	*ordinateur m type "tour"*
desktop computer	*ordinateur m de bureau*
device	*dispositif m, unité f physique*
diagnostic program	*programme m de diagnostic*
digit	*chiffre m*
digital	*numérique*
direct access	*accès m direct*
directory	*répertoire m*
disk	*disque m*
disk capacity	*capacité f du disque*
disk drive	*lecteur m de disques*
diskette	*disquette f*
document	*document m*
dongle	*boîtier m de sécurité*
DOS ®	*DOS ®, SED m (système m d'exploitation sur disques)*
dot matrix printer	*imprimante f par points*
double-density disk(ette)	*disquette f double densité*
down	*en panne*
download *vb*	*transférer*

you can do that using cut and paste *vous pouvez le faire à l'aide du bloc-notes*

downtime	temps *m* d'arrêt
drive	unité *f*, dispositif *m* d'entraînement
DTP (desktop publishing)	PAO *f* (publication *f* assistée par ordinateur)
dumb terminal	terminal *m* passif
dump *n*	vidage *m*
dump *vb*	vider
edit *vb*	éditer
EGA (enhanced graphics adaptor)	adaptateur *m* de graphique amélioré
electronic mail	courrier *m* électronique
end user	utilisateur(-trice) *m(f)* final(e)
enter	introduire
erase *vb*	effacer
error message	message *m* d'erreur
escape	échappement *m*
expert system	système *m* expert (SE *m*)
fault-tolerant	insensible aux défaillances
fibre-optic cable	câble *m* à fibre optique
fibre-optic link	liaison *f* par fibre optique
fibre optics	fibre *f* optique
file *n*	fichier *m*
file *vb*	classer, stocker
filename	nom *m* de fichier
floppy disk	disquette *f*
font	police *f*
format *vb (disk)*	formater
formatting	formatage *m*
form feeder	dispositif *m* de changement de page
function key	touche *f* de fonction
garbage	données *fpl* invalides
gigabyte	gigaoctet *m*
gigaflops	un milliard d'opérations en virgule flottante par seconde
GIGO (garbage in garbage out)	qualité *f* d'entrée égale qualité *f* de sortie
(global) search and replace	recherche *f* et remplacement *m* (automatiques)
graphics	traitement *m* graphique
hacking	effraction *f* informatique
hard disk	disque *m* dur
hardware	matériel *m*, hardware *m*
help menu	menu *m* d'assistance

high-density disk(ette)	disquette f haute densité
high resolution	(à) haute définition f
hot key	touche f directe
housekeeping	gestion f (des disques)
hybrid system	système m hybride
icon	icône f
idle time	temps m mort
incompatible	incompatible
indent	commencer en retrait
information retrieval	recherche f documentaire
information technology (IT)	informatique f
ink jet printer	imprimante f à jet d'encre
input n (process)	entrée f
input vb	introduire, entrer
input (data)	données fpl en entrée
insert vb	insérer
install	installer
integrated accounting package	logiciel m intégré de comptabilité
intelligent terminal	terminal m intelligent
interface	interface f
interrupt	interrompre
I/O (input/output)	E/S (entrée/sortie)
IT (information technology)	informatique f
joystick	manche m à balai
justify left/right	justifier à gauche/à droite
key n	touche f
keyboard	clavier m
key in	introduire au clavier
keypad	clavier m
keystroke	frappe f
kilobyte	kilo-octet m
LAN (local area network)	RLE m (réseau m local d'entreprise)
language	langage m
laptop (computer)	portatif m
laser disk	disque m laser
laser printer	imprimante f à laser
LCD (liquid crystal display)	afficheur m à cristaux liquides
letter quality	qualité f "courrier"
light pen	crayon m optique
line feed	changement m de ligne
line spacing	interligne m
load vb	charger
log	enregistrer
logic	logique f

log in/on	*entrer (dans le système)*
log off/out	*sortir (du système)*
machine-readable	*exploitable sur machine*
magnetic disk	*disque m magnétique*
magnetic tape	*bande f magnétique*
mailbox	*boîte f aux lettres*
mainframe	*unité f centrale*
main memory	*mémoire f centrale (MC f)*
margin	*marge f*
MAT (machine-assisted translation)	*TAO f (traduction f assistée par ordinateur)*
megabyte (Mb)	*méga-octet m (Mo m)*
memory	*mémoire f*
menu	*menu m*
merge *n*	*fusion f*
merge *vb*	*fusionner*
microchip	*puce f*
microcomputer	*micro-ordinateur m*
microdrive	*unité f de microdisquette*
microprocessor	*microprocesseur m*
microsecond	*microseconde f*
millisecond	*milliseconde f*
mips (millions of instructions per second)	*millions mpl d'instructions par seconde*
MIS (management information system)	*SIG m (système m intégré de gestion)*
mobile data system	*système m de données mobile*
model *(of hardware)*	*modèle m*
modem	*modem m*
module	*module m*
monitor	*moniteur m*
mouse	*souris f*
multi-tasking	*traitement m multitâche*
multi-user system	*configuration f multiposte*
nanosecond	*nanoseconde f*
network *n*	*réseau m*
network *vb*	*interconnecter*
off-line	*(en mode) autonome*
on-line	*en ligne*
operating system	*système m d'exploitation*
optical character reader (OCR)	*lecteur m optique*
optical character recognition (OCR)	*lecture f optique*
output *n (process)*	*sortie f*
output *vb*	*sortir*

output (data)	données fpl de sortie
overwrite	recouvrir
package	progiciel m
pagination	pagination f
paperless office	bureau m automatisé
password	mot m de passe
PC (personal computer)	PC m
peripheral n	périphérique m
peripheral adj	périphérique
pirate vb	pirater
pirate copy	copie f pirate
pixel	pixel m
plotter	traceur m
port	point m d'accès
portable (computer)	portable m
printer	imprimante f
print-out	listing m
processor	processeur m
program n	programme m
program vb	programmer
programmer	programmeur(-euse) m(f)
programming	programmation f
programming language	langage m de programmation
prompt	message m (de guidage)
protect	protéger
protocol	protocole m
qwerty keyboard	clavier m QWERTY
rack-mounted unit	appareil m monté en armoire
RAM (random access memory)	RAM f, mémoire f vive
random access	accès m sélectif or aléatoire
real time	temps m réel
reboot	réinitialiser, réamorcer
record	article m
reformat	reformater
response time	temps m de réponse
retrieve	retrouver
RISC (reduced instruction set computing)	traitement m avec jeu d'instructions réduit
ROM (read-only memory)	mémoire f fixe

the package includes hardware, software and consultancy *le forfait comprend le matériel, le logiciel et le service-conseil*
the package is designed for all levels of users *le progiciel est destiné aux utilisateurs de tous niveaux*
now press "return"/any key *appuyez sur "return"/n'importe quelle touche*

run time	*durée f d'exploitation*
scratch file	*fichier m de travail*
screen	*écran m*
SCSI (small computer systems interface)	*SCSI f*
search and replace	*recherche f et remplacement m*
shared facility	*installation f commune*
shareware	*shareware m*
simulation	*simulation f*
soak test	*rôdage m*
soft copy	*présentation f visuelle*
software	*logiciel m, software m*
software engineer	*ingénieur m en logiciel*
software engineering	*ingénierie f du logiciel*
software house	*société f de services et de conseils en informatique (SSCI f)*
software package	*progiciel m*
sort *vb*	*trier*
space bar	*barre f d'espacement*
speech generation	*génération f de parole*
speech recognition	*reconnaissance f de la parole*
speech synthesis	*synthèse f vocale*
spellchecker	*contrôle m orthographique*
spreadsheet	*feuille f de calcul (électronique)*
stand-alone	*autonome*
storage	*mise f en mémoire*
string	*chaîne f*
style sheet	*feuille f de style*
syntax error	*erreur f de syntaxe*
system	*système m*
system operator	*opérateur m du système, serveur m*
systems analysis	*analyse f fonctionnelle*
systems analyst	*analyste m(f) fonctionnel(le)*
teletext	*télétexte m*
template	*patron m*
terminal	*terminal m*
test data	*données fpl d'essai*
text editor	*éditeur m de texte(s)*
time-sharing	*temps m partagé*

you can scroll up or down using the arrow keys *pour le défilement vertical, utilisez les flèches*
we need a software package which ... *il nous faut un progiciel qui ...*

toolkit	valise f
touch-sensitive	à effleurement
tpi (tracks per inch)	pistes fpl par pouce
update n	mise f à jour
update vb	mettre à jour
upgrade	augmenter la puissance
upgradeable	extensible
user	utilisateur(-trice) m(f)
user-friendly	convivial(e)
user-name	nom m de l'utilisateur
utility software	logiciel m utilitaire
validate	valider
VDU (visual display unit)	console f de visualisation
VGA (video gate array) card	carte f VGA
videodisc	vidéodisque m
video game	jeu m vidéo
Viewdata ®	vidéotex m
virus	virus m
WAN (wide area network)	grand réseau m
wildcard	caractère m de remplacement
window	fenêtre f
wordcount	nombre m de mots
word processing	traitement m de texte
word processor	machine f de traitement de texte
wordwrap	retour m (automatique) à la ligne
working disk	disque m de travail
work station	poste m de travail
worm drive	unité f à disques inscriptibles une seule fois
write-protected	protégé(e) contre l'écriture
WYSIWYG (what you see is what you get)	ce que vous voyez est ce que vous aurez

the system needs to be totally upgraded il faut augmenter la puissance de tout le système
to write to a disk écrire sur un disque

See also **MEETINGS AND NEGOTIATIONS**

PRACTICAL PREPARATIONS BEFORE GIVING THE TALK

What time will I be speaking? *à quelle heure commence mon intervention?*

Could I have 25 copies of this please? *je voudrais 25 copies de ceci, s'il vous plaît*

Could I have 25 copies of each of these? *je voudrais 25 copies de chaque*

I need them by 9 o'clock *il me les faut pour 9 heures*

I'd like this typed up *je voudrais faire taper ceci*

Everyone needs one copy of each of these *il faut une copie de chaque pour chaque personne*

Please hand these round *pourriez-vous distribuer ceux-ci/celles-ci s'il vous plaît?*

Has the ... been set up? *est-ce que le/la/les ... est/sont installé(e)(s)?*

Could you help me set up the ...? *pourriez-vous m'aider à installer le/la/les ...?*

Can you show me how to work the ...? *pouvez-vous me montrer comment fonctionne le/la ...?*

There isn't/aren't any ... *il n'y a pas de ...*

Who is dealing with the refreshments/the technical side of things? *qui est-ce qui s'occupe des rafraîchissements/de l'aspect technique?*

I'd like to record/film the talk *je voudrais enregistrer/filmer l'intervention*

The room seems rather small/warm/cold/stuffy *la salle semble un peu petite/un peu surchauffée/insuffisamment chauffée/mal aérée*

INTRODUCING YOURSELF

Good morning/afternoon/evening, Ladies and Gentlemen *Mesdames, Mesdemoiselles, Messieurs, bonjour/bonsoir*

Let me introduce myself *permettez-moi de me présenter*

My name is ..., and I'm ... with Contax *je m'appelle ..., et je suis ... chez Contax*

Let me welcome you to ... *je vous souhaite la bienvenue à/au/en ...*

I'm very pleased to be here/to be in ... *c'est un grand plaisir pour moi d'être ici/d'être à/au/en ...*

Please make allowances for my French *je vous prie de me pardonner mon français*

My French is rather rusty, but I will do my best *mon français est* *assez rouillé, mais je ferai de mon mieux*

Please stop me if there is anything you don't understand *veuillez m'arrêter au cas où vous ne comprendriez pas quelque chose*

YOUR JOB

My official job title is ... *mon titre officiel est ...*

My role within the company/department is to ... *mon rôle au sein de la société/du service consiste à ...*

I deal with all matters regarding ... *je m'occupe de tout ce qui concerne ...*

I am responsible for ensuring that ... *je suis chargé(e) de veiller à ce que ...*

It is my job to ensure that ... *mon travail est de veiller à ce que ...*

I report directly to head office *je suis directement rattaché(e) au siège social*

These departments report directly to me/us *ces services dépendent directement de moi/nous*

I started the job in 1990 *j'ai démarré dans ce poste en 1990*

I have been with the company since March/for eighteen months *je travaille dans cette société depuis mars/depuis dix-huit mois*

I am based at our offices/plant in ... *je suis basé(e) dans nos bureaux/notre usine de ...*

See also **COMPANY STRUCTURES**

INTRODUCING YOUR COMPANY OR DEPARTMENT

As you know, we are in the field of ... *comme vous le savez, nous sommes dans le domaine de ...*

We are a subsidiary of ... *nous sommes une filiale de ...*

We are the parent company of a group comprising ... *nous sommes la société mère d'un groupe comprenant ...*

We are affiliated with ... *nous sommes affiliés à ...*

We have 20 branches in the UK *nous avons 20 succursales/agences au Royaume-Uni*

We operate in 30 countries across 3 continents *nous travaillons dans 30 pays répartis sur 3 continents*

The company employs 3000 people worldwide *notre société a un effectif de 3000 employés répartis dans le monde entier*

There are 20 people in the department/company *il y a 20 personnes dans le service/la société*

See also **COMPANY STRUCTURES** *and* **INDUSTRIES AND TYPES OF COMPANY**

YOUR COMPANY OR DEPARTMENT'S PERFORMANCE

Our turnover was over £1 million last year *l'an dernier, nous avons fait un chiffre d'affaires de plus d'un million de livres sterling*

We sold 100,000 units worldwide/in the UK *nous avons vendu 100.000 unités dans le monde entier/au Royaume-Uni*

Last year we produced over a million units *l'an dernier, nous avons produit plus d'un million d'unités*

There was an increase/decrease in sales of 10% last year *l'an dernier, les ventes ont augmenté/baissé de 10%*

Production is rising/falling fast *la production augmente/baisse rapidement*

We are reasonably satisfied with this performance *nous sommes assez satisfaits de cette performance*

We are not very satisfied with this performance *nous ne sommes pas très satisfaits de cette performance*

We are currently enjoying a period of relative/fast growth *pour le moment, nous sommes dans une période de croissance relative/rapide*

The whole sector is depressed at the moment *tout le secteur est déprimé en ce moment*

We are suffering the effects of a recession at the moment *en ce moment, nous subissons les effets de la récession*

We intend to improve (still further) on this performance *nous avons l'intention d'améliorer (encore) cette performance*

See also **ACCOUNTS AND PAYMENTS, BANKING AND FINANCE, BUYING AND SELLING, ECONOMICS, MANUFACTURING** *and* **PROJECT MANAGEMENT** *for specific vocabulary*

THE STRUCTURE OF THE TALK

First(ly) *premièrement/d'abord*
Secondly *deuxièmement/ensuite*
Thirdly *troisièmement/(et) puis*
Fourth *quatrièmement/(et) puis*
Finally *pour terminer*

AN INITIAL SUMMARY

I'm going to be talking about ... *je vais parler de ...*
I would like to talk about ... *j'aimerais parler de ...*
I would like to analyse/present ... *j'aimerais analyser/présenter ...*

I will begin with an introduction to the subject *je vais commencer par une introduction sur le sujet*

I will begin by giving you an overview of the situation *je vais commencer par vous donner une vue d'ensemble de la situation*

I will begin with a short historical note *je vais commencer par quelques mots sur le passé*

Then I will move on to ... *puis je passerai à ...*

After that, I will deal with ... *ensuite, je parlerai de ...*

I will conclude with ... *je conclurai par ...*

I will try to anticipate future developments *je tenterai d'anticiper sur les développements dans l'avenir*

And I will be happy to answer your questions at the end *et j'aurai grand plaisir à répondre à vos questions à la fin*

MOVING ON TO THE BODY OF THE TALK

First, let us look at ... *voyons d'abord ...*

This brings me to my next point *ceci m'amène à la question suivante*

Next, I would like to examine ... *ensuite, je voudrais examiner ...*

Let me now move on to the question of ... *passons maintenant à la question de ...*

At this point, we must consider ... *à ce stade, il nous faut examiner ...*

To digress for a moment *en guise de parenthèse*

Let me just add a footnote to this *permettez-moi d'ajouter une note (explicative)*

To return to my earlier point *pour revenir à ce que je disais tout à l'heure*

As I mentioned a moment ago *comme je l'ai mentionné il y a un moment*

MAKING A POINT

As we all know ... *comme tout le monde le sait ...*

I must emphasize that ... *il faut que j'insiste sur le fait que ...*

This is a very important point *c'est un point très important*

The question is ... *la question est (de savoir) ...*

The problem is ... *le problème est ...*

Let us not forget that ... *n'oublions pas que ...*

It is all too easy to forget that ... *on oublie trop facilement que ...*

These are the points to remember *voici les points à retenir*

The main argument against/in favour of this is ... *le principal argument contre/en faveur de ceci est ...*

These are the facts to date *ce sont les faits jusqu'à présent*

EXPRESSING AN OPINION

In my opinion *à mon avis* **Personally** *personnellement*
It seems to me that ... *il me semble que ...*
From my/our point of view *d'après moi/nous*
I/we believe that ... *je pense/nous pensons que ...*
We are sure that ... *nous sommes certain(e)s que ...*
Things are likely to change soon *il est probable que les choses vont bientôt changer*
I/we entirely approve of this *je suis/nous sommes tout à fait d'accord avec cela*
We are all very enthusiastic about the proposals *nous sommes tous très enthousiasmé(e)s par ces propositions*
I am/we are very much in favour of going ahead with the plans *je suis/nous sommes tout à fait d'accord pour faire démarrer ces projets*
I/we don't think that it would work *je ne crois pas/nous ne croyons pas que cela marcherait*
I/we can't support this idea *je ne peux pas/nous ne pouvons pas appuyer cette idée*
We are not too happy about these developments *nous ne sommes pas très content(e)s de cette évolution*
We are not at all sure that ... *nous ne sommes pas du tout sûr(e)s que ...*
I am not in a position to comment on this matter *je ne suis pas à même de commenter à ce sujet*
I wouldn't like to give an opinion on that *je n'aimerais pas me prononcer là-dessus*
I really have nothing to add *je n'ai vraiment rien à ajouter*

EXPRESSING INTENTIONS

I/we intend to take action on this immediately *j'ai/nous avons l'intention d'agir immédiatement (à ce sujet)*
My/our intention is to ... *j'ai/nous avons l'intention de ...*
I am/we are thinking of implementing the decisions before the end of the year *je pense/nous pensons appliquer les décisions avant la fin de l'année*
We really have to get things moving immediately *il faut vraiment que nous mettions les choses en route sans délai*
We don't intend to ... *nous n'avons pas l'intention de ...*
We are not thinking of carrying out the changes yet *nous ne pensons pas effectuer les changements pour le moment*
It probably won't come to that *on n'en arrivera probablement pas là*

EXPLANATIONS

In view of ... *étant donné(e)*
In view of the fact that ... *étant donné le fait que ...*
As a result of ... *par suite de ...*
Thanks to ... *grâce à ...*
For lack of ... *faute de ...*
On the grounds that ... *en raison du fait que ...*
This was caused by external factors *ceci est dû à des facteurs externes*
It was therefore necessary to act fast *il fallait donc agir sans délai*
The problem goes back to the oil crisis *le problème remonte à la crise pétrolière*
It's like this: *voilà de quoi il s'agit:*

SUMMING UP

Let me summarize the main points again *permettez-moi de résumer à nouveau les points principaux*
Finally, I would just like to say ... *pour terminer, je voudrais simplement dire ...*
Are there any questions? *y a-t-il des questions?*
Well, if there are no more questions, I will stop here *eh bien, s'il n'y a plus de questions, je vais m'arrêter ici*
Thank you (all) for your attention *je vous remercie (tous) pour votre attention*

ASKING QUESTIONS

I'd like to ask a question *j'aimerais poser une question*
How much/many ...? *combien de ...?*
How often ...? *à quelle fréquence ...?*
Who? *qui?* **When?** *quand?* **Why?** *pourquoi?*
Could you give us a few more details about ...? *pourriez-vous nous donner quelques détails supplémentaires sur ...?*
Can I just pick you up on something you said earlier? *puis-je revenir sur quelque chose que vous avez dit tout à l'heure?*
I'm not sure I understood your point about ... Could you clarify it please? *je ne suis pas certain(e) d'avoir bien compris ce que vous disiez sur ... Puis-je vous demander de clarifier?*
Where can I get more information about ...? *où puis-je trouver de plus amples renseignements sur ...?*
Can you give any examples of that? *pourriez-vous en donner des exemples?*

ANSWERING QUESTIONS

Could you repeat that please? *pourriez-vous répéter ceci, s'il vous plaît?*

I didn't quite hear that *je n'ai pas bien entendu ceci*

Would you mind speaking a little more slowly? *puis-je vous demander de parler un peu plus lentement?*

Could you repeat that in English please? *pourriez-vous répéter ceci en anglais, s'il vous plaît?*

Can I answer that question later? *puis-je répondre plus tard à cette question?*

Good question *c'est une question intéressante*

That's a difficult question but I'll do my best to answer it *c'est une question difficile, mais je ferai de mon mieux pour y répondre*

I think it's best if ... answers that for you *je crois que le mieux serait de demander à ... de vous répondre là-dessus*

I can't give you an exact answer, I'm afraid *je regrette de ne pas pouvoir vous donner une réponse précise*

Can I get back to you on that one? *est-ce que je pourrais vous donner une réponse plus tard?*

Let me clarify that for you *permettez-moi de clarifier cela*

You're quite right *vous avez tout à fait raison*

I agree entirely *je suis tout à fait d'accord*

I'm not sure I can agree with you there *je ne suis pas sûr(e) d'être d'accord avec vous sur ce point*

I take your point, but ... *je vois ce que vous voulez dire, mais ...*

USING VISUAL AIDS

Could we have the lights off, please? *peut-on éteindre la lumière s'il vous plaît?*

Here you can see ... *ici, vous voyez ...*

Please look at figure one/two *veuillez regarder la figure numéro un/deux*

This chart illustrates ... *ce tableau illustre ...*

These are the figures for ... *voici les chiffres pour ...*

This gives you a clear picture of ... *ceci vous donne une idée précise de ...*

The handouts in front of you will give you a better idea of this *la documentation que vous trouverez devant vous vous donnera une idée plus précise là-dessus*

As you can see in this diagram/photograph *comme vous le voyez dans ce diagramme/sur cette photo*

I have brought a short film/a few slides with me to illustrate this

j'ai apporté un court film/quelques diapositives afin d'illustrer ceci

PROBLEMS WITH EQUIPMENT AND MATERIALS

The ... isn't working *le/la/les ... ne marche(nt) pas*
Can you hear me all right? *est-ce que vous m'entendez bien?*
I am sorry about the quality of these photocopies *veuillez excuser la qualité de ces photocopies*
Please bear with me *veuillez m'excuser un instant*

ADDITIONAL VOCABULARY

abstract	*résumé m*
afternoon session	*séance f de l'après-midi*
agenda	*ordre m du jour*
audience	*auditoire m*
audio-visual aids	*supports mpl audio-visuels*
bar chart	*graphique m en tuyaux d'orgue*
(black) board	*tableau m (noir)*
case study	*étude f de cas*
cassette	*cassette f*
cassette player	*magnétophone m*
chart	*graphique m*
conference	*conférence f*
conference centre	*centre m de conférences*
conference hall	*salle f de conférences*
conference room	*salle f de conférences*
convention	*convention f*
data	*données fpl*
debate n	*débat m*
delegate n	*participant(e) m(f)*
diagram	*diagramme m*
discussion	*discussion f*
eraser *(for board)*	*éponge f*
evening session	*séance f du soir*
exhibition hall	*salle f d'exposition*
felt pen	*feutre m*
figure one/two	*figure f numéro un/deux*
flipchart	*tableau m à feuilles mobiles*
flowchart	*grapique m d'évolution*
graph	*graphique m*
hall	*salle f*
handout	*documentation f*
illustration	*illustration f*

keynote speaker	*intervenant m chargé du discours-programme*
keynote speech	*discours-programme m*
lectern	*lutrin m*
light	*lumière f*
meeting	*réunion f*
meeting room	*salle f de réunion*
microphone	*microphone m*
morning session	*séance f du matin*
notepaper	*papier m*
notes	*notes fpl*
overhead projector	*rétroprojecteur m*
PA system	*système m de sonorisation*
photocopy *n*	*photocopie f*
photograph	*photo f*
pie chart	*graphique m circulaire, camembert m*
podium	*podium m*
pointer	*baguette f*
presentation	*exposé m*
press conference	*conférence f de presse*
progress report	*rapport m d'activité*
projector	*projecteur m*
refreshments	*rafraîchissements mpl*
screen	*écran m*
seminar	*colloque m*
slide	*diapositive f*
slide projector	*projecteur m de diapositives*
speak	*parler*
speaker	*intervenant(e) m(f)*
speech *(the talk)*	*discours m, intervention f*
speech *(your notes)*	*notes fpl (de discours)*
talk	*intervention f, discours m*
teleconference	*tenir une téléconférence*
time limit	*délai m fixé*
trade fair	*foire-exposition f*
transparency	*transparent m*
TV monitor	*moniteur m de TV*
video camera	*caméscope m*
video (cassette)	*vidéo(cassette) f*
video conference	*visioconférence f*
video recorder	*magnétoscope m*
whiteboard	*tableau m blanc*
working group	*groupe m de travail*
workshop	*atelier m*

See also **BANKING AND FINANCE** *and* **THE EUROPEAN COMMUNITY**

absolute monopoly	*monopole m absolu*
absorption	*absorption f*
acquisition	*acquisition f*
active partner	*commandité(e) m(f)*
adverse trade balance	*balance f commerciale déficitaire*
affiliated company	*filiale f*
amalgamate	*fusionner*
amalgamation	*fusion f*
anti-dumping duty	*droits mpl anti-dumping*
anti-trust legislation	*loi f anti-trust*
asset-stripping	*réalisation f de l'actif de l'entreprise (en difficulté)*
associated company	*société f affiliée*
balance of payments	*balance f des paiements*
balance of trade	*balance f commerciale*
bankrupt *adj*	*en faillite, failli(e)*
barter *n*	*troc m*
bilateral trade	*commerce m bilateral*
black economy	*économie f souterraine*
black market	*marché m noir*
boom	*boom m*
borrowing	*emprunt m*
break-up value	*valeur f de liquidation*
capital	*capital m*
capital allowance	*provision f pour amortissement*
capital expenditure	*dépenses fpl d'investissment*
capital goods	*biens mpl d'équipement*
capital-intensive	*à forte proportion de capitaux*
capital investment	*dépenses fpl d'investissement*
capital movement	*mouvements mpl de capitaux*
capital structure	*structure f financière*
cartel	*cartel m*
cash reserves	*liquidités fpl*
centralized economy	*économie f centralisée*
collateral	*nantissement m*
collective ownership	*propriété f collective*
conglomerate	*conglomérat m*
consortium	*consortium m*

to absorb a loss *éponger une perte*
a **favourable/unfavourable Budget** *un budget de l'État favorable/défavorable*

consumer	*consommateur(-trice) m(f)*
controlled economy	*économie f dirigée*
cooperative *n*	*coopérative f*
co-ownership	*copropriété f*
cost of living index	*indice m du coût de la vie*
cost-push inflation	*inflation f par les coûts*
credit squeeze	*encadrement m du crédit*
cutback	*réduction f*
deflation	*déflation f*
deflationary	*déflationniste*
demand-pull inflation	*inflation f par la demande*
denationalize	*dénationaliser*
depression	*dépression f, crise f*
devaluation	*dévaluation f*
devalue	*dévaluer*
development area	*zone f d'aménagement*
diseconomies of scale	*déséconomies fpl d'échelle*
disinflation	*désinflation f*
disinvest	*désinvestir*
disinvestment	*désinvestissement m*
disposable personal income	*revenu m disponible*
dollar area	*zone f dollar*
dump *vb*	*vendre à perte à l'extérieur*
dumping	*dumping m*
earned income	*revenu m du travail*
earnings	*revenu m*
economic climate	*conjoncture f économique*
economic growth	*croissance f économique*
economics	*économie f*
economic trend	*conjoncture f économique*
economic warfare	*guerre f économique*
economies of scale	*économies fpl d'échelle*
economist	*économiste m/f*
economize	*économiser*
economy	*économie f*
embargo	*embargo m*
excess capacity	*capacité f excédentaire*
excess supply	*suroffre f*
exchange control	*contrôle m des changes*
Exchange Rate Mechanism (ERM)	*mécanisme m de change*

the economic development of a region/country *le développement
économique d'une région/d'un pays*
a downturn in the economy *un passage à la baisse de l'économie*

excise duties	*impôts mpl prélevés par la régie*
fiscal measures	*mesures fpl fiscales*
fiscal policy	*politique f fiscale*
foreign investment	*investissement m à l'étranger*
free enterprise	*libre entreprise f*
free trade	*libre-échange m*
full employment	*plein emploi m*
galloping inflation	*inflation f galopante*
gold reserves	*réserves fpl d'or*
gold standard	*étalon-or m*
government intervention	*intervention f de l'État*
government stock	*titres mpl d'État*
gross domestic product (GDP)	*produit m intérieur brut (PIB m)*
gross national product (GNP)	*produit m national brut (PNB m)*
growth rate	*taux m de croissance*
horizontal integration	*intégration f horizontale*
hyperinflation	*hyperinflation f*
incomes policy	*politique f des revenus*
income tax	*impôt m sur le revenu*
inflation	*inflation f*
infrastructure	*infrastructure f*
Inland Revenue (IR)	*fisc m britannique*
interest rate	*taux m d'intérêt*
invest (in)	*investir (dans)*
investment	*investissement m, placement m*
investment grant	*subvention f d'équipement*
invisible exports	*exportations fpl invisibles*
invisible imports	*importations fpl invisibles*
labour costs	*coût m de la main-d'œuvre*
labour-intensive	*intensif(-ive) en main-d'œuvre*
labour market	*marché m du travail*
laissez-faire policy	*politique f du laissez-faire*
macroeconomics	*macroéconomie f*
market economy	*économie f de marché*

there has been a sharp/gradual fall in ... *il y a eu une baisse soudaine/ progressive de ...*

to float EC currencies against the dollar *laisser flotter les devises de la CE par rapport au dollar*

to allow the exchange rate of sterling to float *laisser flotter le taux de change de la livre sterling*

a healthy/unhealthy economy *une économie saine/peu solide*

the economy is being held back by ... *l'économie est ralentie par ...*

interest rates are falling/rising *les taux d'intérêt sont en baisse/en hausse*

to go into liquidation *déposer son bilan*

market forces	*tendances fpl du marché*
merge *vb*	*fusionner*
merger	*fusion f*
microeconomics	*microéconomie f*
mixed economy	*économie f mixte*
mobility of labour	*mobilité f de la main-d'œuvre*
monetarism	*monétarisme m*
monetarist	*monétariste m/f*
monetary policy	*politique f monétaire*
money supply	*masse f monétaire*
monopoly	*monopole m*
monopsony	*monopsone m*
nationalization	*nationalisation f*
nationalize	*nationaliser*
nationalized industry	*industrie f nationalisée*
natural resources	*ressources fpl naturelles*
non-profit-making	*à but non-lucratif*
oligopoly	*oligopole m*
overcapitalized	*surcapitalisé(e)*
overheated economy	*surchauffe f de l'économie*
overproduction	*surproduction f*
overspend	*trop dépenser*
paper money	*monnaie f de papier*
petrodollar	*pétrodollar m*
planned economy	*économie f planifiée*
price control	*contrôle m des prix*
price-fixing	*entente f sur les prix*
prices and incomes policy	*politique f des prix et des revenus*
price war	*guerre f des prix*
private (limited) company	*société f privée*
privately-owned	*privé(e)*
private sector	*secteur m privé*
privatization	*privatisation f*
privatize	*privatiser*
productivity	*productivité f*
protectionism	*protectionnisme m*
public limited company	*société f anonyme*
public ownership	*propriété f de l'État*
public sector	*secteur m public*
public utility	*service m public*
public works	*travaux mpl publics*

to let market forces take effect *laisser agir les tendances du marché*
the outlook is bright/gloomy *les perspectives sont brillantes/sombres*

recession	*récession f*
redevelop	*réaménager*
redevelopment	*réaménagement m*
reflation	*relance f économique*
regional development grant	*subvention f pour l'aménagement du territoire*
resale price maintenance (RPM)	*vente f au détail à prix imposé*
reserve currency	*monnaie f de réserve*
retail price index	*indice m des prix de détail*
revaluation	*réévaluation f*
sanctions	*sanctions fpl*
seasonally-adjusted figures	*chiffres mpl corrigés des variations saisonnières*
shift in demand	*déplacement m de la demande*
silent partner	*commanditaire m*
sinking fund	*fonds m d'amortissement*
sleeping partner	*commanditaire m*
sluggish	*stagnant(e)*
slump *n*	*crise f*
slump *vb*	*s'effondrer*
socioeconomic	*socio-économique*
socioeconomic group	*catégorie f socio-professionnelle*
special development area (SDA)	*zone f d'aménagement prioritaire*
stabilization	*stabilisation f*
stagflation	*stagflation f*
stagnation	*stagnation f*
standard of living	*niveau m de vie*
state-owned	*nationalisé(e)*
subsidize	*subventionner*
subsidy	*subvention f*
supply and demand	*l'offre f et la demande*
support buying	*achats mpl de soutien*
take over *vb*	*reprendre*
takeover *n*	*rachat m*
takeover bid	*offre f publique d'achat (OPA f)*
threshold agreement	*accord m d'indexation des salaires*
trade barrier	*barrière f douanière*

to call in the receivers *faire appel à l'administrateur judiciaire*
to go into receivership *être en règlement judiciaire*
there has been a sharp/gradual rise in ... *il y a eu une hausse soudaine/ progressive de ...*
trade in goods and services *le commerce de biens et services*

undercapitalized	*sous-capitalisé(e)*
under-employment	*sous-emploi m*
unemployment	*chômage m*
unit cost	*coût m unitaire*
unit price	*prix m unitaire*
venture capital	*capital-risque m*
vertical integration	*intégration f verticale*
visible exports	*exportations fpl visibles*
visible imports	*importations fpl visibles*
wage-price spiral	*spirale f prix-salaires*
wage restraint	*contrôle m des salaires*

an upturn in the economy *un redressement de l'économie*

See also **FRENCH ABBREVIATIONS AND INSTITUTIONS**

This is a general abbreviations list. Individual topics contain abbreviations specific to that topic.

When citing company names, it is not usual to translate the abbreviations in the names, e.g. Co, Corp, Inc, Ltd, plc. The translations given here are the equivalents in French.

The use of capital letters and full stops in abbreviations and acronyms may vary.

A/A *(articles of association)*	*statuts* mpl *d'une société*
AAR *(against all risks)*	*contre tous risques*
a/c *(account)*	*C (compte* m*)*
a/c *(account current)*	*CC (compte* m *courant)*
acv *(actual cash value)*	*valeur* f *effective au comptant*
a/d *(... after date)*	*à ... d'échéance*
ADC *(Advice of Duration and Charge)*	*IDP* f *(indication* f *de durée et de prix)*
ad val *(ad valorem)*	*A/V (ad valorem; selon valeur)*
af *(advance freight)*	*fret* m *payé d'avance*
AGM *(annual general meeting)*	*AG* f *(assemblée* f *générale)*
AI *(artificial intelligence)*	*IA* f *(intelligence* f *artificielle)*
AIDA *(Attention, Interest, Desire, Action)*	*AIDA* f *(Attention, Intérêt, Désir, Action)*
aka *(also known as)*	*alias*
am *(ante meridiem)*	*du matin*
AO(C)B *(any other (competent) business)*	*autres matières* fpl *à l'ordre du jour*
approx. *(approximately)*	*env (environ)*
APR *(annual(ized) percentage rate)*	*taux* m *(d'intérêt) annuel*
AR *(account rendered)*	*compte* m *remis*
AR *(annual return)*	*rapport* m *annuel*
A/R *(all risks (insurance))*	*(assurance* f*) tous risques*
A/s *(account sales)*	*compte* m *de ventes*
a/s *(... after sight)*	*à ... de vue*
asap *(as soon as possible)*	*aussitôt que possible*
ASR *(automatic send and receive)*	*expédition* f *et réception* f *automatiques*
asst *(assistant)*	*assistant(e)* m *(*f*)*
av *(average)*	*moyenne* f
B/D *(bank draft)*	*traite* f *bancaire*
B/E *(bill of entry)*	*rapport* m *en douane*
B/E *(bill of exchange)*	*lettre* f *de change*

B/L *(bill of lading)*	*connt (connaissement m)*
BO *(branch office)*	*succursale f, agence f*
B/P *(bills payable)*	*eàp mpl (effets mpl à payer)*
B/R *(bills receivable)*	*eàr mpl (effets mpl à recevoir)*
B/S *(balance sheet)*	*bilan m*
B/S *(bill of sale)*	*acte m de vente*
BST *(British Summer Time)*	*heure f d'été britannique*
© *(copyright)*	*© (copyright m)*
c *(circa)*	*env (environ)*
CA *(chartered accountant)*	*expert-comptable m*
c.a. *(current assets)*	*actif m*
C/A *(current account)*	*CC (compte m courant)*
c & f *(cost and freight)*	*C & F (coût et fret)*
carr *(carriage)*	*port m*
cat *(catalogue)*	*catalogue m*
CB *(cash book)*	*livre m de caisse*
cc *(carbon copy)*	*copie(s) f(pl) à*
CD *(cash discount)*	*remise f au comptant*
c.d. *(cum dividend)*	*c.att. (coupon m attaché)*
CET *(Central European Time)*	*heure f d'Europe centrale*
cf *(compare)*	*cf (voir)*
CH *(customs house)*	*poste m de douane*
CIA *(cash in advance)*	*paiement m d'avance*
CIF *(cost, insurance and freight)*	*CAF (coût, assurance, fret)*
CIF & C *(cost, insurance, freight and commission)*	*CAF & C (coût, assurance, fret et commission)*
CIF & I *(cost, insurance, freight and interest)*	*CAF & I (coût, assurance, fret et intérêts)*
CN *(credit note)*	*avoir m*
Co *(company)*	*Cie (compagnie f)*
c/o *(care of)*	*c/o; a/s (aux bons soins de)*
COD *(cash on delivery, collect on delivery)*	*CR (contre remboursement)*
contd *(continued)*	*suite f*
Corp *(corporation)*	*Sté (société f)*
Coy *(company)*	*Cie (compagnie f)*
C/P *(charter-party)*	*charte-partie f*
cwo *(cash with order)*	*paiement m à la commande*
D/A *(deed of arrangement)*	*concordat m*
D/A *(deposit account)*	*compte m de dépôt*
D/A *(documents against acceptance)*	*documents mpl contre acceptation*
DAP *(documents against payment)*	*DP mpl (documents mpl contre paiement)*
DBA *(doing business as)*	*ayant pour nom commercial*

DCF *(discounted cash flow)*	*cash-flow m actualisé*
DD *(demand draft)*	*bon m à vue*
dept *(department)*	*dépt (département m)*
dis *(discount)*	*remise f*
ditto	*id (idem)*
D/N *(debit note)*	*note f de débit*
doz *(dozen)*	*douz. (douzaine f)*
D/P *(deferred payment)*	*paiement m différé*
D/R *(deposit receipt)*	*récépissé m de dépôt*
ea *(each)*	*chacun(e)*
E&OE *(errors and omissions excepted)*	*se & o (sauf erreur ou omission)*
e.g.	*p. ex. (par exemple)*
EGM *(extraordinary general meeting)*	*AGE f (assemblée f générale extraordinaire)*
enc, encl *(enclosed, enclosure)*	*PJ f(pl) (pièce(s) f(pl) jointe(s))*
esp *(especially)*	*particulièrement*
est *(estimate)*	*estimation f*
est *(estimated)*	*estimé(e)*
est, estd *(established)*	*fondé(e)*
et al	*et autres*
etc	*etc*
et seq	*et suivant(e)s*
excl *(excluding)*	*non-compris(e)*
excl *(exclusive)*	*non-compris(e)*
ext(n) *(extension)*	*poste m*
FAQ *(free alongside quay)*	*FLQ (franco long du quai)*
FAS *(free alongside ship)*	*FLB (franco long du bord)*
FD *(free delivered at dock)*	*livraison f franco à quai*
FIFO *(first in first out)*	*PEPS (premier entré premier sorti)*
fig *(figure)*	*fig. (figure f)*
FO *(firm offer)*	*offre f ferme*
FOB *(free on board)*	*FOB, FAB (franco à bord)*
FOC *(free of charge)*	*gratuitement*
FOT *(free of income tax)*	*exonéré(e) d'impôt m sur le revenu*
FP *(fully paid)*	*entièrement libéré(e)*
FT index	*indice m FT*
GA *(general average)*	*avarie f commune*
GDP *(gross domestic product)*	*PIB m (produit m intérieur brut)*
GM *(general manager)*	*DG m/f (directeur(-trice) m(f) général(e))*
GNP *(gross national product)*	*PNB m (produit m national brut)*
gov(t) *(government)*	*gvt (gouvernement m)*
gr wt *(gross weight)*	*poids m brut*

gtd, guar *(guaranteed)*	*garanti(e)*
h *(hour(s))*	*h (heure(s) f(pl))*
HO *(Head Office)*	*siège m social*
hon *(honorary)*	*honoraire*
HP *(hire purchase)*	*vente f à crédit*
HP *(horsepower)*	*CV (cheval m vapeur)*
HQ *(headquarters)*	*siège m social*
hr *(hour(s))*	*h (heure(s) f(pl))*
ib, ibid *(ibidem)*	*ibid (ibidem)*
i/c *(in charge (of))*	*resp (responsable (de))*
i.e.	*c-à-d (c'est-à-dire)*
Inc *(Incorporated)*	*SA (société f anonyme)*
incl *(including, inclusive)*	*compris(e)*
inst *(instant)*	*ct (courant)*
int *(interest)*	*intérêt m*
inv *(invoice)*	*facture f*
IOU *(an I owe you)*	*reconnaissance f de dette*
IT *(income tax)*	*impôt m sur le revenu*
IT *(information technology)*	*informatique f*
J/A *(joint account)*	*compte m conjoint*
Jr, jun *(junior)*	*Jr.*
k *(thousand)*	*mille*
kph *(kilometres per hour)*	*km/h mpl (kilomètres mpl à l'heure)*
L/C *(letter of credit)*	*LC (lettre f de crédit)*
LIFO *(last in first out)*	*DEPS (dernier entré premier sorti)*
loc cit	*loc cit*
lpm *(lines per minute)*	*lignes/mn (lignes fpl à la minute)*
Ltd *(limited)*	*SARL or SA (société f à responsabilité limitée or société f anonyme)*
M *(million)*	*M (million m)*
max *(maximum)*	*max (maximum m)*
MD *(managing director)*	*DG m/f (directeur(-trice) m(f) général(e))*
Messrs	*MM (Messieurs mpl)*
min *(minimum)*	*min (minimum m)*
min *(minute)*	*mn, min (minute f)*
misc *(miscellaneous)*	*divers*
MO *(mail order)*	*VPC f (vente f par correspondance)*
MO *(money order)*	*mandat m postal*
mo *(month)*	*m (mois m)*
mon *(monetary)*	*monétaire*
Mr	*M. (Monsieur m)*

MRP *(manufacturer's recommended price)* — *prix m de vente conseillé*

Mrs — *Mme (Madame f)*

Ms — *Mme or Mlle (Madame f or Mademoiselle f)*

N/A *(not applicable)* — *n.a. (ne s'applique pas)*

no. *(number)* — *nº (numéro m)*

nr *(near)* — *près (de)*

NS *(not specified)* — *non dénommé*

nt wt *(net weight)* — *poids m net*

O & M *(organization and methods)* — *organisation f et méthodes fpl*

o/d *(on demand)* — *sur demande*

OE *(omissions excepted)* — *sauf omissions*

o.n.o. *(or near(est) offer)* — *déb (à débattre)*

op cit — *op cit*

OR *(operational research)* — *R.O. f (recherche f opérationelle)*

OR *(owner's risk)* — *aux risques mpl et périls mpl du propriétaire*

o/s *(out of stock)* — *épuisé(e)*

PA *(personal assistant)* — *secrétaire m/f particulier(-ière)*

p.a. *(per annum)* — *par an*

P & L A/C *(profit and loss account)* — *compte m pertes et profits*

p & p *(postage and packing)* — *frais mpl de port et d'emballage*

pat *(patent)* — *brevet m (d'invention)*

patd *(patented)* — *breveté(e)*

pat pend *(patent pending)* — *modèle m déposé*

PAYE *(pay as you earn)* — *système de retenue des impôts à la source*

pc, % *(percent)* — *% (pour cent)*

pd *(paid)* — *payé*

PERT *(programme evaluation and review technique)* — *méthode f "PERT"*

ph *(per hour)* — */h ((de) l'heure)*

plc *(public limited company)* — *SARL or SA (société f à responsabilité limitée or société f anonyme)*

pls *(please)* — *SVP (s'il vous plaît)*

pm *(post meridiem)* — *de l'après-midi; du soir*

PN *(promissory note)* — *B/O (billet m à ordre)*

PO *(postal order)* — *mandat m postal*

PO Box — *BP f (boîte f postale)*

POS *(point of sale)* — *point m de vente*

pp *(pages)* — *PP (pages fpl)*

pp *(per procurationem)*   *p.p. (par procuration)*
PR *(public relations)*   *relations fpl publiques*
PRO *(public relations officer)*   *responsable m/f des relations publiques*
pro tem *(pro tempore)*   *temporairement*
prox *(proximo)*   *(du mois) prochain*
PS *(postscript)*   *PS m (post-scriptum m)*
PS *(private secretary)*   *secrétaire m/f particulier(-ière)*
PTO *(please turn over)*   *TSVP (tournez s'il vous plaît)*
Pty *(proprietary (company))*   *sté mère (société f mère)*
pw *(per week)*   *p.sem. (par semaine)*
qv *(quod vide)*   *v. (voir)*
® *(registered trademark)*   *® (marque f déposée)*
re *(regarding)*   *réf. (au sujet de)*
ref *(reference)*   *réf. (référence(s) f(pl))*
RO *(receiving order)*   *ordonnance f de mise sous séquestre*
RP *(reply paid)*   *réponse f payée*
RPM *(resale price maintenance)*   *vente f au détail à prix imposé*
RRP *(recommended retail price)*   *prix m conseillé*
RSVP *(répondez s'il vous plaît)*   *RSVP*
sae *(stamped addressed envelope)*   *enveloppe f affranchie avec adresse*
SD *(sine die)*   *sine die*
SDR *(special drawing rights)*   *DTS mpl (droits mpl de tirage spéciaux)*
SE *(stock exchange)*   *bourse f (des valeurs)*
Sen, Sr *(senior)*   *Sr.*
SI *(Système International (d'Unités))*   *SI m (système m international (d'unités))*
sic   *sic*
SME *(small and medium-sized enterprise)*   *PME f (petite et moyenne entreprise f)*
SN *(shipping note)*   *note f de chargement*
Soc *(society)*   *Sté (société f)*
SOR, S/R *(sale or return)*   *en commission*
STD *(subscriber trunk dialling)*   *automatique m interurbain*
ster, stg *(sterling)*   *livre f sterling*
TB *(treasury bill)*   *bon m du Trésor*
tel *(telephone)*   *tél. (téléphone m)*
TM *(trademark)*   *marque f de fabrique*
ult *(ultimo)*   *du mois dernier*
v *(versus)*   *contre*
v *(vide)*   *v. (voir)*
VAT *(value-added tax)*   *TVA (taxe f à la valeur ajoutée)*

VC *(vice-chairman/woman)*	*vice-président(e)* m *(f)*
viz	*à savoir*
WB *(waybill)*	*récépissé* m
WIP *(work-in-progress)*	*en-cours* m
wk *(week)*	*semaine* f
WP *(word processor)*	*machine* f *de traitement de texte*
wpm *(words per minute)*	*mots/min (mots* mpl *à la minute)*
wt *(weight)*	*pds (poids* m*)*
YAR *(York-Antwerp Rules)*	*règles* fpl *d'York et d'Anvers*
yr *(year)*	*an* m

See also **AT THE HOTEL** *and* **TRAVEL**

MEETING PEOPLE

There are two forms of address in French: the formal *vous* and
the informal *tu*. You are advised to stick to the formal *vous* unless
you know the person well or they themselves initiate the switch to
tu. This may happen over drinks, after successful negotiations, or
if you are invited to your host's home.

The titles *Monsieur, Madame* and *Mademoiselle* are widely
used. If a woman is referred to as *Madame* it does not necessarily
mean that she is married. It is similar to *Ms* in English.

When greeting someone you have never met before use *bonjour, Monsieur* or *bonjour, Madame*, rather than just *bonjour. Bonjour* is fine up to about five o'clock, when you should start using
bonsoir. Handshaking is customary every time you greet or say
goodbye to someone, not just when meeting someone for the first
time. When you are introduced to someone you should acknowledge the introduction by saying *enchanté(e)*.

GREETINGS
Hello *bonjour*
Good morning/good afternoon *bonjour*
Good evening *bonsoir*
Goodnight *bonsoir or bonne nuit**
Goodbye *au revoir*
*bonne nuit is used only just before going to bed

IF YOU'VE NEVER MET
What's your name? *quel est votre nom?*
How do you do? *enchanté(e)* (*the person's name is not used in
    French*)
Pleased to meet you, Mr/Ms Smith *enchanté(e) de faire votre
    connaissance (the person's name is not used in French)*
Here's my (business) card *voici ma carte*
Do you have a (business) card? *avez-vous une carte?*
May I introduce you to ... *je voudrais vous présenter ...*
I don't think we've met. I'm John Smith *permettez-moi de me
    présenter: John Smith*
This is Mr/Mrs ... *je vous présente Monsieur/Madame ...*

IF YOU'VE MET BEFORE
It's nice to see you again! *je suis heureux(-euse) de vous revoir*
How are you? *comment allez-vous?*
(I'm) fine, thank you *(je vais) bien, merci*

I'm/we're pleased you were able to come *je suis heureux(-euse)/ nous sommes heureux(-euses) que vous ayez pu venir*

MAKING YOURSELF UNDERSTOOD
I do not speak much French *je ne parle pas bien français*
I learned French at school *j'ai appris le français à l'école*
Do you speak English? *parlez-vous anglais?*
Would you mind speaking (a bit more) slowly? *pourriez-vous parler (un peu plus) lentement, s'il vous plaît?*
Sorry/pardon? *pardon?*
Could you speak up, please? *pourriez-vous parler plus fort, s'il vous plaît?*
I don't understand *je ne comprends pas*
It doesn't matter *cela n'a pas d'importance*
Can you follow me? *me suivez-vous?*
I understand you quite well *je vous suis très bien*

MAKING GENERAL CONVERSATION

AS HOST
How was your journey/flight? *comment s'est passé votre voyage/vol?*
Did your flight leave on time? *est-ce que vous avez décollé à l'heure?*
Is this your first visit to London/Scotland? *est-ce la première fois que vous venez à Londres/en Écosse?*
You look well *vous avez l'air en pleine forme*
How is Mr/Ms ...? *comment va Monsieur/Madame/Mademoiselle ...?*
How is your family *comment va votre famille?*
How long do you plan to stay in Britain? *combien de temps comptez-vous rester en Grande-Bretagne?*
I have been practising my French since we last met *j'ai travaillé mon français depuis notre dernière rencontre*
Your English is excellent *vous parlez parfaitement l'anglais*
Did you have trouble finding us? *avez-vous eu des difficultés à nous trouver?*
Would you like a cup of coffee/something to drink? *vous prendrez bien un café/quelque chose à boire?*
Where are you staying? *où logez-vous?*
How is business? *comment vont les affaires?*

AS GUEST
My flight was delayed 2 hours *mon vol avait 2 heures de retard*
Thank you for coming to meet me *merci d'être venu(e) à ma ren-*

contre

This is my first visit to your country/town/city *c'est la première fois que je viens dans votre pays/ville*

I'm planning to stay a few days *je compte rester quelques jours*

I'm flying back next week/tomorrow afternoon *je repars la semaine prochaine/demain après-midi*

The weather is so much more pleasant here *le temps est tellement plus agréable ici*

I am staying in the ... hotel *je suis à l'hôtel ...*

IN THE PUB/HOTEL

DRINKS AND DRINKING TERMS

alcohol-free	*non-alcoolisé(e)*
apéritif	*apéritif m*
beer	*bière f*
bitter	*bière f anglaise amère*
bitter lemon	*Schweppes ® m au citron*
brandy	*cognac m*
champagne	*champagne m*
cider	*cidre m*
cocktail	*cocktail m*
Coke ®	*Coca ® m*
crisps	*chips fpl*
dry*	*sec*
fresh orange	*orange f pressée*
gin	*gin m*
gin and tonic	*gin-tonic m*
grapefruit juice	*jus m de pamplemousse*
with ice	*avec des glaçons*
lager	*bière f blonde*
lemon	*citron m*
lemonade	*limonade f*
lime	*citron m vert*
liqueur	*liqueur f*
low-alcohol	*peu alcoolisé(e)*
malt whisky	*whisky m pur malt*
medium dry*	*demi-sec*
mineral water	*eau f minérale*
neat	*sec or sans eau*
orange	*orange f*
peanuts	*cacahuètes fpl*
pineapple juice	*jus m d'ananas*
red wine	*vin m rouge*
rosé wine	*vin m rosé*

rum	*rhum m*
shandy	*panaché m*
sherry	*xérès m*
soda	*soda m*
soft drink	*boisson f non-alcoolisée*
stout	*bière f brune*
straight	*sec or sans eau*
sweet*	*doux*
tonic water	*Schweppes ® m*
vermouth	*vermouth m*
vodka	*vodka f*
white wine	*vin m blanc*
whisky	*whisky m*

*In French, it is more usual to specify the kind of wine you want, for example *un Beaujolais* or *un Muscadet*, rather than to ask for *dry*, *medium* or *sweet* wine.

OFFERING DRINKS

Can I buy you a drink? *puis-je vous offrir quelque chose à boire?*

What would you like to drink? *qu'est-ce que vous prendrez (comme boisson)?*

Would you like an apéritif? *prendrez-vous un apéritif?*

Do you drink it neat? *le prenez-vous sec?*

Would you like ice/lemon in it? *voulez-vous des glaçons/du citron?*

Would you like something to eat? *voulez-vous manger (quelque chose)?*

BUYING DRINKS

I'll have a ..., please *je prendrai un/une ..., s'il vous plaît*

Make mine a double/treble ..., please *je voudrais un double/triple ..., s'il vous plaît*

I don't drink (much) alcohol *je ne bois pas (beaucoup) d'alcool*

Nothing for me, thanks, I'm driving *rien pour moi, merci, je conduis*

No ice, thanks *merci, pas de glaçons*

Do you have any ice? *avez-vous des glaçons?*

Can I have a chilled/an unchilled bottle, please? *je voudrais une bouteille rafraîchie/non-rafraîchie, s'il vous plaît*

SMOKING

Do you smoke? *est-ce que vous fumez?*

Do you mind if I smoke? *est-ce que cela vous gêne si je fume?*

Have you got a light? *avez-vous du feu?*

Can I offer you a light? *voulez-vous du feu?*

Would you like a cigarette? *puis-je vous offrir une cigarette?*
What brand do you smoke? *quelle marque fumez-vous?*
It's very smoky in here *c'est très enfumé ici*
No thanks, I don't smoke *(non) merci, je ne fume pas*

EATING OUT

IN THE RESTAURANT
Never make the mistake of calling *garçon!* when you want to
attract the waiter's attention. This is considered very offensive. To
call a waiter/waitress use *s'il vous plaît.*

ARRIVING AT THE RESTAURANT
A table for two/three, please *une table pour deux/trois, s'il vous
    plaît*
I have/don't have a reservation *j'ai réservé/je n'ai pas réservé*
I have reserved a table for three *j'ai réservé une table pour trois*
Could we have a menu, please? *je voudrais voir la carte, s'il vous
    plaît*

ORDERING
Do you have a set menu? *y a-t-il un menu?*
I'll take the menu at 150F *je prendrai le menu à 150F*
I'd like (the) ... *je prendrai le/la/les ...*
And ... to follow *et ensuite ...*
What do you recommend? *que (me/nous) recommandez-vous?*
May I see the wine list? *je voudrais voir la carte des vins*
Which wine would you recommend with ...? *qu'est-ce que vous
    recommandez comme vin avec ...?*
What is the dish of the day? *quel est le plat du jour?*
What is (the) ...? *qu'est-ce que c'est que le/la ...?*
How is this dish cooked? *comment est préparé ce plat?*
Are there any vegetarian dishes on the menu? *y a-t-il des plats
    végétariens au menu?*
Can I have the ... but without the ...? *est-il possible d'avoir le/la/
    les ..., mais sans ...?*
Is this dish very spicy? *est-ce un plat très relevé?*
Does this have ... in it? *y a-t-il ... dans ce plat?*
Are vegetables included? *est-ce que les légumes sont compris?*
Could you bring some (more) water/bread/butter, please? *je
    voudrais (encore) de l'eau/du pain/du beurre, s'il vous plaît*
What types of cheese do you have? *qu'est-ce que vous avez
    comme fromages?*
Nothing else, thank you *plus rien, merci*

PROBLEMS

This is not what I ordered *ce n'est pas ce que j'ai commandé*
I ordered ... *j'ai commandé ...*
My food is cold *mon repas est froid*
This is off *ce n'est pas frais*
My steak/fish is burnt *mon steak/poisson est brûlé*
You haven't brought me my salad/dessert yet *je n'ai pas encore reçu ma salade/mon dessert*

PAYING

Could I have the bill, please? *puis-je avoir l'addition/la note (s'il vous plaît)?* (*la note* would be used in a smarter restaurant)
The meal was delicious *le repas était délicieux*
Is service included? *est-ce que le service est compris?*
There seems to be a mistake here *il doit y avoir une erreur ici*
What is this sum for? *à quoi correspond cette somme?*

TIPPING

In Belgium and Luxembourg, service charges are usually included in the price but an extra tip may be given for outstanding service. If service is not included, it is usual to leave a tip of 12–15% of the bill.

In France, service is always included in the price unless clearly stated otherwise. Quite often, however, the small change left from paying the bill is given as an extra tip. If service is not included the tip is usually 12–15% of the bill.

In Quebec, the service charge is not included, unless otherwise indicated, and it is customary to leave a tip of 15% of the pre-VAT total.

In Switzerland, service is automatically included in the bill and a tip is not expected.

See also **THE EUROPEAN COMMUNITY**

additive	*additif m*
aerosol spray	*aérosol m*
air pollution	*pollution f de l'air*
anti-pollution measure	*mesure f antipollution*
atmosphere	*atmosphère f*
baseline study	*étude f de départ*
biodegradable	*biodégradable*
biosphere	*biosphère f*
breakdown *(of matter)*	*décomposition f*
CFC (chlorofluorocarbon)	*CFC m (chlorofluorocarbone m)*
clean air	*air m pur*
clean technology	*techniques fpl non-polluantes*
clean up *vb*	*nettoyer*
clean-up campaign	*campagne f de nettoyage*
colouring	*colorant m*
compliance audit	*vérification f de conformité*
conservation	*défense f de l'environnement*
conserve	*préserver*
contaminate	*contaminer*
contamination	*contamination f*
damaging	*nuisible*
decontaminate	*décontaminer*
degradation	*dégradation f*
Department of the Environment (DOE)	*Ministère m britannique de l'environnement*
detergent	*détergent m*
development area	*zone f exploitable*
directive	*directive f*
dump *n*	*décharge f*
dump *vb*	*déverser*
dumping	*déversement m*
ecological	*écologique*
ecologist	*écologiste m/f*
ecology	*écologie f*
emission	*émission f*
energy conservation	*économies fpl d'énergie*
energy-saving device	*dispositif m d'économie d'énergie*
energy-saving policy	*politique f d'économie d'énergie*

to clean up one's act *prendre des dispositions antipollution*
to have a high/low lead content *avoir une teneur en plomb élevée/avoir une faible teneur en plomb*
the effect of this on the environment *l'effet de ceci sur l'environnement*

environment	*environnement m*
environmental assessment	*évaluation f environnementale*
environmental audit	*audit m environnement*
environmental damage	*atteintes fpl à l'environnement*
environmental impact	*impact m sur l'environnement*
environmentalist	*écologiste m/f*
environmental lobby	*groupe m de pression écologiste*
environmentally friendly	*écologique*
environmental management	*gestion f de l'environnement*
environmental statement	*rapport m sur l'environnement*
filter	*filtre m*
fossil fuel	*combustible m fossile*
global warming	*réchauffement m de la planète*
green	*vert(e)*
greenfield site	*site m vierge*
greenhouse effect	*effet m de serre*
greenhouse gas	*gaz m entraînant l'effet de serre*
greening	*orientation f écologique*
green issues	*questions fpl écologiques*
guideline	*directive f*
health hazard	*risque m pour la santé*
herbicide	*herbicide m*
impact *n*	*impact m*
impact (on) *vb*	*avoir un impact (sur)*
insecticide	*insecticide m*
Integrated Pollution Control (IPC)	*contrôle m antipollution intégré*
landfill site	*décharge f*
leakage	*fuite f*
legislation	*législation f*
minimize	*minimiser*
natural resources	*ressources fpl naturelles*
noise pollution	*pollution f par le bruit*
noxious substance	*substance f toxique*
nuclear waste	*déchets mpl nucléaires*
optimum	*optimum m*
outflow	*efflux m*
ozone-friendly	*qui ne détruit pas l'ozone*
ozone-safe	*sans danger pour l'ozone*

to stress the environmental advantages of a product *insister sur les atouts écologiques d'un produit*

this product is "greener" than its competitors *ce produit est "plus vert" que ses rivaux*

the greening of industry *l'orientation de plus en plus écologique de l'industrie*

parameter	*paramètre m*
pesticide	*pesticide m*
phosphates	*phosphates mpl*
pollutant	*polluant m*
pollute	*polluer*
polluted	*pollué(e)*
pollution	*pollution f*
pollution-free *(product, process)*	*non-polluant(e)*
preservation	*préservation f*
propellant	*fluide m pulseur*
protect	*protéger*
radioactivity	*radioactivité f*
recyclable	*recyclable*
recycle	*recycler*
recycled	*recyclé(e)*
recycling plant	*usine f de traitement*
regulator	*organisme m législateur*
residue	*reste m*
resource utilization	*exploitation f des ressources*
reusable	*réutilisable*
smoke	*fumée f*
spoil *n*	*rejet m*
spoil *vb*	*gâcher*
standards	*normes fpl*
sustainable development	*développement m soutenable*
toxic	*toxique*
toxicity	*toxicité f*
toxin	*toxine f*
treat	*traiter*
waste	*déchets mpl*
waste disposal	*élimination f des déchets*
waste management	*gestion f des déchets*
waste minimization	*minimisation f des déchets*
waste product	*déchet m*
water pollution	*pollution f des eaux*

this product helps to protect the environment *ce produit contribue à la protection de l'environnement*

this packaging contains 90% recycled material *cet emballage est constitué à 90% de matériaux recyclés*

it is our aim to reduce emissions by 25% (by next year) *nous visons à réduire les émissions de 25% (d'ici l'année prochaine)*

to respect all the regulations governing pollution levels *respecter toutes les règlementations liées aux niveaux de pollution*

this chemical has a very high/low toxicity level *ce produit chimique possède un niveau de toxicité très élevé/faible*

See also **THE ENVIRONMENT, INSTITUTIONS AND ORGANIZA-TIONS** *and* **FRENCH ABBREVIATIONS AND INSTITUTIONS**

associated states	*états mpl associés*
CERN (Conseil Européen pour la Recherche Nucléaire)	*CERN m*
Channel Tunnel	*tunnel m sous la Manche*
collaborative project	*projet m collaboratif*
Common Agricultural Policy (CAP)	*Politique f agricole commune (PAC f)*
Common Budget	*Budget m communautaire*
Common External Tariff (CET)	*tarif m douanier commun*
Common Market	*Marché m commun*
community law	*droit m communautaire*
continental	*continental(e)*
continental Europe	*Europe f continentale*
Council of Europe	*Conseil m de l'Europe*
Council of Ministers	*Conseil m des Ministres*
directive	*directive f*
directorate	*(conseil m d)'administration f*
Directorate General (DG)	*Direction f Générale (DG f)*
EC (European Community)	*CE f (Communauté f européenne)*
ECU (European Currency Unit)	*écu m*
EEC (European Economic Community)	*CEE f (Communauté f économique européenne)*
EEC directive	*directive f de la CEE*
EEC national	*ressortissant(e) m(f) de la CEE*
EEC passport	*passeport m de la CEE*
EEC passport-holder	*titulaire m/f d'un passeport de la CEE*
EEC regulations	*règlements mpl de la CEE*
EEC subsidy	*subvention f de la CEE*
ESPRIT (European Strategic Programme for Research & Development in Information Technology)	*ESPRIT m*

we want/have better access to European markets *nous voulons/avons un meilleur accès aux marchés européens*
with the opening of the Channel Tunnel *avec l'ouverture du Tunnel sous la Manche*
the external value of the ECU *la valeur externe de l'écu*
weights of currencies in the ECU *le poids des devises au sein de l'écu*
we will accept payment in ECUs *nous accepterons les règlements en écus*
to enter the EEC *entrer dans la CEE*

EURATOM	*EURATOM f, Communauté f européenne de l'énergie atomique (CEEA f)*
EUREKA (European Research & Coordination Agency)	*EUREKA f*
euro-ad	*pub f paneuropéenne*
Eurobeach	*plage f conforme aux normes européennes*
Eurobond	*euro-obligation f*
Eurobond issue	*émission f d'euro-obligations*
Eurocheque	*eurochèque m*
Eurocheque card	*carte f eurochèque*
Eurocrat	*eurocrate m/f*
Eurocurrency	*eurodevise f*
Eurocurrency credit	*crédit m en eurodevises*
Eurocurrency market	*marché m des eurodevises*
Eurodeposit	*eurodépôt m*
eurodollar	*eurodollar m*
EUROENVIRON	*EUROENVIRON m*
Euromarket	*euromarché m*
Euro MP	*député m européen*
Europe	*Europe f*
European *n*	*Européen(ne) m(f)*
European *adj*	*européen(ne)*
European Bank for Reconstruction and Development (EBRD)	*Banque f européenne de la reconstruction et du développement (BERD f)*
European Broadcasting Union (EBU)	*Union f européenne de radiodiffusion (UER f)*
European Coal and Steel Community (ECSC)	*Communauté f européenne du charbon et de l'acier (CECA f)*
European Commission	*Commission f des CE*
European Community (EC)	*Communauté f européenne (CE f)*
European Court of Auditors	*Cour f des Comptes (des CE)*
European Court of Justice (ECJ)	*Cour f de Justice des communautés européennes (CJCE f)*
European Development Fund (EDF)	*Fonds m européen de développement (FED m)*
European directive	*directive f européenne*

to take out a eurodollar loan *contracter un emprunt en eurodollars*
we are a very European company *nous sommes une société très européenne*

European Economic Community (EEC)	*Communauté f économique européenne (CEE f)*
European Free Trade Area	*Zone f européenne de libre échange*
European Free Trade Association (EFTA)	*Association f européenne de libre échange (AELE f)*
European Investment Bank (EIB)	*Banque f européenne d'investissement (BEI f)*
Europeanize	*européaniser*
European Monetary Cooperation Fund (EMCF)	*Fonds m européen de coopération monétaire (FECOM m)*
European Monetary System (EMS)	*Système m monétaire européen (SME m)*
European Monetary Union (EMU)	*union f monétaire européenne*
European Parliament (EP)	*Parlement m européen (PE m)*
European Regional Development Fund (ERDF)	*Fonds m européen de développement régional (FEDER m)*
European Social Fund	*Fonds m social européen*
European Space Agency (ESA)	*Agence f spatiale européenne (ASE f)*
European Union	*Union f européenne*
European Unit of Account (EUA)	*Unité f de compte européenne (UCE f)*
Europhile	*europhile m/f*
Europort	*Europort m*
Eurosterling	*euro-sterling m*
Eurotunnel	*eurotunnel m*
Exchange Rate Mechanism (ERM)	*mécanisme m de change*
federal	*fédéral(e)*
federalism	*fédéralisme m*
federation	*fédération f*
free trade	*libre-échange m*
green pound	*livre f verte*
guideline	*directive f*
hard ECU	*écu m fort*

we are hoping to expand our business with continental Europe *nous espérons développer nos affaires avec l'Europe continentale*
free movement of labour and capital throughout Europe *la libre circulation de la main-d'œuvre et des capitaux en Europe*
this product/measure respects all the EC guidelines on ... *ce produit/cette mesure respecte toutes les directives de la CE sur ...*

intra-community trade	*commerce m intracommunautaire*
Member States	*États mpl membres*
MEP (Member of the European Parliament)	*membre m du Parlement européen*
Organization for Economic Cooperation and Development (OECD)	*Organisation f de coopération et de développement économiques (OCDE f)*
pan-European	*paneuropéen(ne)*
single (European) market	*marché m unique, grand marché m (européen)*
subsidize	*subventionner*
subsidy	*subvention f*
trade barrier	*barrière f douanière*

to look towards Europe for business *se tourner vers le reste de l'Europe pour les affaires*
within the single market *au sein du marché unique*
to take advantage of the abolition of trade barriers *profiter de l'abolition des barrières douanières*

See also **THE EUROPEAN COMMUNITY**

When citing company names, it is not usual to translate the abbreviations in the names, such as SA, SARL. The translations given here are the equivalents in English.

The use of capital letters and full stops in abbreviations and acronyms may vary.

For a guide to pronouncing the letters of the alphabet in French, see page viii.

A2 *(Antenne 2 f)*	*French TV channel*
a.c. *(année f courante)*	*this year*
ach. *(achète)*	*buy(s)*
adr. *(adresse f)*	*address*
AELE *f (Association f européenne de libre échange)*	*EFTA (European Free Trade Association)*
AF *(Air France)*	*Air France*
AF *f (Assemblée f fédérale)*	*Swiss Parliament*
AFNOR *f (Association f française de normalisation)*	*French industrial standards authority*
AFP *f (Agence f France-Presse)*	*French press agency*
AG *f (assemblée f générale)*	*AGM (annual general meeting)*
ag. *(agence f)*	*agency; branch; office*
agce *f (agence f)*	*agency; branch; office*
AGE *f (assemblée f générale extraordinaire)*	*EGM (extraordinary general meeting)*
AID *f (Association f internationale pour le développement)*	*IDA (International Development Association)*
AIEA *f (Agence f internationale de l'énergie nucléaire)*	*IAEA (International Atomic Energy Agency)*
AM *f (assurance f maladie)*	*health insurance*
AN *f (Assemblée f nationale)*	*French Parliament*
ANPE *f (Agence f nationale pour l'emploi)*	*French department of employment; job centre*
APL *f (aide f personnalisée au logement)*	*French government aid for house-buyers*
appt *m (appartement m)*	*apt (apartment, flat)*
apr. *(après)*	*after*
AR *m (accusé m de réception)*	*acknowledgement of receipt*
AR *m (aller m (et) retour)*	*return (ticket)*
arr(t) *m (arrondissement m)*	*district (of Paris)*
Arts *mpl* **et Métiers**	*French school of engineering, technology and administration*
AS *fpl (assurances fpl sociales)*	*National Insurance*

a/s *(aux soins de)* — c/o *(care of)*

ASBL *f (association f sans but lucratif)* — non-profit-making organization

ASE *f (Agence f spatiale européenne)* — ESA *(European Space Agency)*

ASSEDIC *f (Association f pour l'emploi dans l'industrie et le commerce)* — French unemployment benefits department

AV *m (avis m de virement)* — advice of bank transfer

A/V *(ad valorem; selon valeur f)* — ad val *(ad valorem)*

avt *(avant)* — before

Banque *f* **Mondiale** — WB *(World Bank)*

Bat. *(bâtiment m)* — building

bcp *(beaucoup)* — a lot

BEI *f (Banque f européenne d'investissement)* — EIB *(European Investment Bank)*

BERD *f (Banque f européenne de la reconstruction et du développement)* — EBRD *(European Bank for Reconstruction and Development)*

BIRD *f (Banque f internationale pour la reconstruction et le développement)* — IBRD *(International Bank for Reconstruction and Development)*

BIT *m (Bureau m international du travail)* — ILO *(International Labour Organization)*

B/O *(billet m à ordre)* — PN *(promissory note)*

BP *f (boîte f postale)* — PO Box

BPF *(bon pour francs)* — value in francs *(BPF appears on cheques before the space for the amount to be inserted)*

BRI *f (Banque f des règlements internationaux)* — BIS *(Bank for International Settlements)*

bt. *(brut)* — gross

BTP *mpl (bâtiments mpl et travaux mpl publics)* — construction industry

BVP *m (Bureau m de vérification de la publicité)* — ASA *(Advertising Standards Authority)*

C *(compte m)* — a/c *(account)*

CA *m (chiffre m d'affaires)* — turnover

CA *m (conseil m d'administration)* — board of directors

CAC *f:* **indice CAC** *(Compagnie f des agents de change)* — French equivalent of the FT index, Dow Jones average

c-à-d *(c'est-à-dire)* — i.e.

CAF *(coût, assurance, fret)* — CIF *(cost, insurance and freight)*

CAF & C *(coût m, assurance, fret et commission)* — CIF & C *(cost, insurance, freight and commission)*

CAF & I *(coût m, assurance, fret et intérêts)* — CIF & I *(cost, insurance, freight and interest)*

CAM *f (carte f à mémoire)* — smart card

CAO *f (conception f assistée par ordinateur)* — CAD *(computer-aided design)*

c.att. *(coupon m attaché)* — c.d. *(cum dividend)*

CB *f (Carte f Bleue ®)* — credit card

CBI *f (Carte f Bleue Internationale ®)* — international credit card

CC *m (compte m courant)* — C/A *(current account)*

CCI *f (Chambre f de commerce et d'industrie)* — chamber of commerce and industry

CCI *f (Chambre f de commerce internationale)* — ICC *(International Chamber of Commerce)*

CCP *m (compte m courant postal; compte m chèque postal)* — Post Office current account

CD *m (comité m directeur)* — steering committee

CDD *m (contrat m à durée déterminé)* — fixed-term employment contract

CDF, C.d.F. *mpl (Charbonnages mpl de France)* — French national coal company

CDI *m (centre m des impôts)* — tax office

CE *m (comité m d'entreprise)* — works council

CE *f (caisse f d'épargne)* — savings bank

CE *f or fpl (Communauté(s) f(pl) européenne(s))* — EC *(European Community)*

CEA *m (Commissariat m à l'énergie atomique)* — French atomic energy authority

CECA *f (Communauté f européenne du charbon et de l'acier)* — ECSC *(European Coal and Steel Community)*

CEDEX *(Courrier m d'entreprise à distribution exceptionnelle)* — accelerated postal service for bulk users

CEE *f (Communauté f économique européenne)* — EEC *(European Economic Community)*

CEEA *f (Communauté f européenne de l'énergie atomique)* — Euratom *(European Atomic Energy Community)*

CERN *m (Conseil m européen pour la recherche nucléaire)* — CERN

CFA *m:* **franc CFA** *(Communauté f financière africaine)* — CFA franc

CFAO *f (conception f de fabrication assistée par ordinateur)* — CAM *(computer-aided manufacture)*

CFCE *m (Centre m français du Commerce Extérieur)* — French Board of Trade

CFDT f *(Confédération f française et démocratique du travail)* — French trade union

CFF m *(Chemin m de fer fédéral)* — Swiss railways

CFL m *(Chemin m de fer luxembourgeois)* — Luxembourg railways

CFP m *(Centre m de formation professionnelle)* — professional training centre

CFP f *(Compagnie f française des pétroles)* — French national oil company

CFTC f *(Confédération f française des travailleurs chrétiens)* — French trade union

CGC f *(Confédération f générale des cadres)* — French management union

CGPME f *(Confédération f générale des petites et moyennes entreprises)* — confederation of small and medium-sized businesses

CGT f *(Confédération f générale du travail)* — French trade union

ch. *(charges fpl)* — (service) charges, fees

ch. *(cherche)* — seeks

cial *(commercial)* — commercial

Cie *(compagnie f)* — Co. (company)

CIJ f *(Cour f internationale de justice)* — ICJ (International Court of Justice)

CJCE f *(Cour f de justice des communautés européennes)* — ECJ (European Court of Justice)

CLT f *(Compagnie f Luxembourgeoise de Télévision)* — Luxembourg TV company

CNAM m *(Conservatoire m national des arts et métiers)* — French school of engineering, technology and administration

CNC m *(comité m national de la consommation)* — national consumers' council

CNCL f *(Commission f nationale de la communication et des libertés)* — French independent broadcasting authority

CNE f *(Caisse f nationale d'épargne)* — national savings bank

CNES m *(Centre m national d'études spatiales)* — French space research centre

CNIL f *(Commission f nationale de l'informatique et des libertés)* — French body governing data protection

CNIT m *(Centre m national des industries et des techniques)* — exhibition centre in Paris

CNP *f (Caisse f nationale de prévoyance)* — French savings bank

CNPF *m (Conseil m national du patronat français)* — national council of French employers

CNUCED *f (Conférence f des Nations Unies pour le commerce et le développement)* — UNCTAD (UN Conference on Trade and Development)

CODEVI *m (compte m pour le développement industriel)* — type of French investment account

COFACE *f (Compagnie f française d'assurance pour le commerce)* — French Export Credit Guarantee Department

connt *m (connaissement m)* — B/L (bill of lading)

Conseil *m* **Fédéral** — Swiss Parliament

cps *(caractères mpl par seconde)* — cps (characters per second)

cpt *(comptant)* — cash

cpte *m (compte m)* — a/c (account)

CR *m (compte m rendu)* — report

C.R. *(contre remboursement)* — COD (cash on delivery, collect on delivery)

cse *(cause f)* — cause; case

ct *(courant)* — inst (instant)

C.U. *f (charge f utile)* — payload

CV *m (cheval m vapeur)* — HP (horsepower)

CVS *adj (corrigé des variations saisonnières)* — seasonally adjusted

DA *mpl (documents mpl contre acceptation)* — D/A (documents against acceptance)

DAO *m (dessin m assisté par ordinateur)* — CAD (computer-aided design)

DATAR *f (Délégation f à l'aménagement du territoire et à l'action régionale)* — French regional development agency

déb. *(à débattre)* — o.n.o. (or near(est) offer)

dép. *m (départ m)* — dep. (departure)

dép. *m (département m)* — dept (department)

DEPS *(dernier entré premier sorti)* — LIFO (last in first out)

dépt *m (département m)* — dept (department)

DG *m (directeur m général)* — MD; GM (managing director, chief executive; general manager)

Dir. *f (direction f)* — management

DOM *m (Département m d'outre-mer)* — French overseas "département" (e.g. Guadeloupe, Réunion)

DOM-TOM *mpl (Départements et territoires mpl d'outre-mer)*	*French territories overseas*
douz. *f (douzaine f)*	*doz (dozen)*
DP *mpl (documents mpl contre paiement)*	*DAP (documents against payment)*
DPO *f (direction f par objectifs)*	*management by objectives*
dr. *(droit(e))*	*R (right)*
ds *(dans)*	*in*
DTS *mpl (droits mpl de tirage spéciaux)*	*SDR (special drawing rights)*
EAO *m (enseignement m assisté par ordinateur)*	*CAL (computer-aided learning)*
eàp *mpl (effets mpl à payer)*	*B/P (bills payable)*
eàr *mpl (effets mpl à recevoir)*	*B/R (bills receivable)*
éd. *f (édition f)*	*ed. (edition)*
EDF *f (Électricité f de France)*	*French state electricity company*
édit. *m (éditeur m)*	*publisher; editor*
ENA *f (École f nationale d'administration)*	*French college for senior civil servants*
env *(environ)*	*approx.*
et coll. *(et collaborateurs)*	*et al*
E.-U. *mpl (États-Unis mpl)*	*US (United States)*
EU(A) *mpl (États-Unis (d'Amérique) mpl)*	*US(A) (United States (of America))*
EV *(en ville)*	*in town, in the city*
exp. *(expéditeur m)*	*sender*
FAO *f (fabrication f assistée par ordinateur)*	*CAM (computer-aided manufacture)*
FB *(franc m belge)*	*FB, BF (Belgian franc)*
FECOM *m (Fonds m européen de coopération monétaire)*	*EMCF (European Monetary Co-operation Fund)*
FED *m (Fonds m européen de développement)*	*EDF (European Development Fund)*
FGA *m (Fonds m de garantie automobile)*	*fund financed through insurance premiums to compensate road accident victims*
FIDA *m (Fonds m international de développement agricole)*	*IFAD (International Fund for Agricultural Development)*
FIO *f (fabrication f intégrée par ordinateur)*	*CIM (computer integrated manufacturing)*
FLB *(franco long du bord)*	*FAS (free alongside ship)*
FLQ *(franco long du quai)*	*FAQ (free alongside quay)*
FMI *m (Fonds m Monétaire International)*	*IMF (International Monetary Fund)*

FNSEA f (Fédération f nationale des syndicats d'exploitants agricoles)	French farmers' union
FR3 (France Régions 3)	French TV channel
Frs. (frères mpl)	Bros. (brothers)
FS (franc m suisse)	FS, SF (Swiss franc)
G (gauche)	L (left)
g (gramme m)	g (gram(me))
GAB m (guichet m automatique de banque)	ATM (automated telling machine)
garde m **des Sceaux**	French Minister of Justice
gd (grand)	L, lge (large)
GDF m (Gaz m de France)	French national gas company
GIE m (groupement m d'intérêt économique)	trade association
GRE f (garantie f contre les risques à l'exportation)	guarantee against damage or loss during export
gvt m (gouvernement m)	gov(t) (government)
h ((à l')heure f)	(p)h ((per) hour)
hab. m (habitant m)	inhabitant
hdb. (heures fpl de bureau)	office hours
HEC f (École f des hautes études commerciales)	prestigious French college for management and business studies
Hexagone m	informal name for France
HLM m or f (habitation f à loyer modéré)	council flat or house
HO (hors œuvre)	labour not included
HS fpl (heures fpl supplémentaires)	overtime
HS (hors service)	out of order
HT (hors taxe(s))	exclusive of tax
IA f (intelligence f artificielle)	AI (artificial intelligence)
id (idem)	ditto
IFOP m (Institut m français d'opinion publique)	French market research institute
IGF m (impôt m sur les grandes fortunes)	wealth tax
IUT m (Institut m universitaire de technologie)	technical university
INC m (Institut m national de la consommation)	French consumer research organization
INPI m (Institut m national de la propriété industrielle)	French patent office

INRA m *(Institut m national de la recherche agronomique)*	French agronomical research institute
INSEE m *(Institut m national de la statistique et des études économiques)*	French institute of statistics and economics
INSERM m *(Institut m national de la santé et de la recherche médicale)*	French medical research institute
Inspection f **des Finances**	tax inspectorate
Inspection f **du Travail**	factory inspectorate and body ruling on conditions of employment
IPC m *(Indice m des prix à la consommation)*	CPI (Consumer Price Index)
IRPP m *(impôt m sur le revenu des personnes physiques)*	income tax
ITP m *(ingénieur m des travaux publics)*	civil engineer
J *(jour m)*	day
JO m *(Journal m officiel (de la République Française))*	French government bulletin of laws and official announcements
K *(kilo m)*	kg (kilogram)
Ko *(kilooctet m)*	KB (kilobyte)
LC f *(lettre f de crédit)*	L/C (letter of credit)
LEP m *(livret m d'épargne populaire)*	type of interest-paying account for low earners
LTA f *(lettre f de transport aérien)*	air waybill
M *(million m)*	M (million)
m *(mois m)*	mo (month)
M. *(Monsieur m)*	Mr
Matif m *(Marché m à terme des instruments financiers)*	regulating body of French stock exchange
MD *(marque f déposée)*	® (registered trademark)
Me *(Maître m)*	term of address for lawyers etc
MF *(millions mpl de francs)*	millions of francs
MIDEM m *(Marché m international du disque et des éditions musicales)*	French music industry trade fair
Mlle *(Mademoiselle f)*	Miss, Ms
MM *(Messieurs mpl)*	Messrs
Mme *(Madame f)*	Mrs, Ms
mn. *(minute f)*	min (minute)
MO f *(main-d'œuvre f)*	labour costs
Mo *(méga-octet m)*	MB (megabyte)
Mo *(métro m)*	metro (station)

M.P. *m (mandat m postal)* — postal order, money order

n.a. *(ne s'applique pas)* — N/A (not applicable)

nb *m (nombre m)* — no. (number)

n.c. *(non communiqué)* — unknown

n.c. *(non coté)* — not listed, not quoted

n.d. *(non daté)* — undated

n.d. *(non disponible)* — unavailable

N.D.L.R. *(note f de la rédaction)* — editor's note

NF *(norme f française)* — French approved standard of manufacture

**n° ** *m (numéro m)* — no. (number)

NPI *m(pl) (nouveau(x) pays m(pl) industrialisé(s))* — newly industrialized country (countries)

N/Réf *(notre référence f)* — our ref

NSP *(ne sais pas)* — don't know

OCDE *f (Organisation f de co-opération et de développement économique)* — OECD (Organization for Economic Cooperation and Development)

OIC *f (Organisation f internationale du commerce)* — ITO (International Trade Organization)

OIT *f (Organisation f internationale du travail)* — ILO (International Labour Organization)

ONU *f (Organisation f des nations unies)* — UN (United Nations)

ONUDI *f (Organisation f des Nations Unies pour le développement industriel)* — UNIDO (UN Industrial Development Organization)

OPA *f (offre f publique d'achat)* — takeover bid

OPAEP *f (Organisation f des pays arabes exportateurs de pétrole)* — OAPEC (Organization of Arab Petroleum Exporting Countries)

OPE *f (offre f publique d'échange)* — takeover bid where bidder offers shares in his company for shares in target company

OPEP *f (Organisation f des pays exportateurs de pétrole)* — OPEC (Organization of Petroleum-Exporting Countries)

OS *m (ouvrier m spécialisé)* — semiskilled worker

OTAN *f (Organisation f du traité de l'Atlantique Nord)* — NATO (North Atlantic Treaty Organization)

PAC *f (Politique f agricole commune)* — CAP (Common Agricultural Policy)

PAF *m (paysage m audiovisuel français)* — collective term for all French TV and radio

PAO *f (publication f assistée par ordinateur)* — DTP (desktop publishing)

PAP *m (prêt m pour l'accession à la propriété)* — home buyers' loan, mortgage

PC *m (permis m de construire)* — planning permission

pcc *(pour copie conforme)* — certified accurate

PCV: appeler en PCV *(percevoir)* — to make a reverse-charge call (in France, this facility is only available for international calls)

PDG *m (président-directeur m général)* — chairman and chief executive officer

pds *m (poids m)* — wt (weight)

p.ê. *(peut-être)* — perhaps

PE *m (Parlement m européen)* — EP (European Parliament)

PEL *m (plan m d'épargne logement)* — savings plan providing cheaper mortgage

PEPS *(premier entré premier sorti)* — FIFO (first in first out)

PER *m (plan m d'épargne retraite)* — personal pension plan

p. ex. *(par exemple)* — e.g. (for example)

p.i. *(par intérim)* — interim, acting

PIB *m (produit m intérieur brut)* — GDP (gross domestic product)

PJ *f(pl) (pièce(s) f(pl) jointe(s))* — enc, encl (enclosed, enclosure)

PL *m (poids m lourd)* — HGV (heavy goods vehicle)

PLV *f (publicité f sur le lieu de vente)* — POS material

p.m. *(pour mémoire)* — for the record

PME *f(pl) (petite(s) et moyenne(s) entreprise(s) f(pl))* — SME (small and medium-sized business(es))

PMI *f(pl) (petite(s) et moyenne(s) industrie(s) f(pl))* — small and medium-sized industries

PNB *m (produit m national brut)* — GNP (gross national product)

p.o. *(par ordre)* — pp (per procurationem)

Ponts *mpl* **et chaussées** — French department of civil engineering; French school of civil engineering

PP *(pages fpl)* — pp. (pages)

p.p. *(par procuration)* — pp (per procurationem)

PR *f (poste restante f)* — poste restante

pr *(pour)* — for

à prox. *(à proximité f)* — nr (near)

PS *m (post-scriptum m)* — PS

p.sem. *(par semaine f)* — pw (per week)

PTMA *m (poids m total maximum autorisé)* — maximum permitted load

PTT *fpl (Postes Télécommunications et Télédiffusion fpl)* — French post office

PV *m (procès-verbal m)*	minutes; parking ticket
PVD *m (pays m en voie de développement)*	developing country
px *m (prix m)*	price
qqch. *(quelque chose)*	sth (something)
qqe(s) *(quelque(s))*	some
qqn *(quelqu'un)*	s.o. (someone)
Quai *m* **d'Orsay**	French foreign office
RAS *(rien à signaler)*	nothing to report
RATP *f (Régie f autonome des transports parisiens)*	Paris transport authority
RBE *m (revenu m brut d'exploitation)*	gross profit (of a farm)
R-D *f (recherche-développement f)*	R & D (research and development)
RDA *f (République f démocratique allemande)*	GDR (German Democratic Republic, East Germany)
RDB *m (revenu m disponible brut)*	total income (of a family etc)
rdc *m (rez-de-chaussée m)*	ground floor
réf. *f (référence(s) f(pl))*	ref (reference)
réf. *(au sujet m de)*	re (regarding)
RER *m (Réseau m express régional)*	Paris region high-speed train service
RES *m (rachat m de l'entreprise par ses salariés)*	management buyout
resp *(responsable (de))*	i/c (in charge (of))
RF *f (République f française)*	French Republic
RFA *f (République f fédérale d'Allemagne)*	FRG (Federal Republic of Germany)
R.F.I. *f (Radio f France International f)*	French overseas radio, like the BBC World Service
RFO *f (Radio-Télévision f Française d'Outre-mer)*	French overseas broadcasting service
RIB *m (relevé m d'identité bancaire)*	slip provided by bank showing account numbers, holder's name etc
RIP *m (relevé m d'identité postal)*	slip provided by post office showing details of post office account
RLE *m (réseau m local d'entreprise)*	LAN (local area network)
RMI *m (revenu m minimum d'insertion)*	French income support
RN *f (route f nationale)*	A road

R.O. *f (recherche f opérationelle)* — OR (operational research)

RP *f (recette f principale)* — main post office

RP *f (région f parisienne)* — Paris region

RSVP *(répondez s'il vous plaît)* — RSVP

RV *m (rendez-vous m)* — appointment

SA *f (société f anonyme)* — Ltd, plc (limited company)

SACEM *f (Société f des auteurs, compositeurs et éditeurs de musique)* — French body responsible for collecting and distributing music royalties

SAMU *m (Service m d'assistance médicale d'urgence)* — French ambulance service

SARL *f (société f à responsabilité limitée)* — Ltd, plc (limited company (with non-negotiable shares))

SAV *m (service m après-vente)* — after-sales service

SC *(service m compris)* — service included

s/c *(sous couvert de)* — c/o (care of)

SEITA *f (Société f nationale d'exploitation des tabacs et allumettes)* — French national tobacco and match company

S.E.M. *f (société f d'économie mixte)* — partly privatized company

se & o *(sauf erreur f ou omission f)* — E&OE (errors and omissions excepted)

SERNAM *m (Service m national de messagerie)* — French rail delivery service

SFI *f (Société f financière internationale)* — IFC (International Finance Corporation)

SFP *f (Société f française de production et de création audiovisuelle)* — French TV and film production company

SGDG *(sans garantie du gouvernement)* — without government warranty

SICAV *f (Société f d'investissement à capital variable)* — open-ended investment trust; share in such a trust

SICOB *m (Salon m international d'informatique, télématique, communication, organisation du bureau et bureautique)* — Paris office technology trade fair

SIG *m (système m intégré de gestion)* — MIS (management information system)

SIRET *m (système m informatique du répertoire des entreprises et établissements)* — French computerized register of companies

SMAG *m (salaire m minimum agricole garanti)* — guaranteed minimum agricultural wage in France

SME m (Système m monétaire européen)	EMS (European Monetary System)
SMIC m (salaire m minimum interprofessionnel de croissance)	index-linked guaranteed minimum wage in France
SMIG m (salaire m mininum interprofessionnel garanti)	guaranteed minimum wage in France
SNC (service m non compris)	service not included
SNC f (société f en nom collectif)	general partnership
SNCB f (Société f nationale des chemins de fer belges)	Belgian Railways
SNCF f (Société f nationale des chemins de fer français)	French national railways
s.o. (sans objet)	no longer applicable
SOFRES f (Société f française d'enquêtes pour sondage)	French opinion poll company
SSR f (Société f suisse romande)	Swiss French-language broadcasting company
Sté (Société f)	Co. (company)
SVP (s'il vous plaît)	pls (please)
SVT m (spécialiste m en valeurs de trésor)	Government Broker
T (tonne f)	t (tonne)
TAO f (traduction f assistée par ordinateur)	MAT (machine-aided translation)
TCA f (taxe f sur le chiffre d'affaires)	tax on turnover
TDF f (Télévision f de France)	French broadcasting authority
TEG m (taux m effectif global)	APR (annual percentage rate)
tél. (téléphone m)	tel (telephone)
TF1 (Télévision f française un)	French TV channel
TG f (Trésorerie f générale)	French local government finance office
TGV m (train m à grande vitesse)	high-speed train
tlj (tous les jours)	every day
TOM m (Territoire m d'outre-mer)	French colony
TP mpl (travaux mpl publics)	public works
TP m (Trésor m public)	public revenue office
TPG m (Trésorier-payeur m général)	paymaster
tps m (temps m)	time
ts (tous)	all
TSVP (tournez s'il vous plaît)	PTO (please turn over)
tt (tout)	all, everything
TTC (toutes taxes fpl comprises)	inclusive of tax
ttes (toutes)	all

TUP *m (titre m universel de paiement)*	*payment slip*
TVA *f (taxe f à la valeur ajoutée)*	*VAT (value-added tax)*
U *(unité f)*	*unit (10000 ff)*
UCE *f (Unité f de compte européenne)*	*EUA (European Unit of Account)*
UER *f (Union f européenne de radiodiffusion)*	*EBU (European Broadcasting Union)*
UFC *f (Union f fédérale des consommateurs)*	*national consumer group*
UIT *f (Union f internationale des télécommunications)*	*ITU (International Telecommunications Union)*
URSSAF *f (Union f pour le recouvrement des cotisations de la sécurité sociale et des allocations familiales)*	*French national insurance body*
UTA *f (Union f des transporteurs aériens)*	*French international airline*
v. *(voir)*	*v (vide)*
vd *(vend)*	*sell(ing)*
VF *f (version f française)*	*French version (of a film)*
VO *f (version f originale)*	*original language version (of a film)*
VPC *f (vente f par correspondance)*	*MO (mail order)*
V/Réf *(votre référence f)*	*your ref*
VRP *m (voyageur m représentant placier)*	*rep (sales representative)*
XP *(exprès payé)*	*express paid*
ZAC *f (zone f d'aménagement concerté)*	*urban development area (financed by public money)*
ZAD *f (zone f d'aménagement différé)*	*future development area (where the local authority has first option on land for sale)*
ZEP *f (zone f d'environnement protégé)*	*protected area where no development is permitted*
ZI *f (zone f industrielle)*	*industrial estate*
ZIF *f (zone f d'intervention foncière)*	*zone where government has first option on property for sale*
ZUP *f (zone f à urbaniser en priorité)*	*priority urban development area*

See also **ENTERTAINING, MAKING CONTACT** *and* **TRAVEL**

There is no official system of classification in operation for hotels in Belgium but details of hotels and rates are available from the Belgian Tourist Office, Premier House, 2 Gayton Road, Harrow, Middlesex HA1 2XX. Tel: 081 861 3300. Fax: 081 427 6760.

In France, hotels are graded officially from 1 star to 4 stars (*étoiles*) with a luxury category of *4 étoiles luxe*. Details of hotels and rates are available from the French Government Tourist Office, 178 Piccadilly, London W1V OAL. Tel: 071 491 7622. Fax: 071 493 6594.

Hotels in Luxembourg may request classification and will be graded on an official scale of 1 to 5 stars (*étoiles*). Not all hotels are classified. The Luxembourg Tourist Office, 36 Piccadilly, London W1V 9PA will supply details of hotels and rates. Tel: 071 434 2800. Fax: 071 734 1205.

In Quebec, hotels are graded by the Ministry of Tourism on a scale of 1 to 6 fleur-de-lys. NE means that the hotel is new or has not yet been evaluated. For further details of hotels and rates, contact Quebec Tourism, Quebec House, 59 Pall Mall, London SW1Y 5JH. Tel: 071 930 8314. Fax: 071 930 7938.

For details of hotels and rates in Switzerland, you should contact the Swiss National Tourist Office, Swiss Centre, Swiss Court, London W1V 8EE. Tel: 071 734 1921. Fax: 071 437 4577.

MAKING A RESERVATION

I'd like to make a reservation *je voudrais faire une réservation*
What are your room rates? *quels sont les prix des chambres?*
How much is a room per night, with breakfast? *quel est le prix d'une chambre par nuit, avec petit déjeuner?*
Which credit cards do you take? *Quelles cartes de crédit acceptez-vous?*
I'd like a single room with bath/shower for two nights *je voudrais une chambre à un lit avec salle de bains/douche pour deux nuits*
If possible, I would like a room with a view of ... *si c'est possible, je voudrais une chambre avec vue sur ...*
I'd like a room which isn't too noisy, please *j'aimerais une chambre calme, s'il vous plaît*
Please send me a brochure about your hotel *veuillez m'envoyer un prospectus sur votre hôtel*
Can you suggest another hotel that might have a vacancy? *pourriez-vous me conseiller un autre hôtel qui aurait une chambre de libre?*

CHECKING IN/OUT

I have a reservation in the name of ... *j'ai fait une réservation au nom de ...*

I confirmed my booking by phone/fax/letter *j'ai confirmé ma réservation par téléphone/par fax/par écrit*

Can I see the room? *puis-je voir la chambre?*

Which floor is my room on? *à quel étage se trouve ma chambre?*

When will my room be ready? *quand est-ce que ma chambre sera prête?*

Please have my luggage taken up/brought down *pourriez-vous faire monter/descendre mes bagages?*

Has anyone else from Smith & Co checked in yet? *est-ce que quelqu'un d'autre de chez Smith & Cie est déjà arrivé?*

I'll be staying for 3 days *je vais rester trois jours*

I'd like to stay an extra night/two extra nights *je voudrais rester une nuit de plus/deux nuits de plus*

I shall be leaving tomorrow at 9 o'clock *je partirai demain à 9 heures*

What time must I vacate the room? *à quelle heure faut-il libérer la chambre?*

I'd like to pay my bill *je voudrais régler ma note*

I'd like an itemized bill *je voudrais une note détaillée*

Can I pay by credit card/with traveller's cheques? *acceptez-vous les cartes de crédit/les travellers?*

Please send the bill to ... *veuillez envoyer la note à ...*

Has my bill been settled? *est-ce que ma note a été réglée?*

HOTEL SERVICES

Do you have ... in the hotel? *y a-t-il ... dans l'hôtel?*

Where's the ...? *où est le/la ...?/où sont les ...?*

Do you provide transport to the airport/station/city centre? *assurez-vous le transport pour l'aéroport/la gare/le centre-ville?*

(When) does the hotel close at night? *(à quelle heure) est-ce que l'hôtel ferme le soir?*

What is the voltage here? *quel est le voltage (ici)?*

Put it on my bill *mettez-le sur ma note*

I'd like a six o'clock alarm call *je voudrais qu'on me réveille à six heures*

Can I leave this in the safe? *puis-je laisser ceci dans le coffre-fort?*

I'd like ... cleaned/washed/polished/ironed *je voudrais faire nettoyer/laver/cirer/repasser ...*

I'd like this letter typed up/photocopied *je voudrais faire taper/photocopier cette lettre*

May I have an extra ...? *puis-je avoir un(e) autre ...?*
Can I leave my luggage here and collect it later? *est-ce que je peux laisser mes bagages ici? Je viendrai les reprendre plus tard*
Please call a porter/taxi *pourriez-vous m'appeler un porteur/un taxi?*

MEALS

When do you stop serving breakfast/lunch/dinner? *jusqu'à quelle heure sert-on le petit déjeuner/le déjeuner/le dîner?*
Do you provide room service? *est-il possible de prendre les repas dans la chambre?*
May I see the breakfast/lunch/dinner/snack menu? *je voudrais voir le menu pour le petit déjeuner/le déjeuner/le dîner/les snacks*
I'd like breakfast/lunch/dinner in my room *je voudrais prendre le petit déjeuner/le déjeuner/le dîner dans ma chambre*
Do you serve English breakfasts? *est-il possible d'avoir un petit déjeuner anglais?*
I'm dining alone – can you recommend a good restaurant? *je suis seul(e) pour dîner; pourriez-vous me recommander un bon restaurant?*

See also **ENTERTAINING**

MESSAGES/COMMUNICATIONS

What do I dial for outside/overseas calls? *quel numéro faut-il faire pour les lignes extérieures/internationales?*
Give me 334 8895 please *pourriez-vous me passer le 334-88-95 (s'il vous plaît)?*
Where can I send a fax from? *d'où est-ce que je peux envoyer un fax?*
What is the hotel's fax/phone/telex number? *quel est le numéro de fax/téléphone/télex de l'hôtel?*
I'd like this letter posted/faxed *je voudrais poster cette lettre/envoyer cette lettre par fax*
Are there any messages for ...? *y a-t-il un message pour ...?*
Please forward any messages to ... *veuillez faire suivre tous les messages à ...*
I can be contacted at this number *on peut me joindre à ce numéro*

I'm expecting a Mr Smith. Please call me when he arrives *j'attends la visite de M Smith. Pourriez-vous me prévenir de son arrivée?*

Please send him/her up *faites-le/la monter, s'il vous plaît*

Please tell him/her I'll be down in a moment *dites-lui que j'arrive dans un instant, s'il vous plaît*

See also **MAKING CONTACT**

PROBLEMS

My room is noisy/dirty *ma chambre est bruyante/sale*

My room is too cold/too hot *il fait froid/trop chaud dans ma chambre*

I'd like a different room, please *j'aimerais changer de chambre, s'il vous plaît*

There is no ... in my room *il n'y a pas de ... dans ma chambre*

The ... in my room is not working *le/la/les ... ne fonctionne(nt) pas dans ma chambre*

The ... in my room is broken *le/la ... est cassé(e) dans ma chambre*

I ordered ... and it has not been delivered/brought up *j'ai commandé ... et on ne me l'a/les a pas encore apporté(s)*

Please cancel my order *veuillez annuler ma commande*

I've locked myself out of my room *je suis enfermé(e) dehors de ma chambre*

I've lost my key *j'ai perdu ma clef*

ADDITIONAL VOCABULARY

adjacent rooms	*chambres fpl voisines*
air conditioning	*climatisation f*
alarm call	*see phrase in* **HOTEL SERVICES** *above*
balcony	*balcon m*
bank	*banque f*
bar	*bar m*
bath	*bain m*
bed	*lit m*
blanket	*couverture f*
breakfast	*petit déjeuner m*
business service centre	*service m affaires*
car park	*parking m*
chambermaid	*femme f de chambre*
check in *vb*	*s'inscrire (à la réception)*

check out *vb*	*régler sa note*
check-out time	*heure f limite d'occupation*
coffee shop	*salon m de thé*
conference facilities	*installations fpl et équipement m de conférences*
conference room	*salle f de conférences*
connecting rooms	*chambres fpl attenantes*
dining room	*salle f à manger*
doorman	*portier m*
double room	*chambre f pour deux personnes*
emergency exit	*issue f de secours*
en suite bathroom	*salle f de bains attenante*
envelope	*enveloppe f*
executive room	*chambre f de grand standing*
fire exit	*issue f de secours*
foyer	*hall m*
full board	*pension f complète*
function suite	*appartement m de réunion*
garage	*garage m*
hairdresser	*coiffeur(-euse) m(f)*
hairdryer	*sèche-cheveux m*
half board	*demi-pension f*
hot water	*eau f chaude*
key	*clef f*
landing	*palier m*
laundry service	*blanchisserie f*
lift	*ascenseur m*
lobby	*hall m*
lounge	*salon m*
manager	*gérant(e) m(f)*
meeting room	*salle f de réunion*
mini-bar	*mini-bar m*
motel	*motel m*
nightclub	*boîte f de nuit*
night porter	*gardien m de nuit*
non-smoking room	*chambre f pour non-fumeurs*
note paper	*papier f à lettres*
operator	*standardiste m/f*
pillow	*oreiller m*
porter	*porteur m*
private bathroom	*salle f de bain particulière*
quilt	*édredon m*
receipt	*reçu m*
reception	*réception f*
receptionist	*réceptionniste m/f*

register *n*	*registre m*
register *vb*	*s'inscrire*
restaurant	*restaurant m*
room	*chambre f*
room rates	*tarif m des chambres*
room service	*service m des chambres*
safe	*coffre-fort m*
sauna	*sauna m*
secretarial services	*services mpl de secrétariat*
sheet *(for bed)*	*drap m*
shower	*douche f*
single room	*chambre f à un lit*
soap	*savon m*
suite	*appartement m*
swimming pool	*piscine f*
switchboard	*standard m*
television	*télévision f*
towel	*serviette f*
twin beds	*lits mpl jumeaux*
valet service	*pressing m*
washbasin	*lavabo m*
writing paper	*papier m à lettres*

See also **ACCOUNTS AND PAYMENTS** *and* **STOCK MANAGEMENT**

accredited agent	*agent m accrédité*
advice note	*avis m d'expédition*
agency	*agence f*
agent	*agent m*
agent's commission	*commission f de l'agent*
air cargo	*fret m aérien*
air consignment note	*lettre f de transport aérien (LTA f)*
air freight	*fret m aérien*
air waybill	*lettre f de transport aérien (LTA f)*
anti-dumping duty	*droits mpl anti-dumping*
banker's reference	*références fpl bancaires*
bilateral trade	*commerce m bilatéral*
bill of entry	*déclaration f de douane*
bill of exchange	*lettre f de change*
bill of lading	*connaissement m*
blocked currency	*monnaie f non-convertible*
bond *vb*	*entreposer*
bonded goods	*marchandises fpl en douane*
bonded warehouse	*entrepôt m des douanes*
breakage	*casse f*
broken lot	*articles mpl dépareillés*
bulk buying	*achat m en gros*
bulk cargo	*cargaison f en vrac*
c & f (cost and freight)	*C et F (coût et fret)*
cargo	*cargaison f*
carriage forward	*en port dû*
carriage free	*franco de port*
carriage inwards	*port m à la charge de l'acheteur*
carriage outwards	*port m à la charge du vendeur*
carriage paid	*en port payé*
carrier	*transporteur m*
carton	*carton m*
cartonned	*mis(e) en carton*
certificate of origin	*certificat m d'origine*
certificate of shipment	*certificat m d'expédition*
certificate of value	*certificat m de valeur*

please contact our agent in Brussels *veuillez vous adresser à notre agent de Bruxelles*
goods held in bond *marchandises en entrepôt de douane*
to take goods out of bond *dédouaner les marchandises en entrepôt*

channels of distribution	*circuits m de distribution*
CIF (cost, insurance and freight)	*CAF (coût, assurance, fret)*
CIF & C (cost, insurance, freight and commission)	*CAF & C (coût, assurance, fret et commission)*
CIF & I (cost, insurance, freight and interest)	*CAF & I (coût, assurance, fret et intérêts)*
clean bill of exchange	*lettre f de change sans réserves*
clean bill of lading	*connaissement m sans réserves*
clearance	*dédouanement m, déclaration f*
clearance certificate	*lettre f de mer, certificat m de douane*
COD (cash on delivery)	*livraison f contre remboursement (CR)*
collect	*enlever*
collection	*enlèvement m*
community transit form	*fiche f de transit communautaire*
confirmed irrevocable letter of credit	*lettre f de crédit irrévocable confirmé*
confirming house	*commissionnaire m*
consign	*expédier*
consignee	*destinataire m/f*
consignment *(incoming)*	*arrivage m*
consignment *(leaving)*	*envoi m*
consignment note	*bordereau m d'expédition*
consignor	*expéditeur(-trice) m(f)*
consular invoice	*facture f consulaire*
container	*conteneur m*
containerization	*conteneurisation f*
containerize	*conteneuriser*
container ship	*porte-conteneurs m*
countertrading	*commerce m compensé*
country of origin	*pays m d'origine*
courier	*coursier m*
courier service	*messagerie f*
crate	*caisse f*
creditworthiness	*solvabilité f*

the goods will be collected/delivered on 31 May *les marchandises seront enlevées/livrées le 31 mai*

the goods are ready for collection *les marchandises sont prêtes à être enlevées*

the consignment consists of ... *l'envoi consiste en ...*

to send goods on consignment *envoyer des marchandises en dépôt*

in duplicate/triplicate/in 5 copies *en deux/trois/cinq exemplaires*

it will take 24 hours for the goods to clear customs *il faudra 24 heures pour le dédouanement des marchandises*

customs	*douane f*
customs broker	*agent m en douane*
customs clearance	*passage m en douane*
customs declaration	*déclaration f de douane*
customs duty	*droits mpl de douane*
customs entry	*passage m en douane*
customs form	*formulaire m de déclaration en douane*
customs official	*douanier(-ière) m(f)*
customs receipt	*récépissé m des douanes*
customs registered number	*numéro m d'immatriculation douanière*
customs regulation	*réglementation f douanière*
customs union	*union f douanière*
damaged	*endommagé(e)*
deck cargo	*pontée f*
delay	*retard m*
deliver	*livrer*
deliverable state	*état m livrable*
delivered price	*prix m tout compris*
delivery	*livraison f*
delivery note	*bon m de livraison*

to obtain customs clearance for a shipment *obtenir le dédouanement de l'expédition*

we are still waiting for customs clearance *nous attendons toujours le dédouanement*

we will take care of the customs formalities *nous prendrons les formalités de douane en charge*

we would be grateful if you could take care of the customs formalities *nous vous serions obligés de prendre les formalités de douane en charge*

please send us a customs receipt *veuillez nous envoyer un récépissé des douanes*

the goods were damaged in transit *les marchandises ont été endommagées en transit*

what is the reason for the delay? *quelle est la raison du retard?*

to deliver something on time/late *livrer quelque chose à temps/avec du retard*

we can deliver the goods immediately *nous pouvons vous livrer immédiatement*

I am afraid that we cannot accept goods delivered after ... *je regrette, mais nous ne pourrons pas accepter les marchandises livrées après (le) ...*

please allow ... days/weeks for delivery *il faut compter un délai de livraison de ... jours/semaines*

we are still awaiting delivery of the goods *nous attendons toujours la livraison des marchandises*

delivery time	*délai m de livraison*
demurrage	*surestarie f*
depository	*dépôt m*
depot	*dépôt m*
destination	*destination f*
dispatch	*expédier*
dispatch department	*service m des expéditions*
distribute	*distribuer*
distribution	*distribution f*
distribution centre	*centre m de distribution*
distribution costs	*coûts mpl de distribution*
distribution network	*réseau m de distribution*
distributor	*distributeur(-trice) m(f)*
dock(s)	*bassin(s) m(pl)*
dock *vb*	*accoster*
dock dues	*droits mpl de bassin*
docket	*bordereau m*
documents against acceptance (D/A)	*documents mpl contre acceptation (DA mpl)*
documents against payment (D/P)	*documents mpl contre paiement (DP mpl)*
documentary bill of exchange	*lettre f de change documentaire*
documents of title	*titres mpl de propriété*
domestic sales	*ventes fpl sur le marché intérieur*
driver	*chauffeur m*
drop shipment	*livraison f directe*
duty-free	*hors taxe*
duty-paid price	*prix m dédouané*
embargo	*embargo m*
estimated time of arrival (ETA)	*heure f estimée d'arrivée*
Europallet	*europalette f*
exceed	*dépasser*
ex dock	*à quai*
ex factory	*départ usine*
export(s)	*exportation(s) f(pl)*

the goods were dispatched on 31 May *les marchandises ont été expédiées le 31 mai*

please advise us of the documentation required *veuillez nous indiquer les documents requis*

the duty will be paid by the purchaser/consignee *les droits seront acquittés par l'acheteur/le dépositaire*

exports are 10% up/down on last year *les exportations ont augmenté/ diminué de 10% par rapport à l'an dernier*

we hope to increase our exports by 30% *nous espérons augmenter nos exportations de 30%*

export *vb*	*exporter*
export agent	*commissionnaire-exportateur(-trice) m(f)*
Export Credit Guarantee Department (ECGD)	*service m de garantie financière à l'exportation*
export drive	*campagne f d'exportations*
exporter	*exportateur(-trice) m(f)*
export house	*entreprise f d'exportation*
export invoice	*facture f à l'exportation*
export licence	*licence f d'exportation*
export manager	*directeur(-trice) m(f) du service d'exportations*
export trade	*exportation f*
express delivery	*livraison f exprès*
ex ship	*ex navire*
ex works	*départ usine*
fair-trade agreement	*accord m de libre échange réciproque*
FAQ (free alongside quay)	*FLQ (franco long du quai)*
FAS (free alongside ship)	*FLB (franco long du bord)*
FD (free delivered at dock)	*livraison f franco à quai*
first-class post	*courrier m (à tarif) normal*
FOB (free on board)	*FOB, FAB (franco à bord)*
FOR (free on rail)	*FOR (franco wagon)*
forwarding agent	*transitaire m*
franco	*franco*
free currency	*devise f convertible*
free of tax	*exonéré(e) d'impôts*
free to receiving station	*franco gare de réception*
freight *n*	*fret m*
freight *vb*	*(faire) transporter*
freight forward	*en port dû*
freight forwarder	*transitaire m*
freight forwarding	*opérations fpl de transit*
freight inward	*port m payé par le destinataire*
freight train	*train m de marchandises*
General Agreement on Tariffs and Trade (GATT)	*GATT m*
goods	*marchandises fpl*

to export 1,000 units p.a. to Africa *exporter 1.000 unités par an en Afrique*
oil-exporting/grain-exporting countries *pays exportateurs de pétrole/de céréales*
30% of our production is for the export market *30% de la production est destiné à l'exportation*

goods in transit	*marchandises fpl en transit*
goods received note	*bon m de réception des marchandises*
goods train	*train m de marchandises*
handling charge	*frais mpl de manutention*
harbour dues	*droits mpl de port*
haulage	*transport m routier*
haulage contractor *(firm)*	*entreprise f de transport routier*
haulage contractor *(person)*	*entrepreneur m de transport routier*
haulage (cost)	*frais mpl de transport*
HS number	*numéro m SH*
import(s)	*importation(s) f(pl)*
import *vb*	*importer*
import ban	*interdiction f d'importer*
import duty	*droits mpl d'entrée*
importer	*importateur(-trice) m(f)*
import-export *(business)*	*import-export m*
importing	*importation f*
import levy	*taxe f douanière*
import licence	*licence f d'importation*
import quota	*contingent m d'importation*
import surcharge	*surtaxe f à l'importation*
import tariff	*droits mpl de douane à l'importation*
impound	*confisquer*
in bond	*en entrepôt des douanes*
in-bond price	*prix m en entrepôt (des douanes)*
Incoterms	*termes mpl de commerce international*
insurance certificate	*attestation f d'assurance*
in transit	*en transit*
joint venture	*entreprise f en participation*
late delivery	*retard m de livraison*
lay days	*estaries fpl*

the goods have been held up at Customs *les marchandises ont été retenues à la douane*

the ship has been held up by the weather *le bateau a été retardé par le mauvais temps*

to import products into Britain *importer des produits en Grande-Bretagne*

I represent a British import-export company *je représente une société d'import-export britannique*

to apply for/get an import licence *faire une demande pour/obtenir une licence d'importation*

the import licence has been refused *la licence d'importation a été refusée*

lead time	*délai m de livraison*
load *n*	*chargement m*
load *vb*	*charger*
loading bay	*aire f de chargement*
loading dock	*quai m de chargement*
lorry	*camion m*
loss in transit	*freinte f*
low-loader	*semi-remorque f à plate-forme surbaissée*
manifest	*manifeste m*
maritime law	*droit m maritime*
merchantman	*navire m marchand*
non-acceptance	*non-acceptation f*
non-delivery	*défaut m de livraison*
notification	*avis m*
packet tying machine	*machine f à ficelage*
pallet	*palette f*
palletization	*palettisation f*
palletize	*palettiser*
palletized carton	*carton m sur palette*
parcel post	*service m colis postaux*
payload	*charge f utile (CU f)*
perishable goods	*denrées fpl périssables*
port of entry	*port m d'entrée*
post-free	*port payé, franco (de port)*
post-paid	*port payé*
pro-forma invoice	*facture f pro forma*
Red Star International ®	*Red Star International ®*
re-export	*réexporter*
road haulage	*transport m routier*
rolling and wrapping machine	*machine f d'enroulement et d'empaquetage*
sail *vb*	*partir*
sample	*échantillon m*

the goods should be packed using ... *les marchandises devront être emballées dans ...*

how would you prefer the order to be packed/shipped? *quel type de conditionnement/transport désirez-vous pour votre commande?*

there is a penalty of ... for late delivery *il y a une pénalité de ... pour les livraisons effectuées avec du retard*

is that price FOB or CIF? *ce prix est-il FOB ou CAF?*

please confirm safe receipt of the goods *veuillez nous confirmer la bonne réception des marchandises*

we received the consignment safely on 2 August *nous avons reçu votre envoi en bon état le 2 août*

scheduled flight	*vol m régulier*
second-class post	*courrier m à tarif réduit*
ship *n*	*navire m*
ship *vb*	*expédier*
shipment *(load)*	*cargaison f*
shipowner	*armateur m*
shipper *(transports goods)*	*expéditeur(-trice) m(f)*
shipper *(organizes transport)*	*chargeur m*
shipping	*expédition f*
shipping agent	*agent m maritime*
shipping company	*compagnie f de navigation*
shipping department	*service m des expéditions*
shipping documents	*documents mpl d'expédition*
shipping note	*note f de chargement*
ship's manifest	*manifeste m*
ship's report	*manifeste m*
shockproof	*résistant(e) aux chocs*
shrink-wrap	*emballer sous film plastique*
sole agent	*agent m exclusif*
stamp duty	*droits mpl de timbre*
supercargo	*subrécargue m*
tachograph	*tachygraphe m*
tariff barrier	*barrière f douanière*
tax exemption	*exonération f d'impôts*
tax haven	*paradis m fiscal*
trade barrier	*barrière f douanière*
trade mission	*mission f commerciale*
trade reference	*référence f commerciale*
tranship	*transborder*
transhipment	*transbordement m*
truck	*camion m*
trucking company	*entreprise f de transport (routier)*
van	*camionnette f*
VAT (value-added tax)	*TVA f (taxe f à la valeur ajoutée)*
vessel	*navire m*
warehouse	*entrepôt m*
warrant	*garantie f*
waterproof	*imperméable*
weight limit	*poids-limite m*

to send goods by air/post/rail/road/sea *expédier des marchandises par avion/la poste/chemin de fer/la route/voie maritime*
we make three shipments per month to Switzerland *nous faisons trois expéditions par mois pour la Suisse*

aeronautical industry	industrie f aéronautique
agribusiness	agro-industries fpl
arms trade	armement m
banking	banque f
business (world of)	affaires fpl
car industry	industrie f automobile
caterer	traiteur m
catering (industry)	restauration f
chemical industry	industrie f chimique
civil engineering	génie m civil
commerce	commerce m
computing	informatique f
construction industry	(industrie f du) bâtiment m
consultancy	cabinet-conseil m
copy shop	bureau m de photocopie
distillery	distillerie f
diversification	diversification f
electronics	électronique f
engineering	ingénierie f
entertainment industry	industrie f du spectacle
fashion industry	mode f
finance	finances fpl
food industry	industrie f alimentaire
food processing	industrie f alimentaire
growth industry	industrie f en pleine expansion
heavy industry	industrie f lourde
industrial capacity	capacité f industrielle
industrial estate	zone f industrielle
industrialist	industriel m
industry	industrie f
information industry	secteur m de l'information
iron and steel industry	sidérurgie f
light industry	industrie f légère
manufacturing	fabrication f
manufacturing sector	secteur m de la fabrication
metallurgy	métallurgie f
mining	exploitation f minière
music industry	industrie f de la musique

what's your field? dans quel domaine travaillez-vous?
the company is moving into the field of ... la société passe au domaine de ...
this sector of industry is growing/declining ce secteur de l'industrie est en expansion/en déclin
I'm in ... je travaille dans le/la/les ...
to work in industry travailler dans l'industrie

nationalize	*nationaliser*
nuclear industry	*secteur m nucléaire*
oil industry	*secteur m pétrolier*
petroleum industry	*secteur m pétrolier*
pharmaceutical industry, pharmaceuticals	*industrie f pharmaceutique*
power industry	*secteur m de l'énergie*
printing industry	*imprimerie f*
private (limited) company	*société f privée*
privately-owned	*privé(e)*
private sector	*secteur m privé*
privatize	*privatiser*
processing industry	*secteur m de la transformation*
public company	*société f anonyme*
public sector	*secteur m public*
publishing	*édition f*
registered company	*société f inscrite au registre du commerce*
service industry	*société f de services*
shipbuilding	*construction f navale*
state-owned	*nationalisé(e)*
steel industry	*sidérurgie f*
subsidiary (company)	*filiale f*
telecommunications	*télécommunications fpl*
tertiary industry	*entreprise f du tertiaire*
tertiary sector	*secteur m tertiaire*
textile industry, textiles	*(industrie f) textile m*
timber industry	*filière f bois*
tobacco industry	*tabac m*
tourist industry	*tourisme m*
translation agency	*bureau m de traduction*
travel agency	*agence f de voyages*
travel industry	*secteur m du tourisme*
winemaking	*viticulture f*

in Britain, this is a privatized/state-owned industry *en Grande-Bretagne, c'est une industrie privatisée/nationalisée*

See also **THE EUROPEAN COMMUNITY**

International organizations or institutions usually have an official French version of their name. Wherever possible, we have given this French name as a translation. Where the English name of a British or American organization will be recognized by French speakers, we have given this English name as a translation. If the English name will not be recognized, and there is no French name, we have provided a French definition of the organization. When discussing such organizations, it is best to cite the English name, followed by the French definition.

American National Standards Institute (ANSI)	*institut m américain de normalisation (ANSI m)*
American Standards Association (ASA)	*association f américaine de normalisation (ASA f)*
Association for Payment Clearing Services (APACS)	*association f britannique des services de compensation*
Association of British Ports (ABP)	*association f des ports britanniques*
Association of South-East Asian Nations (ASEAN)	*Association f des nations de l'Asie du Sud-Est (ASEAN f)*
Bank for International Settlements (BIS)	*Banque f des règlements internationaux (BRI f)*
Bank of England	*Banque f d'Angleterre*
Bay Street	*Bay Street (la bourse de Toronto)*
BBC	*BBC f*
Big Eight *(accounting firms)*	*les huit grands cabinets mpl d'expertise comptable*
Big Four (Banks)	*les quatre grandes banques fpl anglaises*
Board of Trade	*Ministère m britannique du commerce*
British Airports Authority (BAA)	*autorités fpl aéroportuaires britanniques*
British Airways (BA)	*British Airways f (BA f)*
British Exporters' Association (BEXA)	*association f des exportateurs britanniques*
British Overseas Trade Board (BOTB)	*direction f britannique des relations économiques extérieures*
British Standards Institution (BSI)	*association f britannique de normalisation*

please send me details of your organization's activities *veuillez m'envoyer des renseignements sur les activités de votre organisation*

Central Office of Information (COI)	*centre m national britannique d'information*
Chamber of Commerce	*Chambre f de commerce*
Civil Aviation Authority (CAA)	*direction f britannique de l'aviation civile*
COMEX	*bourse f de matières premières de New York*
Common Fund for Commodities (CFC)	*Fonds m commun pour les produits de base*
Confederation of British Industry (CBI)	*conseil m national du patronat britannique*
Consumers' Association	*association f britannique de défense du consommateur*
Department of Trade and Industry (DTI)	*Ministère m britannique de l'industrie et du commerce*
Export Credit Guarantee Department (ECGD)	*service m de garantie financière à l'exportation*
Food and Agriculture Organization of the United Nations (FAO)	*Organisation f des Nations Unies pour l'alimentation et l'agriculture (FAO f)*
Foreign Office (FO)	*Ministère m britannique des affaires étrangères*
General Agreement on Tariffs and Trade (GATT)	*GATT m*
Group of 3 (G3)	*Groupe m des trois*
Group of 5 (G5)	*Groupe m des cinq*
Group of 7 (G7)	*les sept grands mpl*
Group of 10 (G10)	*Groupe m des dix*
HM Customs (HMC)	*douanes fpl (de Sa Majesté)*
Independent Broadcasting Authority (IBA)	*commission f britannique de radiotélévision commerciale*
Independent Television Commission (ITC)	*commission f britannique des télévisions indépendantes*
Inland Revenue (IR)	*fisc m britannique*
Internal Revenue Service (IRS)	*fisc m des États-Unis*
International Atomic Energy Agency (IAEA)	*Agence f internationale de l'énergie atomique (AIEA f)*

it would be wiser to contact ... before going ahead *il vaudrait mieux s'adresser à ... avant de commencer*

the organization that deals with this is the ... *l'organisation qui s'en occupe est ...*

what is the equivalent organization in France/Paris? *quelle est l'organisation équivalente en France/à Paris?*

there is no equivalent body in Britain *il n'existe pas d'équivalent à cet organisme en Grande-Bretagne*

International Bank for Reconstruction and Development (IBRD)	*Banque f internationale pour la reconstruction et le développement (BIRD f)*
International Chamber of Commerce (ICC)	*Chambre f de commerce internationale (CCI f)*
International Court of Justice (ICJ)	*Cour f internationale de justice (CIJ f)*
International Development Association (IDA)	*Association f internationale pour le développement (AID f)*
International Finance Corporation (IFC)	*Société f financière internationale (SFI f)*
International Fund for Agricultural Development (IFAD)	*Fonds m international de développement agricole (FIDA m)*
International Labour Organization (ILO)	*Organisation f internationale du travail (OIT f)*
International Monetary Fund (IMF)	*Fonds m monétaire international (FMI m)*
International Standards Organization (ISO)	*Organisation f des normes internationales (ISO f)*
International Telecommunications Union (ITU)	*Union f internationale des télécommunications (UIT f)*
International Trade Organization (ITO)	*Organisation f internationale du commerce (OIC f)*
Lloyd's of London	*la Lloyd's de Londres*
Monopolies and Mergers Commission	*commission f britannique d'enquête sur les monopoles*
Office of Fair Trading (OFT)	*service m gouvernemental britannique de la protection des consommateurs*
Organization for Economic Cooperation and Development (OECD)	*Organisation f de coopération et de développement économiques (OCDE f)*
Organization of Arab Petroleum Exporting Countries (OAPEC)	*Organisation f des pays arabes exportateurs de pétrole (OPAEP f)*
Organization of Petroleum Exporting Countries (OPEC)	*Organisation f des pays exportateurs de pétrole (OPEP f)*

I am sure that the local Chamber of Commerce would be able to help *je suis sûr que la Chambre de Commerce locale pourrait nous or vous aider*

is there an office of ... in London? *y a-t-il une agence de ... à Londres?*

Trades Union Congress (TUC)	*confédération f des syndicats britanniques*
UN Conference on Trade and Development (UNCTAD)	*Conférence f des Nations Unies pour le commerce et le développement (CNUCED f)*
UN Industrial Development Organization (UNIDO)	*Organisation f des Nations Unies pour le développement industriel (ONUDI f)*
Wall Street	*Wall Street m (la Bourse de New York)*
World Bank	*Banque f mondiale*

this organization is roughly the same as your ... *cette organisation correspond plus ou moins à votre ...*

accident	accident m
accidental	accidentel(le)
accident insurance	assurance f contre les accidents
act of God	cas m de force majeure
actuarial	actuariel(le)
actuarial tables	table f de mortalité
actuary	actuaire m/f
adjust	ajuster
adjuster (general insurance)	expert m en assurances
adjuster (maritime insurance)	répartiteur m d'avaries
adjustment (loss)	règlement m
airworthiness	navigabilité f
all-risks policy	assurance f tous risques
annuity	rente f
assess	évaluer
assessor	contrôleur(-euse) m(f)
assurance company	compagnie f d'assurance-vie
average	avarie f
average clause	clause f d'avaries
award n	dommages-intérêts mpl
barratry	baraterie f
beneficiary	bénéficiaire m/f
blanket policy	assurance f tous risques
broker	courtier m
buildings insurance	assurance f sur l'immeuble
cancel	résilier
car insurance	assurance-automobile f
cash bonus	prime f en espèces
cash surrender value	valeur f de rachat
cessation of risk	cessation f du risque
claim n	déclaration f de sinistre
claim vb	faire une déclaration de sinistre
claimant	requérant(e) m(f)
claims department	service m des sinistres
clause	clause f
commencement of risk	commencement m du risque
compensation	indemnité f
comprehensive insurance	assurance f tous risques

I would like to cancel my policy, no. 315/M *je voudrais résilier ma police nº 315/M*

to put in a claim *faire une déclaration de sinistre*

to handle a claim *s'occuper d'une déclaration de sinistre*

the company cannot settle your claim until you have answered the following queries *la société ne pourra pas vous indemniser tant que vous n'aurez pas répondu aux questions suivantes*

comprehensive policy	*assurance f tous risques*
contributory pension scheme	*régime m de retraite avec retenues sur le salaire*
cover *n*	*couverture f*
cover *vb*	*couvrir*
cover note	*attestation f provisoire d'assurance*
damage *n*	*dégâts mpl*
damage *vb*	*endommager*
damage survey	*expertise f d'avarie*
double indemnity	*double indemnité f*
endowment assurance	*assurance f à capital différé*
endowment policy	*assurance f à capital différé*
estimator	*expert m*
excess clause	*franchise f*
exemption clause	*clause f d'exonération*
extent of cover	*étendue f de la couverture*
fidelity bond	*assurance f contre les détournements*
fire and theft policy	*assurance f vol et incendie*
fire damage	*dégâts mpl causés par le feu*
fire-damaged	*endommagé(e) par le feu*
fire insurance	*assurance-incendie f*
force majeure clause	*clause f de force majeure*
fraudulent claim	*déclaration f frauduleuse*
free of particular average (FPA)	*franc(franche) d'avarie particulière*
freight insurance	*assurance f sur fret*
friendly society	*mutuelle f*
general average loss	*perte f d'avaries communes*
graduated pension	*retraite f proportionnelle*
green card	*carte f verte internationale*
health insurance	*assurance f maladie*
(home) contents insurance	*assurance f mobilier-habitation*
house insurance	*assurance f habitation*
indemnity insurance	*assurance f de compensation*

we require a policy that covers ... *nous voulons une police qui couvre ...*
what is covered by the policy? *qu'est-ce qui est couvert par la police?*
this is not covered by the policy *ceci n'est pas couvert par la police*
I enclose a cover note *vous trouverez ci-joint une attestation provisoire d'assurance*
please send me a cover note and full details of the policy *veuillez m'envoyer une attestation provisoire d'assurance et tous les détails sur la police*
the policy comes into force as of ... *la police sera en vigueur à partir du ...*

insurance	*assurance f*
insurance agent *or* broker	*agent m d'assurances*
insurance certificate	*attestation f d'assurance*
insurance claim	*déclaration f de sinistre*
insurance company	*compagnie f d'assurance*
insurance manager	*directeur(-trice) m(f) de compagnie d'assurances*
insurance premium	*prime f d'assurance*
insure (oneself)	*(s')assurer*
insured *n, adj*	*assuré(e) (m(f))*
insurer	*assureur m*
knock-for-knock agreement	*convention f entre assureurs par laquelle chacun dédommage son propre client*
liability	*responsabilité f*
liability insurance	*assurance f responsabilité civile*
liable	*responsable*
life annuity	*rente f viagère*
life expectancy	*espérance f de vie*
life insurance	*assurance-vie f*
Lloyd's agent	*agent m d'assurance Lloyd's*
Lloyd's Certificate of Marine Insurance	*attestation f d'assurance maritime de Lloyd's*
Lloyd's List	*Lloyd's list m*
Lloyd's of London	*la Lloyd's de Londres*
loading	*majoration f de prime*
lump sum settlement	*indemnisation f par versement unique*
malicious damage	*dommage m causé avec intention de nuire*
marine insurance	*assurance f maritime*
marine survey	*expertise f maritime*
medical insurance	*assurance f maladie*
motor insurance	*assurance-automobile f*
mutual insurance company	*(compagnie f d'assurance) mutuelle f*
negligence	*négligence f*

to insure something/someone against something *assurer quelque chose/ quelqu'un contre quelque chose*

you need to insure the goods against fire/theft/damage/loss *vous devez assurer les marchandises contre l'incendie/le vol/les dégâts/la perte*

your company car is not insured for personal use *votre voiture de fonction n'est pas assurée pour l'usage privé*

you/the goods are insured for £25,000 *vous êtes assuré(s)/les marchandises sont assurées pour 25.000 livres sterling*

negligent	*négligent(e)*
new for old	*remplacement m (par du neuf)*
no-claims bonus	*bonus m*
non-contributory pension scheme	*régime m de retraite sans retenues*
non-disclosure	*réticence f*
occupational pension scheme	*régime m de retraite professionnelle*
other party	*partie f adverse*
particular average loss	*perte f d'avarie particulière*
perishable goods	*denrées fpl périssables*
policy	*police f (d'assurance)*
policy-holder	*assuré(e) m(f)*
premium	*prime f*
product liability insurance	*assurance f responsabilité produit*
proposal form	*formulaire m de proposition d'assurance*
reinsurance	*réassurance f*
reinsurance pool	*consortium m de réassurance*
reinsure	*réassurer*
renew	*renouveler*
renewal	*renouvellement m*
replacement cost	*coût m de remplacement*
replacement value	*valeur f de remplacement*
risk	*risque m*
salvage n *(payment)*	*prime f de sauvetage*
salvage n *(what is saved)*	*matériel m sauvé*
salvage *vb*	*sauver, récupérer*
salvage costs	*frais mpl de récupération*
seaworthiness	*navigabilité f*
settle	*régler*
small print	*petits caractères mpl*
storm damage	*dégâts mpl causés par une tempête*
storm insurance	*assurance f tempête*
subrogation	*substitut m (de créancier)*
surrender *vb*	*racheter*
surrender value	*valeur f de rachat*
temporary cover	*couverture f provisoire*
term insurance	*assurance f à terme*
theft	*vol m*

high-risk/low-risk activity *activité f à risque élevé/à faible risque*
to take out insurance against *prendre une assurance contre*

third-party insurance	*assurance f au tiers*
total loss	*sinistre m total*
transport insurance	*assurance f transport*
travel insurance	*assurance-voyage f*
underwrite	*souscrire, garantir*
underwriter	*assureur m*
unlimited liability	*responsabilité f illimitée*
void *adj*	*nul(le)*
whole-life insurance	*assurance f en cas de décès*
with particular average (WPA)	*avec avarie particulière*
with-profits endowment assurance	*assurance f à capital différé avec bénéfice*

to have unlimited cover *avoir une couverture illimitée*
fair wear and tear *usure f normale*

See also **BANKING AND FINANCE**

above par	*au-dessus du pair*
account *(period)*	*terme m*
allotment	*attribution f*
A shares	*actions fpl ordinaires (sans droit de vote)*
asking price	*prix m demandé*
bearer bonds	*obligations fpl au porteur*
bearish	*à la baisse*
bear market	*marché m baissier*
below par	*au-dessous du pair*
benchmark	*repère m*
Big Bang	*big bang m*
blue-chip investment	*investissement m de premier ordre*
bonus issue	*émission f d'actions gratuites*
bonus share	*action f gratuite*
broker	*agent m de change*
brokerage	*courtage m*
B shares	*action f ordinaire à droit de vote limité*
bucket shop	*agence f (de courtage) louche*
bullish	*à la hausse*
bull market	*marché m haussier*
business news summary	*chronique f économique*
called-up capital	*capital m appelé*
call option	*option f d'achat*
closing price	*cours m de clôture*
commission	*commission f*
commodity exchange	*bourse f de marchandises*
common stock	*action f ordinaire*
consols	*rentes fpl consolidées*
contango	*report m*
contract note	*avis m d'exécution*
convertible loan stock	*titres mpl convertibles*
crash	*krach m*
current yield	*rendement m courant*
dealer	*courtier(-ière) m(f)*
dealing	*transactions fpl*

the market is buoyant *le marché est soutenu*
to buy 1,000 shares in a company *acquérir 1.000 actions d'une société*
the share closed at 105 pence *l'action valait 105 pence à la clôture*
to corner the market (in ...) *accaparer le marché (de ...)*

dividend	*dividende m*
dividend cover	*rapport m dividendes-résultat*
Dow-Jones Average	*indice m Dow-Jones*
earnings per share	*bénéfice m par action*
equities	*actions fpl ordinaires*
equity capital	*capitaux mpl propres*
Eurobond	*euro-obligation f*
ex dividend	*ex-dividende*
ex rights	*ex-droits*
falling market	*marché m à la baisse*
flotation *(of a company)*	*lancement m (en Bourse)*
flotation *(of shares)*	*émission f*
forward contract	*promesse f d'achat à terme*
FT Index	*indice m boursier du "Financial Times"*
fully-paid share	*action f entièrement libérée*
futures	*opérations fpl à terme*
gilt-edged securities	*valeurs fpl sûres*
gold reserves	*réserves fpl d'or*
Government Broker	*spécialiste m/f en valeurs de trésor (SVT m/f)*
government stock	*titres mpl d'État*
Hang Seng Index	*indice m Hang Seng*
holding company	*holding m*
insider dealing	*délit m d'initié(s)*
investment	*placement m*
investment income	*revenu m de placement*
investment portfolio	*portefeuille m de titres*
investment trust	*société f de placements*
investor	*investisseur(-euse) m(f)*
irredeemable	*irremboursable*
issue *n*	*émission f*
issue *vb*	*émettre*
issued capital	*capital m émis*
jobber	*négociant(e) m(f) en titres*
joint-stock company	*société f par actions*
listed company	*société f cotée en Bourse*

to float shares on the open market *émettre des actions en Bourse*
to sell one's holding in a company *vendre ses actions d'une société*
we would like to invest £10,000 in shares/commodities *nous aimerions placer 10.000 livres sterling dans des actions/matières premières*
we have £10,000 available to invest *nous avons 10.000 livres sterling à placer*
a sound/unsound investment *un placement sûr/peu sûr*

majority shareholder	*actionnaire m/f majoritaire*
majority shareholding	*participation f majoritaire*
minority shareholder	*actionnaire m/f minoritaire*
minority shareholding	*participation f minoritaire*
money market	*marché m financier*
Nikkei Index	*indice m Nikkei*
non-voting shares	*actions fpl sans droit de vote*
offer price	*prix m d'émission*
opening price	*cours m d'ouverture*
option	*option f*
ordinary share	*action f ordinaire*
overcapitalize	*surcapitaliser*
oversubscribed	*sursouscrit(e)*
parent company	*société f mère*
partly-paid share	*action f partiellement libérée*
par value	*valeur f nominale*
personal equity plan (PEP)	*plan m d'épargne-capitalisation personnel*
portfolio	*portefeuille m*
preference shares	*actions fpl privilégiées*
preferred ordinary shares	*actions fpl ordinaires privilégiées*
privatization	*privatisation f*
privatize	*privatiser*
put option	*option f de vente*
rally *vb*	*reprendre*
rate of return	*taux m de rendement*
redeemable	*remboursable*
return on investments (ROI)	*rentabilité f des investissements*
rights issue	*émission f préférentielle*
risk capital	*capital-risque m*
securities	*valeurs fpl, titres mpl*
share	*action f*
share capital	*capital m social*
share certificate	*titre m d'action*
shareholder	*actionnaire m/f*

the bottom has fallen out of the market *le marché s'est effondré*
to invest overseas *investir à l'étranger*
how are our shares in ... performing? *comment se comportent nos actions de ...?*
a newly-privatized company *une société privatisée tout récemment*
to go public *être admis(e) à la cote*
the shares are quoted on the stock exchange *les actions sont cotées en Bourse*
they have acquired a majority shareholding in ... *ils ont acquis la majorité des parts chez ...*

share index	*indice m de la Bourse*
share issue	*émission f d'actions*
share price	*cours m de l'action*
shell company	*société-écran f*
short (seller)	*vendeur(-euse) m(f) à découvert*
shorts *(securities)*	*titres mpl à court terme*
slump *n (of share prices)*	*effondrement m*
slump *vb*	*s'effondrer*
speculate	*spéculer*
speculation	*spéculation f*
speculator	*spéculateur(-trice) m(f)*
spot price	*prix m sur place*
stag	*loup m*
statutory meeting	*assemblée f statutaire*
statutory report	*rapport m réglementaire*
stock	*actions fpl*
stockbroker	*agent m de change*
stock exchange	*bourse f (des valeurs)*
stockholder	*actionnaire m/f*
stock market	*Bourse f*
stocks and shares	*valeurs fpl (mobilières), titres mpl*
subscriber	*souscripteur m*
subscription	*souscription f*
takeover bid	*offre f publique d'achat (OPA f)*
TESSA (Tax Exempt Special Savings Account)	*compte m d'épargne spécial exonéré d'impôts*
tranche	*tranche f*
transaction	*opération f*
transfer of shares	*transfert m d'actions*
trend	*tendance f*
turn *n*	*bénéfice m*
undated stock	*valeur f mobilière sans échéance*
underwrite *(share issue)*	*garantir*
underwriter	*preneur m ferme*
unissued capital	*capital m non-émis*

the share price has risen/fallen 25 pence since we bought the stock *le cours des actions est monté/a baissé de 25 pence depuis que nous avons acheté ces titres*

to attract small investors *attirer les petits actionnaires*

the issue is oversubscribed/fully subscribed *l'émission est sursouscrite/ entièrement souscrite*

a good time to buy/sell *le moment d'acheter/de vendre*

we will forward details of the transaction to you as soon as possible *nous vous enverrons les détails de l'opération dès que possible*

unit trust	*société f d'investissement à capital variable (SICAV f)*
unlisted company	*société f non-cotée (en Bourse)*
unlisted securities market (USM)	*second marché m de Londres*
venture capital	*capital-risque m*
white knight	*sauveteur m d'entreprise*

these shares will yield a high/low return *ces actions rapporteront gros/ peu*

EC citizens can work in any EC country without a work permit and a residence permit (*carte de séjour*) should be granted automatically if you have a job offer. There are very strict restrictions on working in Switzerland for more than a holiday job and it is best to check with the Swiss Embassy about these. You must have a work permit to work in Canada and you should contact the Canadian High Commission for further details.

Salaries are usually expressed per month in mainland Europe and are generally quoted gross. Companies may offer a *treizième mois* or even a *quatorzième mois* (13th or 14th month), i.e. one or two months' salary paid as a bonus at Christmas.

If you are sending your CV to a French-speaking company, it is helpful to translate your job title(s) and qualifications. Employers often expect a photo on a CV and a handwritten letter of application, as handwriting analysis is quite common.

For more employment vocabulary, see **PERSONNEL**
For more information about letter-writing, see **MAKING CONTACT**
For job titles and names of departments, see **COMPANY STRUCTURES**
and the **FRENCH-ENGLISH GLOSSARY**

APPLYING FOR A JOB

OPENING THE LETTER

In reply to your advertisement for a regional sales director/ personal assistant in today's/this week's/this month's Jobs Magazine, I would be grateful if you could send me further details of this post, together with an application form *en réponse à votre annonce pour un poste de directeur des ventes/ secrétaire particulière dans le Magazine de l'Emploi de ce jour/ cette semaine/ce mois, je vous serais obligé(e) de bien vouloir me faire parvenir tous renseignements utiles sur ce poste, ainsi qu'un formulaire de candidature*

I saw your advertisement in today's/this week's/this month's Jobs Magazine, and I would like to apply for the post of ... *j'ai vu votre annonce dans le Magazine de l'Emploi de ce jour/cette semaine/ ce mois, et j'ai l'honneur de poser ma candidature pour le poste de ...*

I am writing to you in the hope that you will be able to offer me employment in the field of ... *je m'adresse à vous dans l'espoir que vous pourrez m'offrir un emploi dans le domaine de ...*

I am writing to enquire about the possibility of joining your company/department for 3 months/6 months on work placement *je vous écris pour me renseigner sur la possibilité de faire un stage de 3 mois/6 mois dans votre entreprise/votre service*

GIVING YOUR BACKGROUND

I have three years' experience of this kind of work *j'ai trois ans d'expérience dans ce type de travail*

I have the qualifications and experience for the job *j'ai les qualifications et l'expérience nécessaires pour ce poste*

I am currently working in the same field *je travaille dans le même domaine actuellement*

I was trained as an engineer *j'ai une formation d'ingénieur*

As you will see from my CV, I have worked in Belgium/Canada before *comme l'indique mon curriculum vitae, j'ai travaillé en Belgique/au Canada*

As well as speaking fluent German, I have a working knowledge of French and can read Italian and Spanish *je parle allemand couramment, j'ai de bonnes connaissances de français, et je lis l'italien et l'espagnol*

WHY YOU WOULD LIKE THE JOB

I am very anxious to work in publishing/advertising *je désire vivement travailler dans l'édition/la publicité*

I would like to work in France for approximately 6 months before starting university/beginning my training course *j'aimerais passer environ 6 mois à travailler en France avant d'aller à l'université/de commencer une formation professionnelle*

I would like to work abroad (again) *j'aimerais travailler (à nouveau) à l'étranger*

I would like to make better use of my languages *j'aimerais faire plus d'usage de mes langues*

I would like to change jobs because ... *j'aimerais changer d'emploi parce que ...*

For personal/professional reasons *pour des raisons personnelles/professionnelles*

CLOSING THE LETTER

I shall be available from the end of April *je serai disponible à partir de la fin avril*

My present salary is ... per annum/per month and I have four weeks holiday with pay *mon salaire actuel est de ... par an/par mois, et j'ai quatre semaines de congés payés*

I am available for interview at any time *je me tiens à votre disposition pour un entretien aux date et heure qui vous conviendront*

Please do not contact my present employers *je vous prie de ne pas contacter mon employeur actuel*

Would you cover my relocation expenses? *seriez-vous disposé à payer mes frais de déménagement?*

Would you help me to find accommodation? *pourriez-vous m'ai-*

der à trouver un logement?

I enclose a stamped addressed envelope for your reply *veuillez trouver ci-joint une enveloppe affranchie avec adresse pour votre réponse*

I enclose an international reply coupon *vous trouverez ci-joint un coupon-réponse international*

I can supply references from my previous employers if you require them *si vous le souhaitez, je vous enverrai les références de mon dernier employeur*

Please find enclosed my completed application form, CV and references *veuillez trouver ci-joint mon formulaire de candidature, mon curriculum vitae et des références*

If you require any further information, please do not hesitate to contact me *n'hésitez pas à me contacter pour tous renseignements complémentaires*

RECRUITING EMPLOYEES ABROAD

We are seeking to recruit ... *nous cherchons à recruter ...*

We have vacancies for ... *nous avons des postes libres de ...*

We are looking for experienced sales personnel *nous sommes à la recherche de personnel de ventes expérimenté*

The successful candidate will be between 25–45 *le candidat sera âgé de 25 à 45 ans de préférence*

Experience in the field is preferable but not essential *de l'expérience dans ce domaine est souhaitable mais pas indispensable*

Knowledge of English and at least one other European language is essential *la connaissance de l'anglais et d'au moins une autre langue européenne est indispensable*

You will be travelling for two months of the year *vous serez en déplacement deux mois par an*

You will have to be capable of working in a team *vous devrez être capable de travailler en équipe*

The closing date for applications is 15 October *la date-limite de candidature est le 15 octobre*

Salary: ... p.a. plus commission/bonuses and a company car *rémunération: ... par an plus commission/primes et voiture de fonction*

Salary on application *rémunération sur candidature*

We will arrange temporary accommodation for you free of charge *nous vous trouverons un logement provisoire gratuit*

We will cover your relocation expenses up to ... *nous vous paierons les frais de déménagement jusqu'à concurrence de ...*

For more details, contact ... *pour tous renseignements complémentaires, veuillez vous adresser à ...*

REPLYING TO AN APPLICANT

Thank you for your letter of application *nous vous remercions de votre lettre de candidature*

I enclose an application form. Please fill it in and return it by 25 September *vous trouverez ci-joint un formulaire de candidature. Veuillez le remplir et nous le retourner d'ici le 25 septembre*

We would like to invite you for an interview at the above address on 26 June at 2pm. Please contact us immediately if this is not convenient *nous avons le plaisir de vous inviter à un entretien à l'adresse ci-dessus le 26 juin à 14H00. Veuillez nous aviser immédiatement si ces heure et date ne vous conviennent pas*

ACCEPTING AND REFUSING

Thank you for your letter of 19 June. I shall be pleased to attend the interview at your offices in London on Thursday 4 July at 10am *je vous remercie de votre lettre en date du 19 juin. Je me ferai un plaisir de venir à un entretien dans votre bureau de Londres le 4 juillet à 10H00*

I am very pleased to say that I would like to accept your offer of the post of ..., commencing 15 June *j'accepte avec grand plaisir votre offre pour le poste de ..., à commencer du 15 juin*

Could you send me details about obtaining a work/residence permit? *pourriez-vous m'envoyer tous renseignements utiles sur l'obtention d'un permis de travail/de séjour?*

I would very much like to accept the post which you have offered me. However, would it be possible to postpone my starting date until 1 March? *j'aimerais vraiment beaucoup accepter le poste que vous m'avez offert. Mais serait-il possible de reporter la date de commencement au 1er mars?*

I would be very glad to accept your offer if you agreed to increase the salary to ... *je serais très heureux(-euse) d'accepter votre offre si vous acceptiez d'augmenter le salaire à ...*

Having given your offer all due consideration, I regret to say that I am forced to decline *après avoir mûrement réfléchi à votre offre, j'ai le regret de vous aviser que je me vois dans l'obligation de la refuser*

INFORMING THE SUCCESSFUL/UNSUCCESSFUL CANDIDATE

We are happy to offer you the post of ... *nous avons le plaisir de vous offrir le poste de ...*

I am enclosing a contract. Please sign it and return it to me *vous trouverez ci-joint un contrat. Veuillez le signer et me le retourner*

Would a starting date of ... be acceptable? *seriez-vous en mesure de commencer le ...?*

We regret to inform you that the post has already been filled *nous avons le regret de vous informer que ce poste est déjà pris*

We regret to inform you that your name has not been put on our shortlist *nous avons le regret de vous informer que votre nom n'a pas été présélectionné*

We will keep your CV and application form on file *nous garderons votre curriculum vitae et candidature dans nos dossiers*

Please do not hesitate to reply to future advertisements for a similar post *n'hésitez pas à répondre à d'autres annonces d'emploi pour des postes semblables*

QUALIFICATIONS

Below is a list of the basic British academic qualifications and their approximate equivalent in France.

O levels, GCSEs, Standard Grades	*BEPC m (brevet m d'études du premier cycle)*
A levels, Higher Grades	*baccalauréat m*
degree (in ...)	*licence f (en ...)*
OND	*BTS m (brevet m de technicien supérieur)*
HND	*DUT m (diplôme m universitaire de technologie)*
MA (in ...)	*maîtrise f (de ...)*
PhD (in ...)	*doctorat m (de ...)*

OTHER FRENCH QUALIFICATIONS

BEP m	*(Brevet m d'études professionnelles)*	skilled worker's qualification
BT m	*(Brevet m de technicien)*	vocational training certificate, taken at approximately 18 years
BTn m	*(Baccalauréat m de technicien)*	A levels in technical and scientific subjects
BTS m	*(Brevet m de technicien supérieur)*	vocational training certificate taken at end of two-year higher education course
CAP m	*(Certificat m d'aptitude professionnelle)*	basic vocational training certificate
DEA m	*(Diplôme m d'études approfondies)*	post-graduate diploma taken before completing a PhD

DESS *m*	*(Diplôme m d'études su-périeures spécialisées)*	one-year course after a Master's degree
DEUG *m*	*(Diplôme m d'études universitaires générales)*	two-year pre-degree course
DUT *m*	*(Diplôme m universitaire de technologie)*	two-year technical pre-degree course

ADDITIONAL VOCABULARY

applicant	*candidat(e) m(f)*
application	*candidature f*
application form	*formulaire m de candidature*
apply (for)	*poser sa candidature (pour)*
aptitude test	*test m d'aptitude*
company car	*voiture f de fonction*
contract	*contrat m*
CV	*curriculum vitae m (CV m)*
graduate recruitment	*recrutement m de jeunes diplômés (universitaires)*
handwritten letter	*lettre f manuscrite*
headhunter	*chasseur m de têtes*
international reply coupon	*coupon-réponse m international*
job description	*description f du poste*
job title	*titre m*
letter of application	*lettre f de candidature*
qualifications	*diplômes mpl*
recruit *vb*	*recruter*
recruitment	*recrutement m*
referee	*répondant(e) m(f)*
reference	*référence f*
relocation expenses	*frais mpl de déménagement*
residence permit	*permis m de séjour*
sae (stamped addressed envelope)	*enveloppe f affranchie avec adresse*
student	*étudiant(e) m(f)*
training	*formation f*
typewritten letter	*lettre f dactylographiée*
unemployed	*au chômage*
vacancy	*poste m vacant*
work permit	*permis m de travail*
work placement	*stage m*

See also **COMPANY STRUCTURES** *and* **PERSONNEL**

John Dawes
89 Short Street
Glossop
Derbys SK13 4AP
Angleterre

Glossop, le 5 juillet 1991

Objet: demande d'emploi de directeur
du service d'exportations

Service du personnel
DLC-Équipements
18 avenue de la Libération
33000 Bordeaux

Messieurs,

En réponse à votre annonce parue cette semaine dans "Commerce et
Industrie", je me permets de poser ma candidature au poste de
directeur du service d'exportations dans votre entreprise.

Je vous prie de bien vouloir trouver ci-joint mon curriculum
vitae et je me tiens à votre disposition pour vous communiquer
tout complément d'information que vous pourriez souhaiter.

Dans l'espoir que vous voudrez bien considérer favorablement ma
demande et dans l'attente de votre réponse, je vous prie de
croire, Messieurs, à l'assurance de mes sentiments respectueux.

John Dawes

John Dawes

Dear Sirs,

Re: Application for the post of Export Director

With reference to your advertisement in this week's "Commerce
et Industrie", I wish to apply for the post of Export Director
in your company.

Please find enclosed my Curriculum Vitae. I shall be happy to
provide any further information you may require.

I hope the enclosed will be to your satisfaction and look
forward to hearing from you.

Yours faithfully

John Dawes

John Dawes

CURRICULUM VITAE

NOM, PRÉNOM	DAWES, John Alexander
ADRESSE	89 Short Street Glossop Derbys, SK13 4AP Angleterre
TÉLÉPHONE	19-44-457 86 46 03 (domicile) 19-44-332 61 791 (bureau)
DATE DE NAISSANCE	15.10.58
LIEU DE NAISSANCE	Sheffield, Angleterre
SITUATION DE FAMILLE	Célibataire
NATIONALITÉ	Britannique
LANGUES PRATIQUÉES	anglais (langue maternelle) français (courant) allemand (parlé, compris) hollandais (lu)

FORMATION

1983 - 1984	Diploma in Industrial Management (diplôme de gestion industrielle), London Polytechnic
1980 - 1981	Master of Business Administration (maîtrise de gestion), Hatfield Polytechnic
1977 - 1980	BSc in Mechanical Engineering (2i) (licence en ingénierie mécanique, mention bien), Sheffield University
mai 1977	4 A levels - French, German, Maths, Physics (niveau BAC: spécialisation en français, allemand, mathématiques et physique)

EXPÉRIENCE PROFESSIONNELLE

depuis juin 1987	Export Manager (Directeur du service d'exportations), Bawring Manufacturing plc, Derby
sept 1984 - mai 1987	Quality Controller (Contrôleur de qualité), Jones Machines, Welwyn Garden City
oct 1981 - mai 1983	Sales Representative (VRP), Smith and Sons, Sheffield
juin 1980 - sept 1980	Trainee Salesman (Vendeur stagiaire), Dupont Frères, Lyon
AUTRES RENSEIGNEMENTS	Bonnes connaissances d'informatique Permis de conduire Nombreux voyages en Europe et aux États-Unis

See also **PERSONNEL** *and* **PROPERTY**

absolute undertaking	*engagement m de responsabilité absolue*
acceptance of goods	*acceptation f des marchandises*
acceptance of offer	*acceptation f de l'offre*
acceptor	*accepteur(-euse) m(f)*
accredited agent	*agent m accrédité*
action	*procès m*
actionable *(claim)*	*recevable*
actionable *(person)*	*passible de poursuites*
adjudicate	*juger*
adjudication	*jugement m*
administration	*administration f*
administrator	*administrateur(-trice) m(f)*
administrative tribunal	*tribunal m administratif*
advocate *n*	*avocat(e) m(f)*
affidavit	*déclaration f (sous serment)*
affirmation	*affirmation f*
agent	*agent m*
aggravated damages	*dommages mpl aggravés*
agreement	*accord m*
agreement to sell	*compromis m de vente*
allow *(claim)*	*reconnaître la recevabilité de*
allow *(time, damages)*	*accorder*
anticipatory breach	*rupture f de contrat par anticipation*
anti-trust legislation	*loi f anti-trust*
appeal *n*	*appel m*
appeal *vb*	*interjeter appel*
appeal court	*cour f d'appel*
appellant	*appelant(e) m(f)*
arbitration clause	*clause f compromissoire*
arbitrator	*arbitre m*
article *(in contract)*	*article m*
articles of association	*statuts mpl d'une société*
ascertained goods	*marchandises fpl déterminées*
assessment (of damages)	*évaluation f (des dégâts)*
assign	*assigner*
assignee	*cessionnaire m/f*
assignment	*cession f*
assignor	*cédant(e) m(f)*

I would like some advice regarding the law covering ... *j'ai besoin de conseils sur la loi couvrant ...*

attachment	saisie f
attorney	avocat(e) m(f), mandataire m/f
Attorney-General (UK)	procureur m général britannique
Attorney-General (US)	ministre m de la Justice américain
award n (sum of money)	dommages-intérêts mpl
award vb	accorder
backdate	antidater
bad faith	mauvaise foi f
bail	caution f
bailee	dépositaire m/f
bailment	dépôt m
bailor	déposant(e) m(f)
bankrupt adj	en faillite, failli(e)
bankrupt n	failli(e) m(f)
go bankrupt	faire faillite
bankruptcy	faillite f
barrister	avocat(e) m(f) (plaidant(e))
bearer	porteur(-euse) m(f)
bearer bill	effet m au porteur
bilateral agreement	accord m bilatéral
bill of sale	contrat m de vente
bona fide	de bonne foi
breach of contract	rupture f de contrat
by(e-)law	règlement m
case	affaire f
causation	causalité f
caveat emptor	mise f en garde de l'acheteur
charge (criminal)	accusation f
charter party	charte-partie f
civil law	droit m civil
clause	clause f
code of practice	déontologie f
codicil	avenant m
commercial law	droit m commercial
common law	droit m coutumier et jurisprudentiel
common mistake	erreur f commune
community law	droit m communautaire
Companies Act	loi f sur les sociétés
company law	droit m des affaires

they did not respect the relevant clause in the contract *ils n'ont pas respecté la clause concernée du contrat*
the law is quite clear on this matter *la loi est très claire à ce sujet*

compensation	*indemnité f*
complainant	*demandeur(-deresse) m(f)*
completion	*achèvement m*
compromise *n*	*compromis m*
compromise *vb*	*faire un compromis*
conditional	*conditionnel(le)*
conditional sale agreement	*accord m de vente sous réserve*
conditions of sale	*conditions fpl de vente*
consignee	*destinataire m/f*
consumer protection	*protection f du consommateur*
contract	*contrat m*
under contract	*sous contrat*
contract law	*droit m contractuel*
contract of employment	*contrat m de travail*
contract of hire	*contrat m de louage*
contract of sale	*contrat m de vente*
contractual liability	*responsabilité f contractuelle*
contractual obligation	*engagement m contractuel*
conveyancing	*rédaction f des actes de cession de propriété*
cooling-off period	*délai m de réflexion*
copyright *n*	*droits mpl d'auteur*
copyright *vb*	*déposer*
costs	*frais mpl d'instance et dépens*
counsel for the defence	*avocat(e) m(f) de la défense*
counter-claim *n*	*demande f reconventionnelle*
counter-claim *vb*	*faire une demande reconventionnelle*
counter-offer *n*	*contre-offre f*
counter-offer *vb*	*faire une contre-offre*
Court of Appeal	*cour f d'appel*
covenant	*contrat m, engagement m*
creditor	*créancier(-ière) m(f)*
criminal law	*droit m pénal*
damages	*dommages-intérêts mpl*
debenture	*obligation f*
debt	*dette f*
debt collection agency	*agence f de recouvrement*

please sign one copy of the contract and return it to us *veuillez signer un exemplaire du contrat et nous le retourner*

we will draw up a contract and submit it to you for inspection *nous rédigerons un contrat et vous le soumettrons pour vérification*

this text is copyright *les droits de reproduction de ce texte sont réservés*

does French/Swiss law cover this? *est-ce que le droit français/suisse couvre ceci?*

debtor	*débiteur(-trice)* m(f)
debtor-creditor-supplier agreement	*accord* m *entre le fournisseur-créditeur et le débiteur*
deed	*acte* m *notarié*
deed of covenant	*acte* m *de donation*
default vb	*manquer à ses engagements*
default notice	*notification* f *de défaut*
defend	*défendre*
defendant	*défendeur(-deresse)* m(f)
defraud	*frauder*
deviation	*déviation* f
directives	*directives* fpl
disenfranchise	*priver d'un droit de représentation*
draft n	*ébauche* f
draft vb	*ébaucher*
effective date	*date* f *d'effet, date* f *d'entrée en vigueur*
embezzle	*détourner (des fonds)*
embezzlement	*détournement* m *de fonds*
employment law	*droit* m *du travail*
enforcement order	*mandat* m *d'exécution*
equitable *(fair)*	*équitable*
equity	*équité* f
escape clause	*clause* f *dérogatoire*
estate	*biens* mpl
exclusion clause	*clause* f *d'exclusion*
exclusive agency agreement	*accord* m *d'agence exclusive*
exemption clause	*clause* f *d'exonération*
ex gratia payment	*gratification* f
expiry date	*date* f *d'expiration*
fee	*honoraires* mpl
fiduciary	*agent* m *fiduciaire*
final demand	*dernier rappel* m
fixed-price contract	*contrat* m *à prix ferme*
formality	*formalité* f
franchise n	*franchise* f
franchise vb	*franchiser*
franchise agreement	*contrat* m *de franchise*
franchisee	*franchisé* m
franchiser	*franchiseur* m
fraud	*fraude* f
gentleman's agreement	*gentleman's agreement* m
good faith	*bonne foi* f
goods and chattels	*biens* mpl *et effets* mpl

guarantee *n*	*garantie f*
guarantee *vb*	*garantir*
under guarantee	*sous garantie*
guarantor	*garant(e) m(f)*
guilty party	*coupable m/f*
hire-purchase agreement	*contrat m de crédit*
illegal	*illégal(e)*
illegality	*illégalité f*
illegally	*illégalement*
incidental damages	*dommages-intérêts mpl accessoires*
indemnity clause	*clause f de dédommagement*
injunction	*injonction f, ordre m*
innocent	*innocent(e)*
innocent party	*innocent(e) m(f)*
insolvency	*insolvabilité f*
intellectual property *(work of art)*	*propriété f littéraire et artistique*
intellectual property *(patent)*	*propriété f industrielle*
international law	*droit m international*
judge *n*	*juge m*
judge *vb*	*juger*
judgement	*jugement m*
jurisdiction	*juridiction f*
justification	*justification f*
lapse of time	*laps m de temps, intervalle m*
law	*loi f*
law court	*cour f de justice*
lawful	*légal(e)*
Law Society	*ordre m des avocats*
lawsuit	*procès m*
lawyer *(company lawyer)*	*juriste m/f*
lawyer *(barrister)*	*avocat(e) m(f)*
lease back	*vendre en cession-bail*
leaseback	*cession-bail f*
leaseback arrangement	*accord m de cession-bail*
legal	*légal(e)*

to operate within/outside the law *agir conformément/contrairement à la loi*

to bring a lawsuit against someone *intenter un procès à quelqu'un*

you will be hearing from our lawyer in the very near future *notre avocat vous contactera incessamment*

to take legal action to recover something *intenter un procès pour recouvrer quelque chose*

we will be forced to take legal action if ... *nous nous verrons dans l'obligation d'entamer des poursuites judiciaires si ...*

legal department	*service m du contentieux*
legality	*légalité f*
legally binding	*juridiquement contraignant(e)*
legal requirement	*obligation f légale*
legatee	*légataire m/f*
letter of intent	*lettre f d'intention*
letters patent	*brevet m d'invention*
liable	*responsable*
liability	*responsabilité f*
licensing agreement	*accord m de licence*
limited liability	*responsabilité f limitée*
litigation	*litige m*
loophole	*point m faible*
magistrate	*magistrat m*
mandate	*mandat m*
mandatory	*obligatoire, mandataire*
maritime law	*droit m maritime*
maritime lawyer	*juriste m/f de droit maritime*
misrepresentation	*fausse déclaration f*
mitigation of loss	*réduction f des pertes*
moratorium	*moratoire m*
negligence	*négligence f*
negligent	*négligent(e)*
negotiable	*négociable*
negotiation	*négociation f*
non-payment	*non-paiement m*
non-performance	*non-exécution f*
notification	*notification f*
nuisance	*infraction f simple*
null and void	*nul(le) et non-avenu(e)*
official receiver	*administrateur m judiciaire,*
	* syndic m de faillite*
out-of-court settlement	*règlement m à l'aimable*
partner	*associé(e) m(f)*
partnership	*association f*
patent *n*	*brevet m d'invention*
patent *vb*	*faire breveter*
patent office	*bureau m des brevets*
patent rights	*propriété f industrielle*

to seek *or* **take legal advice** *consulter un juriste*
to give someone legal advice *donner des conseils juridiques à quelqu'un*
to have a legal right to ... *avoir une autorisation légale pour ...*
to exploit a loophole in the law *exploiter une faille dans la loi*
the contract becomes null and void if ... *le contrat devient nul et non*
*   avenu si ...*

penalty clause	clause f pénale
performance	exécution f
plagiarism	plagiat m
plaintiff	plaignant(e) m(f)
power of attorney	procuration f (écrite)
precedent	précédent m
prima facie case	affaire f recevable
prima facie evidence	commencement m de preuve
principal	auteur m principal (du délit)
promise n	promesse f
promise vb	promettre
promissory note	billet m à ordre
property	biens mpl
proprietary goods	articles mpl de marque
prosecute	poursuivre (en) justice
prosecuting counsel	procureur m
quid pro quo	contrepartie f
ratification	ratification f
ratify	ratifier
receiver	administrateur m judiciaire
receivership	see phrases below
rectification	rectification f
registered trademark	marque f déposée
regulation	règlement m
repossess	reprendre possession de
repossession	reprise f de possession
represent	représenter
representation	représentation f
repudiation	refus m d'honorer, rejet m
required notice	préavis m réglementaire
restrictive trading agreement	clause f de non-concurrence
return order	ordre m de renvoi
revocation	révocation f
revoke	révoquer
rider	clause f additionnelle
right n	droit m
ruling	décision f
sale and lease back	cession-bail f
secured creditor	créancier(-ière) m(f) garanti(e)
security of tenure (in job)	stabilité f de l'emploi, titularisation f

I have a query regarding clause 4 of the contract *j'ai besoin d'une explication sur la clause 4 du contrat*
to go into receivership *être en règlement judiciaire*

security of tenure *(of tenant)*	*droit m d'occupation du logement*
sequestration	*mise f sous séquestre*
settle	*régler*
settlement	*règlement m*
signatory	*signataire m/f*
solicitor *(for divorce, court cases)*	*avocat(e) m(f)*
solicitor *(for sales, wills)*	*notaire m/f*
specimen signature	*spécimen m de signature*
statute	*statut m*
statutory	*statutaire, légal(e)*
subcontract *n*	*contrat m de sous-traitance*
subcontract *vb*	*sous-traiter*
subject to contract	*sous réserve d'un contrat*
subject to confirmation	*sous réserve de confirmation*
termination of contract	*résiliation f de contrat*
third party	*tiers m*
tort	*acte m délictuel*
Trade Descriptions Act	*loi f contre les appellations et la publicité mensongères*
trademark	*marque f de fabrique*
trust	*fidéicommis m*
trustee	*fidéicommissaire m/f*
unascertained goods	*marchandises fpl non-déterminées*
unconditional	*sans conditions*
undersigned	*soussigné(e) m(f)*
unilateral mistake	*erreur f unilatérale*
void	*nul(le)*
voidable contract	*contrat m résiliable*
warrant	*mandat m*
warranty	*garantie f*
under warranty	*sous garantie*
writ	*acte m judiciaire*

to sue (a company) for damages *poursuivre (une société) en dommages et intérêts*
the contract is valid for all countries *le contrat est valide dans tous les pays*
to make void *rendre nul(le)*
to serve a writ on someone *sommer quelqu'un de comparaître en justice*

BY PHONE

DIALLING CODES (UK ONLY)

To Belgium	010 32
To France	010 33
To Luxembourg	010 352
To Quebec	010 418
To Switzerland	010 41

From Belgium	00 44	(when in Bruges, Ostend and Veurne, wait for the dialling tone after the 44)
From France	19 44	(wait for the dialling tone after the 19)
From Luxembourg	00 44	
From Quebec	011 44	
From Switzerland	00 44	

When calling the UK from abroad, remember to knock the initial zero off the British dialling code, e.g. when calling London from France you dial 19 44 71 or 19 44 81.

CALLING FROM A PAYPHONE
You can phone abroad from Belgium using a card phone or from coin boxes displaying the European flag. These will have dialling instructions in English and you can make a reverse-charge call from them by calling the operator on 09.

Most French phone boxes now take a phonecard (*une carte télé-phonique*) rather than coins. It is worth noting that reverse-charge calls can only be made internationally, by calling the operator on 19. The cheap rate is Monday-Friday 21.30–08.00, Saturday after 14.00 and Sunday and public holidays all day.

All call boxes in Luxembourg accept both Belgian and Luxembourg francs and can be used for international calls. Reverse-charge calls can only be made from the post office. For national/international enquiries ring 016/017.

International direct dialling is not available from public payphones in Quebec. The cheap rate is daily from 18.00–21.00. There is also an intermediate rate, Monday-Friday 13.00–18.00 and Saturday 09.00–18.00.

You can phone abroad from all call boxes in Switzerland. All have dialling instructions in English. To make a reverse-charge call ring the operator on 114. For international enquiries ring 121. The cheap rate is Monday-Friday 21.00–08.00 and all day Saturday.

CALLING THE OPERATOR

Could you get me 65 13 22 20, please *je voudrais le 65 13 22 20, s'il vous plaît*

Would you give me Directory Enquiries, please *pourriez-vous me passer les renseignements, s'il vous plaît?*

I'm looking for the phone number of ... *je cherche le numéro de téléphone de ...*

The address is ... *l'adresse est ...*

What is the code for Bordeaux? *quel est l'indicatif pour Bordeaux?*

I'd like to make a reverse-charge call to Glasgow/England *je voudrais faire un appel en PCV à Glasgow/en Angleterre*

I'd like a credit card call to Berlin *je voudrais une communication payable avec carte de crédit pour Berlin*

I want to make an international call *je voudrais une communication pour l'étranger*

Can I dial direct to the Philippines? *est-ce que je peux appeler les Philippines par automatique?*

My call was just cut off. Can you reconnect me? *j'ai été coupé. Pouvez-vous me remettre en ligne?*

THE OPERATOR REPLIES

Quel numéro demandez-vous? *what number do you want?*

D'où appelez-vous? *where are you calling from?*

Pourriez-vous répéter le numéro, s'il vous plaît? *would you repeat the number, please*

Vous pouvez obtenir ce numéro par l'automatique *you can dial the number direct*

Raccrochez et recomposez le numéro *replace the receiver and dial again*

Le 65 13 22 20 ne répond pas *there's no reply from 65 13 22 20*

La ligne est occupée *the line is engaged*

Ça sonne *ringing for you now*

Ça ne répond pas *there's no reply*

C'est à vous *go ahead, caller*

Vous êtes en ligne *go ahead, caller*

GETTING PAST THE SWITCHBOARD

Extension 3045 please *le poste 30 45 s'il vous plaît*

Could I speak to Ms Rousseau, please? *je voudrais parler à Mme Rousseau, s'il vous plaît*

Could you put me through to M. Darbeau, please? *pourriez-vous me passer M. Darbeau, s'il vous plaît?*

Please try the number again *veuillez réessayer ce numéro*

I'll hold *je patiente*

Does anyone speak English? *y a-t-il quelqu'un qui parle anglais?*

THE SWITCHBOARD OPERATOR REPLIES
Qui est à l'appareil? *who is calling, please?*
C'est de la part de qui? *who shall I say is calling?*
Est-ce que vous connaissez le numéro de poste? *do you know the extension number?*
Je vous le passe *I'm putting you through now*
Ne quittez pas *sorry to keep you waiting*
M. Pagot est sur l'autre ligne *Mr Pagot is on the other line*
Vous êtes en communication avec un répondeur automatique *this is a recorded message*
Au bip sonore, veuillez laisser votre message *please speak after the tone*

IF THE PERSON IS OUT
I'll call back later/tomorrow *je rappellerai plus tard/demain*
Is there anyone else I can speak to? *est-ce que je pourrais parler à quelqu'un d'autre?*
Please transfer my call to ... *veuillez transférer mon appel à ...*
Do you have a number where I can reach him/her? *savez-vous où je pourrais le/la contacter?*
When will he/she be in the office? *quand sera-t-il/elle au bureau?*
Can you ask him/her to call me back? *pourriez-vous lui demander de me rappeler?*
Can I leave a message? *puis-je laisser un message?*
Who am I speaking to? *qui est à l'appareil?*

WHEN YOU GET THROUGH
My name is ... *je m'appelle ...*
I'm calling on behalf of ... *j'appelle de la part de ...*
You were recommended to me by ... *vous m'avez été recommandé(e) par ...*
I'm calling about ... *je vous téléphone à propos de ...*

RECEIVING A CALL FROM ABROAD
Speaking *c'est moi-même*
How can I help you? *que puis-je faire pour vous?*
Sorry, I don't speak French *je regrette, je ne parle pas français*
Hold on a moment, please *ne quittez pas*
Who's calling? *qui est à l'appareil?*
He's/she's out at the moment *il/elle n'est pas là pour l'instant*
Please call back in an hour/tomorrow/this afternoon *veuillez rappeler dans une heure/demain/cet après-midi*
Can you speak a little louder/more slowly, please? *pourriez-vous parler un peu plus fort/plus lentement s'il vous plaît?*
This is a very bad line *la ligne est très mauvaise*

SAMPLE TELEPHONE CONVERSATION

STANDARDISTE	: *Établissements Duvalin, bonjour!*	
M FOSTER	: *Allô, bonjour Madame.* **Pourriez-vous me passer** *Monsieur Vercors, s'il vous plaît?*	*could you put me through to ...*
	Il est au poste 342, *service du marketing.*	*he's on extension 342*
STANDARDISTE	: *Oui,* **c'est de la part de qui, s'il vous plaît?**	*can I ask who's calling?*
M FOSTER	: *Monsieur Foster de la société Best Books Ltd.*	
STANDARDISTE	: *Un moment, s'il vous plaît, je vais voir s'il est là.* **Ne quittez pas ...**	*please hold the line ...*
	Allô Monsieur Foster, **je regrette,** *Monsieur Vercors n'est pas dans son bureau,* **mais je peux vous passer sa secrétaire.**	*I'm sorry ...* *but I can put you through to his secretary*
M FOSTER	: *Oui, très bien.*	
MME LEBERT	: *Allô, ici Madame Lebert, secrétaire de Monsieur Vercors.* **Que puis-je faire pour vous?**	*How can I help you?*
M FOSTER	: *Bonjour Madame Lebert.* **Je téléphone au sujet du** *Salon du Livre qui doit commencer le 20 mars prochain. Monsieur Vercors et moi-même avions parlé de nous rencontrer à cette occasion. J'aimerais donc savoir s'il serait possible de fixer une date et un lieu de rencontre, si du moins ses engagements le lui permettent.*	*I'm phoning about ...*
MME LEBERT	: *Très bien.* **Un instant, s'il vous plaît ...**	*one moment, please*
	Voyons ... *Monsieur Vercours est pris toute la journée du 20 mais il est libre le mardi 21 dans la matinée.* **Cela vous conviendrait-il?**	*let's see/let me see ...* *would that suit you?*
M FOSTER	: *Cela me convient parfaitement. Disons rendez-vous à 10 heures dans le hall de réception?*	
MME LEBERT	: *Oui, très bien.* **C'est noté.**	*I've made a note of it*
M FOSTER	: *Merci beaucoup. Au revoir!*	

LETTERS, FAXES AND TELEXES

STANDARD OPENING AND CLOSING FORMULAE

Used when the person is not personally known to you	
Monsieur, Madame, Mademoiselle,	Je vous prie de croire, [...], à l'assurance de mes sentiments distingués (*or* de mes salutations distinguées). Veuillez agréer, [...], l'expression de mes sentiments les meilleurs.
Used only if the person is known to you personally	
Cher Monsieur, Chère Madame, Chère Mademoiselle,	As above plus: Croyez, [...], à l'expression de mes sentiments les meilleurs.

TO ACQUAINTANCES AND FRIENDS

Still fairly formal	
Cher Monsieur, Chère Madame, Chère Mademoiselle,	Recevez, je vous prie, mes meilleures amitiés. Je vous envoie mes bien amicales pensées.
Cher Monsieur, chère Madame, Chers amis,	Je vous adresse à tous deux mon très amical souvenir.
Fairly informal: 'Tu' or 'Vous' forms could be used	
Cher Patrick, Chère Lucienne Chers Philippe et France,	Bien amicalement Cordialement Amitiés

WRITING TO A FIRM OR AN INSTITUTION

Messieurs, Monsieur, Madame,	Je vous prie d'agréer, [...], l'assurance de mes sentiments distingués. Veuillez accepter, [...], l'expression de mes sentiments distingués.

STARTING A LETTER

Thank you for your letter, which I have just received/which was passed to me by X *je vous remercie de votre courrier que je viens de recevoir/qui m'a été transmis par X*

Please accept my apologies for the delay in replying to your letter *je vous prie de m'excuser d'avoir tardé à vous répondre*

With reference to your letter of 31 July *comme suite à votre courrier du 31 juillet*

Further to our conversation of 4 December *comme suite à notre conversation du 4 décembre*

WITHIN THE LETTER

I was interested to hear that ... *j'ai appris avec intérêt que ...*

I regret to inform you that ... *j'ai le regret de vous informer que ...*

I am happy to inform you that ... *j'ai le plaisir de vous informer que ...*

Please find enclosed *veuillez trouver ci-joint*

I am sending under separate cover ... *je vous envoie sous pli séparé ...*

Could you please send us ... *veuillez nous envoyer ...*

We would welcome your views on this matter *nous apprécierions vos commentaires à ce sujet*

I hope you understand our point of view on this matter *j'espère que vous comprendrez notre point de vue sur cette question*

I have received no reply to my letter of 3 August *mon courrier du 3 août est resté sans réponse*

Please acknowledge receipt of this letter *veuillez accuser réception de ce courrier*

ENDING A LETTER

I trust the foregoing is to your satisfaction *j'espère que ce qui précède vous conviendra*

I would be grateful if you could reply by return of post *je vous serais obligé(e) de bien vouloir répondre par retour de courrier*

If there is anything further I can do for you, please do not hesitate to contact me *si je peux vous être utile, n'hésitez pas à me contacter*

Should you have any queries, I shall be pleased to discuss them with you *nous serons heureux de vous fournir tous renseignements utiles*

I look forward to hearing from you ... *en attendant le plaisir de vous lire ...*

THANKS AND BEST WISHES

Thank you for taking the trouble to write to us *nous vous remer-*

LA MAISON RUSTIQUE

Fabrication de mobilier
Zone industrielle de Dampierre
B.P. 531 - 17015 Dampierre Cedex

Tél: 06 28 42 37

Vos réf: HL/SA 50746
Nos réf: MB/AL 16064
Objet: envoi de documentation

Country Kitchens
29 Montgomerie Street
ARDROSSAN KA22 8EQ

Messieurs,

Dampierre, le 13 août 1991

Nous vous remercions de votre lettre du 10 août, ainsi que de
votre demande de renseignements concernant notre gamme de sièges
de cuisine. Nous vous prions de trouver ci-joint une
documentation complète, accompagnée de notre liste de prix.
Toutefois, nous nous permettons d'attirer votre attention sur
nos nouveaux modèles 'Saintonge', qui semblent convenir
particulièrement à vos besoins. Ces modèles sont actuellement
offerts à des prix très avantageux.

Nous nous tenons à votre entière disposition pour toute demande
de renseignements supplémentaires et vous prions d'agréer,
Messieurs, l'assurance de nos sentiments dévoués.

Le Directeur commercial

J. Leclerc

Jean Leclerc

PJ: 1 documentation complète

Dear Sirs,

Re: Catalogue request

Thank you for your letter of 10th August requesting
information on our range of kitchen chairs. Please find
enclosed a complete catalogue along with our price list. We
would like to draw your attention to our new 'Saintonge'
range, which would appear to be particularly suited to your
needs. This range is currently on special offer.

We shall be happy to provide any further information you may
require.

Yours faithfully

J. Leclerc

Enc

Jean Leclerc
Sales Director

cions d'avoir pris la peine de nous écrire
We greatly appreciate the time and trouble you took for us *nous vous sommes très obligés pour le temps et les efforts que vous nous avez consacrés*
I have been asked to thank you on behalf of the managing director for the presentation you gave us *le PDG m'a chargé(e) de vous remercier pour l'exposé que vous nous avez présenté*

AT THE POST OFFICE

Belgian post offices do not combine telephone and telegram services. The main post office in Brussels is at 1 place de la Monnaie. There is a 24-hour post office in Brussels at the Gare du Midi, 48A avenue Fonsny.

The French postal service (PTT) offers telephone and telegram facilities as well as handling mail. The main Paris post office is open 24 hours a day and is at 52 rue du Louvre, 75001. You can also buy stamps in your hotel or in a *café tabac*.

Post office opening times in Luxembourg depend on the size of the office and on the services offered. The times given below are for the main post office only. Many post offices only open in the afternoon.

In Switzerland post offices also offer telephone and telegram facilities and the mail system itself is highly efficient. The main post office in Geneva is located in rue de Lausanne and is open from 06.30 to 23.00 every day.

POST OFFICE OPENING HOURS

In Belgium	Mon-Fri	09.00–12.00	
	and	14.00–15.30	Sat 08.00–12.00
In France	Mon-Fri	08.00–19.00	Sat 08.00–12.00
In Luxembourg	Mon-Sun	06.00–20.00	
	Parcels	08.00–12.00	
	and	17.00–18.00	
In Quebec	Mon-Fri	08.00–17.45	
In Switzerland	Mon-Fri	07.30–12.00	
	and	13.45–18.30	Sat 09.30–11.00

PHRASES USED BY THE CUSTOMER
Where's the nearest post office? *où se trouve le bureau de poste le plus proche?*
Which window/counter sells stamps? *pour acheter les timbres c'est à quel guichet/comptoir?*
Where is the poste restante? *où se trouve la poste restante?*
I'd like ten first-class/second-class stamps, please *je voudrais dix*

timbres à tarif normal/réduit

I'd like some change for the phone/stamp machine/photocopier *je voudrais de la monnaie pour le téléphone/distributeur automatique de timbres/photocopieur*

I'd like a money order for 150F *je voudrais un mandat-poste de 150 francs*

Could I have a receipt? *pourriez-vous me donner un reçu?*

Can I send a fax from here? *est-il possible d'envoyer des télécopies ici?*

Can I make photocopies here? *est-il possible de faire des photocopies ici?*

How long will this letter/parcel take to arrive? *combien de temps mettra cette lettre/ce colis pour arriver?*

What's the quickest/cheapest way of sending this letter/parcel? *quel est le moyen le plus rapide/le moins cher d'expédier cette lettre/ce colis?*

I'd like to send this letter/parcel ... *je voudrais expédier cette lettre/ce colis ...*

by air/surface mail *par avion/courrier ordinaire*

by registered post *en recommandé*

express delivery *par exprès*

special delivery *par exprès*

as printed matter *comme imprimé*

cheap rate *en régime ordinaire/tarif réduit*

Which form should I fill out? *quel formulaire faut-il remplir?*

Could I have a registered post form/customs form/express delivery form? *je voudrais une fiche de recommandé/une fiche douanière/une fiche de courrier exprès*

I don't know the post code. Where can I look it up? *je ne connais pas le code postal. Où puis-je le trouver?*

PHRASES YOU ARE LIKELY TO HEAR

Je regrette, il faut aller au comptoir/guichet 4 *I'm sorry, you'll have to go to counter/window 4*

Par quel régime voulez-vous expédier ceci? *how do you want to send this?*

Remplissez ce formulaire s'il vous plaît *please fill out this form*

Avez-vous une pièce d'identité sur vous? *do you have any identification?*

Mettez le colis sur la balance *put the parcel on the scales, please*

Ce colis n'est pas bien scellé/emballé *this parcel is not sealed/packed correctly*

Que contient ce colis? *what is in the parcel?*

Quelle est la valeur du contenu? *what is the value of the contents?*

ADDITIONAL VOCABULARY

above-mentioned	*mentionné(e) ci-dessus*
acknowledge	*accuser réception de*
address	*adresse f*
airmail	*poste f aérienne*
answer-back code	*indicatif m*
answering machine	*répondeur m automatique*
business address *(of individual)*	*adresse f au bureau*
(of company)	*adresse f du siège social*
Business Reply Service	*service-lecteurs m*
call *n*	*coup m de téléphone*
call *vb*	*appeler*
car phone	*téléphone m de voiture*
cardphone	*téléphone m à carte*
cellular telephone	*téléphone m cellulaire*
cheap rate	*tarif m réduit*
circular	*circulaire f*
compliments slip	*fiche f de transmission*
conference call	*appel m par Réunion-Téléphone ®*
continuation sheet	*feuille f additionnelle*
continuous tone	*tonalité f continue*
cordless telephone	*téléphone m sans fil*
counter staff	*guichetiers(-ières) mpl/fpl*
courier service	*messagerie f*
credit card call	*appel m payé par carte de crédit*
Datapost ®	*Postexpress ®*
"date as postmark"	*"pour la date se référer au cachet de la poste"*
dialling tone	*tonalité f*
dictate	*dicter*
directory enquiries	*renseignements mpl*
draft *vb*	*faire le brouillon de*
draft *(letter) n*	*brouillon m*
engaged tone	*tonalité f "occupé"*
envelope	*enveloppe f*
ex-directory number	*numéro m sur la liste rouge*
express delivery	*exprès m*
extension number	*numéro m de poste*
fax *n*	*télécopie f, fax m*
fax *vb*	*envoyer par télécopie or fax*
fax machine	*télécopieur m*
fax number	*numéro m de télécopieur/fax*
first class post	*courrier m (à tarif) normal*

franking machine	*machine f à affranchir*
Freefone ®	*numéro m vert*
Freepost ®	*franchise f postale*
international reply coupon	*coupon-réponse m international*
letter	*lettre f*
local/long-distance call	*communication f urbaine/ interurbaine*
memo	*note f (de service)*
modem	*modem m*
number unobtainable tone	*tonalité f numéro hors service*
operator	*standardiste m/f*
operator service	*standard m*
pager	*avertisseur m de poche*
parcel	*colis m*
parcel post	*service m de colis postaux*
payphone	*téléphone m public*
peak rate	*tarif m maximal*
personal call	*communication f personnelle*
phone box	*cabine f téléphonique*
phone call	*coup m de téléphone*
phonecard	*carte f téléphonique*
PO Box	*BP (boîte f postale)*
post *vb*	*expédier par la poste*
postage and packing	*frais mpl de port et d'emballage*
postage rate	*tarif m postal*
postal order	*mandat(-poste) m*
post box	*boîte f aux lettres*
post code	*code m postal*
poste restante	*poste f restante*
postmark	*cachet m de la poste*
post office	*bureau m de poste*
post paid	*port payé*
prepaid envelope	*enveloppe f affranchie*
"private"	*"personnel"*
"private and confidential"	*"confidentiel"*
recorded delivery	*envoi m recommandé*
recorded message	*message m enregistré*
re-dial *vb*	*recomposer le numéro*
registered post	*envoi m recommandé*
reply-paid postcard	*carte-réponse f*
reverse-charge call	*communication f en PCV*
ringing tone	*sonnerie f*
second class post	*courrier m à tarif réduit*
send	*envoyer*
stamp	*timbre m*

stamp machine	*distributeur m (automatique) de timbres*
standard rate	*tarif m normal*
surface mail	*courrier m ordinaire*
switchboard	*standard m*
telephone *n*	*téléphone m*
telephone box	*cabine f téléphonique*
telephone/telex directory	*annuaire m téléphonique/des télex*
telex *(message)*	*télex m*
telex *(machine)*	*télex m*
transfer charge call	*communication f en PCV*
trunk call	*communication f interurbaine*
type *vb*	*taper*
undermentioned	*mentionné(e) ci-dessous*
undersigned	*soussigné(e)*
videophone	*visiophone m*
window envelope	*enveloppe f à fenêtre*
Yellow Pages ®	*pages fpl jaunes*

acceptable quality level	*niveau m de qualité acceptable*
allowance	*tolérance f*
assembly line	*chaîne f de montage*
assembly plant	*usine f de montage*
automated	*automatisé(e)*
automation	*automatisation f*
backlog of orders	*accumulation f de commandes en retard*
backlog of work	*travail m en retard*
batch	*lot m*
batch production	*production f par lots*
blueprint	*projet m, plan m directeur*
bottleneck	*goulot m d'étranglement*
bottling plant	*usine f de mise en bouteilles*
breakdown *(of machine)*	*panne f*
brewery	*brasserie f*
built-in obsolescence	*obsolescence f planifiée*
by-product	*sous-produit m*
cannery	*conserverie f*
capital goods	*biens mpl d'équipement*
chemical plant	*usine f chimique*
component	*composant m, élément m*
computer-controlled	*géré(e) par ordinateur*
control system	*système m de contrôle*
custom-built	*fait(e) sur commande*
cutting machine	*machine f à couper*
defect	*défaut m*
defective	*défectueux(-euse)*
depreciate *(machine)*	*se déprécier*
depreciation *(on machine)*	*dépréciation f*
distillery	*distillerie f*
division of labour	*division f du travail*
downtime *(machine)*	*temps m mort*
downtime *(person)*	*temps m d'arrêt*
drill *n*	*perceuse f*
drill *vb*	*percer*
economies of scale	*économies fpl d'échelle*
ergonomics	*ergonomie f*

the plant is running 10% above/below capacity *l'usine fonctionne à 10% au-dessus/en-dessous de sa capacité*
do you have sufficient capacity to handle an order of ...? *avez-vous une capacité suffisante pour honorer une commande de ...?*
there is a manufacturing defect in this consignment *il y a un défaut de fabrication dans cet envoi*

factory	*usine f*
finished goods	*produits mpl finis*
fitter	*monteur(-euse) m(f)*
flaw	*défaut m*
flawed	*imparfait(e)*
flow-line production	*production f à la chaîne*
foundry	*fonderie f*
furnace	*fourneau m*
hiccup	*hoquet m*
idle capacity	*potentiel m inutilisé*
idle time	*temps m mort*
imperfect	*imparfait(e)*
industrial goods	*biens mpl d'équipement*
job	*commande f*
job card	*fiche f de commande*
job number	*numéro m de commande*
joint venture	*entreprise f en participation*
just-in-time manufacturing	*fabrication f "juste-à-temps"*
kite mark	*estampille f de qualité*
latent defect	*vice m caché*
lathe *n*	*tour m*
lead time *(for delivery)*	*délai m de livraison*
lead time *(for manufacture)*	*délai m d'exécution*
licensing agreement	*accord m de licence*
on line	*en production, en service*
off line	*pas en service*
machine *n*	*machine f*
machine *vb*	*usiner*
machine shop	*atelier m d'usinage*
machine tool	*machine-outil f*
machinist	*machiniste m/f*
maintenance shift	*équipe f de maintenance*
man-hour	*heure f travaillée*
man-made	*synthétique*
manufacture *n*	*fabrication f*
manufacture *vb*	*fabriquer*
manufactured goods	*produits mpl manufacturés*
manufacturer	*fabricant m*

please advise me of the lead time for supply of ... *veuillez m'indiquer le délai de livraison pour la fourniture de ...*
to come on line *passer à la production*
to take something off line *interrompre la production de quelque chose*
they are clothes/car manufacturers *ce sont des fabricants de prêt-à-porter/d'automobiles*

manufacturing	*fabrication f*
manufacturing cycle	*cycle m de fabrication*
mass-produced	*fabriqué(e) en série*
mass production	*fabrication f en série*
micrometer	*palmer m, micromètre m*
operating costs	*charges fpl d'exploitation*
operating profit	*bénéfice m d'exploitation*
operation *(of machine)*	*fonctionnement m*
operations	*opérations fpl*
order book	*carnet m de commandes*
output *n*	*production f, rendement m*
output *vb*	*produire*
overcapacity	*surcapacité f*
overproduction	*surproduction f*
packaging *(process)*	*conditionnement m*
packaging *(wrapper)*	*emballage m*
parameter	*paramètre m*
piece rate	*tarif m à la pièce*
plant *(machinery)*	*installations fpl*
plant *(factory)*	*usine f*
pottery *(factory)*	*poterie f*
press *(machine in factory)*	*presse f*
primary products	*produits mpl de base*
process *n*	*procédé m*
process *vb*	*traiter*
processing plant	*usine f de transformation*
product	*produit m*
product design	*conception f du produit*
production	*production f*
production control	*contrôle m de (la) production*
production line	*chaîne f (de fabrication)*
production planning	*planification f de la production*
production problem	*problème m de production*
productivity	*productivité f*
progress *(through factory)*	*progression f*
pump *n*	*pompe f*
quality control	*contrôle m de qualité*
quality controller	*contrôleur(-euse) m(f) de la qualité*

the factory is operational 24 hours a day *l'usine est opérationnelle 24 heures sur 24*
we would like to place an order for ... *nous voulons commander ...*
to increase/reduce output *augmenter/réduire la production*
to output 30,000 units per day *produire 30.000 unités par jour*

raw materials	*matières fpl premières*
recycled	*recyclé(e)*
refinery	*raffinerie f*
robot	*robot m*
robotics	*robotique f*
running costs	*frais mpl de fonctionnement*
safety standards	*normes fpl de sécurité*
semi-automated	*semi-automatisé(e)*
service centre	*atelier m de réparation*
shop floor	*ateliers mpl*
shrink-wrap	*emballer sous film plastique*
shrink-wrapped	*sous emballage plastique*
shrink-wrapping	*emballage m plastique*
shut-down *n*	*fermeture f*
shut down *vb*	*fermer*
specialization	*spécialisation f*
standardization	*standardisation f*
steelworks	*aciérie f*
stoppage *(in work)*	*arrêt m*
stoppage *(strike)*	*arrêt m de travail*
on stream	*en production, en service*
subassembly	*montage m préparatoire*
substandard	*de qualité inférieure*
throughput	*capacité f de traitement*
time clock	*pointeuse f*
tool	*outil m*
turnaround time	*temps m d'immobilisation*
undermanning	*manque m de main-d'œuvre*
unit cost	*coût m unitaire*
unit price	*prix m unitaire*
vacuum-packed	*emballé(e) sous vide*
waste *n*	*déchets mpl*
waste *vb*	*gaspiller*
wear and tear *(on machine)*	*usure f*

the factory has an excellent record on delivery/quality/safety *l'usine a d'excellents antécédents pour ce qui concerne les livraisons/la qualité/la sûreté*

the factory has high/low running costs *les frais d'exploitation de l'usine sont élevés/modestes*

a large-scale/small-scale manufacturer *un fabricant à grande/petite échelle*

to come on stream *passer à la production*

is it possible to arrange a tour of the factory? *est-il possible d'organiser un tour de l'usine?*

would you like to visit our factory? *souhaitez-vous faire le tour de notre usine?*

work in progress	*travaux mpl en cours*
works	*usine f*
workshop	*atelier m*

See also **ADVERTISING AND MEDIA** *and* **BUYING AND SELLING**

advertise	*faire de la publicité (pour)*
advertisement	*réclame f, publicité f*
advertising campaign	*campagne f de publicité*
advertising manager	*directeur(-trice) m(f) de la publicité*
advertising strategy	*stratégie f publicitaire, politique f de commercialisation*
after-sales service	*service m après-vente (SAV m)*
appeal	*attrait m*
artwork	*maquette f*
attitude survey	*étude f de comportement*
audience research	*étude f d'opinion*
available market	*débouchés mpl disponibles*
bad PR	*relations fpl publiques médiocres*
bar chart	*diagramme m en tuyaux d'orgue*
blind test	*test m en aveugle*
blurb	*texte m publicitaire*
brand	*marque f*
brand acceptance	*accueil m réservé à une marque*
brand awareness	*notoriété f de la marque*
brand image	*image f de marque*
brand loyalty	*fidélité f à la marque*
brand manager	*directeur(-trice) m(f) de produit*
brief *n*	*instructions fpl*
brief *vb*	*donner des instructions à*
bring out	*lancer*
brochure	*brochure f, prospectus m*
built-in obsolescence	*obsolescence f planifiée*
buyer's market	*marché m à la baisse*
buying behaviour	*comportement m des acheteurs*

who is the campaign aimed at? *à qui est destinée la campagne?*
is it possible to arrange a tour of the factory? *est-il possible d'organiser un tour de l'usine?*
we would be happy to arrange ... at your convenience *nous serions heureux d'organiser ... quand cela vous conviendra*
please arrange accommodation for our guests *vous voudrez bien vous occuper de l'hébergement de nos invités?*
to arrange for guests to be met/taken care of *faire chercher les invités/ organiser l'accueil et l'escorte des invités*
to increase/reinforce brand awareness *augmenter/consolider la notoriété de la marque*
what is your brief? *quelles sont vos instructions?*
our brief is to ... *nous nous proposons de ...*

canvass	*prospecter, démarcher*
canvasser	*démarcheur(-euse)* m(f)
captive market	*marché* m *captif*
catalogue	*catalogue* m
circular	*prospectus* m
client	*client(e)* m(f)
competition	*concurrence* f
concessionaire	*concessionnaire* m/f
consumer behaviour	*comportement* m *des consommateurs*
consumer credit	*crédit* m *à la consommation*
consumer durables	*biens* mpl *de consommation durables*
consumer goods	*biens* mpl *de consommation*
consumer market	*marché* m *des consommateurs*
control group	*groupe* m *témoin*
convenience goods	*produits* mpl *de consommation courante*
corporate entertaining	*divertissement* m *offert* or *réception* f *donnée par la société*
corporate identity	*image* f *de l'entreprise*
corporate image	*image* f *de marque de l'entreprise*
corporate logo	*logo* m *de l'entreprise*
corporate planning	*planification* f *de l'entreprise*
corporate strategy	*stratégie* f *de l'entreprise*
customer	*client(e)* m(f)
customer profile	*profil* m *de la clientèle*
cut-throat competition	*concurrence* f *acharnée*
demand n	*demande* f
demand forecasting	*prévisions* fpl *de demande*
derived demand	*demande* f *induite*
desk research	*recherche* f *documentaire*
direct-mail advertising	*publicité* f *directe par correspondance*
direct marketing	*marketing* m *direct*
direct selling	*vente* f *directe*

to capture 40% of the market *s'approprier 40% du marché*
to corner the market (in ...) *accaparer le marché (de ...)*
to project a strong corporate image *projeter une forte image de marque de la société*
to create a demand for a product *créer la demande pour un produit*
the demand for ... has increased (dramatically) *la demande pour ... s'est accrue (de façon spectaculaire)*

distributor	*distributeur(-trice) m(f)*
distributor policy	*politique f de distribution*
diversification	*diversification f*
diversify	*diversifier*
down-market *adj*	*bas de gamme*
end product	*produit m fini*
end user	*utilisateur(-trice) m(f) final(e), consommateur(-trice) m(f)*
exhibition centre	*hall m d'exposition*
falling market	*marché m à la baisse*
feasibility study	*étude f de faisabilité*
feature *n*	*caractéristique f*
feedback	*feed-back m, réactions fpl*
field research	*recherche f sur le terrain*
follow-up *n*	*relance f*
freebie	*cadeau m*
fringe market	*débouché m marginal*
gimmick	*astuce f publicitaire*
good PR	*bonnes relations fpl publiques*
growth market	*secteur m de croissance*
guesstimate	*estimation f au jugé*
halo effect	*effet m de la bonne image de marque*
house style	*stylisme m maison*
hype *n*	*matraquage m publicitaire*
hype *vb*	*lancer à grand renfort de publicité*
image	*image f de marque*
impact	*impact m*
impulse buying	*achat m spontané or d'impulsion*
impulse purchase	*achat m spontané or d'impulsion*
indirect demand	*demande f indirecte*
junk mail	*imprimés mpl publicitaires*
launch *n*	*lancement m*
launch *vb*	*lancer*
liaise (with)	*assurer la liaison (avec)*
lifestyle	*style m de vie*
logo	*logo m*
loss leader	*article m sacrifié*

to go down-market *viser le grand public*
to flood the market (with ...) *inonder le marché (de ...)*
the market for ... is growing very fast *les débouchés pour ... s'accroissent très rapidement*
who is coming to the launch? *qui viendra au lancement?*

mailing list	*liste f d'adresses*
mailshot	*mailing m, publipostage m*
market *n*	*marché m*
market *vb*	*commercialiser*
marketable	*vendable*
market analysis	*analyse f du marché*
market demand	*besoins mpl du marché*
market development manager	*chef m du développement des marchés*
market forces	*tendances fpl du marché*
marketing	*marketing m, commercialisation f*
marketing concept	*concept m de commercialisation*
marketing intelligence	*informations fpl commerciales*
marketing manager	*chef m du marketing*
marketing mix	*marketing mix m, marchéage m*
marketing plan	*plan m de commercialisation*
market leader	*entreprise f or produit m en tête du marché*
market penetration	*pénétration f du marché*
market potential	*potentiel m du marché*
market price	*prix m marchand*
market profile	*caractéristiques fpl du marché*
market research	*étude f de marché*
market rigging	*manipulation f des prix*
market share	*part f du marché*
market test	*opération f témoin*
market trends	*tendances fpl du marché*
market value	*valeur f marchande*
mass-market *adj*	*grand public adj inv*

would you like to be on our mailing list? *souhaitez-vous recevoir régulièrement notre documentation?*

please add our name to your mailing list *veuillez nous envoyer régulièrement votre documentation*

is there a market for ...? *y a-t-il des débouchés pour ...?*

there is no market for this product *il n'y a pas de débouché pour ce produit*

to be on the market *être en vente*

the bottom has fallen out of the market *le marché s'est effondré*

the competition has priced itself out of the market *la concurrence pratique des prix trop élevés pour le marché*

our products have found a ready market *nous avons facilement trouvé un marché pour nos produits*

what is the marketing strategy for these products? *quelle est la stratégie de commercialisation de ces produits?*

to have a 30% market share *détenir 30% du marché*

media research	*étude f des médias*
merchandising	*merchandising m,*
	marchandisage m
mid-market	*de niveau moyen*
mock-up	*maquette f*
new business manager	*directeur(-trice) m(f) des*
	nouveaux contrats
niche	*créneau m*
niche marketing	*marketing m de créneau*
open day	*journée f portes ouvertes*
open house	*opération f portes ouvertes*
own brand	*marque f du distributeur*
packaging	*emballage m*
photo call	*photo-call m*
photo opportunity	*occasion f pour une photo*
pie chart	*graphique m circulaire,*
	"camembert" m
pilot scheme	*projet m pilote*
point of sale (POS)	*lieu m de vente, point m de vente*
point-of-sale advertising	*publicité f sur le lieu de vente*
point-of-sale material	*matériel m de publicité sur le lieu*
	de vente, matériel m PLV
postal survey	*étude f de marché par courrier*
PR (public relations)	*RP fpl (relations fpl publiques)*
premium offer	*prime f*
press call	*appel m de presse*
press officer	*attaché(e) m(f) de presse*
press release	*communiqué m de presse*
PR exercise	*opération f de relations*
	publiques
price-cutting	*réductions fpl de prix*
price maintenance agreement	*accords mpl de maintien des prix*
pricing policy	*politique f des prix*
PR man/woman	*responsable m/f des relations*
	publiques
product	*produit m*
product manager	*chef m de produit*

to perform well (against the competition) *être performant(e) (par rapport
   à la concurrence)*
to present the company's viewpoint *présenter le point de vue de la société*
**you can contact our press officer on 350 1306. He/she will be pleased to
   deal with your enquiry** *vous pouvez contacter notre attaché(e) de presse
   au n⁰ 3501306. Il/elle se fera un plaisir de vous renseigner*

product range	*gamme f de produits*
promote	*promouvoir*
promotion	*promotion f*
proprietary brand	*marque f déposée*
prospectus	*prospectus m*
PR people	*responsables m/fpl des relations publiques*
public *n*	*public m*
publicity	*publicité f*
publicity event	*opération f publicitaire*
publicize	*faire connaître*
public relations (PR)	*relations fpl publiques (RP fpl)*
public relations consultant	*conseiller(-ère) m(f) en relations publiques*
public relations event	*opération f de relations publiques*
public relations firm	*agence f de relations publiques*
public relations officer	*responsable m/f des relations publiques*
reply-paid postcard	*carte-réponse f*
retail outlet	*point m de vente*
retail price	*prix m de détail*
sales campaign	*campagne f de ventes*
sales conference	*réunion f du service commercial*
sales drive	*campagne f de promotion des ventes*
sales figures	*chiffre m d'affaires*
seller's market	*marché m à la hausse*
shift in demand	*déplacement m de la demande*
showcard	*affiche f cartonnée*
showroom	*magasin m or salle f d'exposition*
spin-off	*nouveau débouché m*
spokesman/woman	*porte-parole m inv*
stand	*stand m*
standard of living	*niveau m de vie*
static market	*marché m stagnant*
target market	*marché m cible*
target marketing	*marketing m orienté*

the general public *le grand public*
it's good for public relations to ... *c'est bon pour les relations publiques de ...*

please send details of the results of the marketing campaign *veuillez m'envoyer les résultats détaillés de la campagne de commercialisation*
we are targeting young people *nous visons les jeunes*

teaser	*annonce f mystère*
telemarketing	*télémarketing m*
testimonial	*recommandation f*
trade fair	*foire(-exposition) f commerciale*
unique selling point (USP)	*avantage m unique*
unofficial market	*marché m parallèle*
unsolicited goods	*produits mpl non-sollicités*
up-market *adj*	*haut de gamme, de luxe*
user-friendly	*facile à utiliser, convivial(e)*
visitor	*visiteur(-euse) m(f)*
wrapper	*enveloppe f*
wrapper *(on book)*	*jaquette f*

the market is unsettled *le marché est instable*
to go up-market *viser un public haut de gamme*
X and Y will be visiting the plant/our offices on 2 August *X et Y visiteront l'usine/viendront à nos bureaux le 2 août*

See also **CONFERENCES AND PUBLIC SPEAKING**

MEETINGS

SETTING UP THE MEETING

Please suggest a convenient time and date for our meeting *veuillez m'indiquer une date et heure qui vous conviendraient*

I shall be free to meet you some time during the week commencing 20 March *je serai disponible pour un rendez-vous la semaine du 20 mars*

I'm afraid I can't manage the date/time you suggest *je regrette mais la date/l'heure que vous proposez ne me convient pas*

I will be happy to meet you at your office at the time you suggest *je serai heureux(-euse) de venir vous voir à votre bureau quand cela vous conviendra*

I will be in Brussels on 2 February and would be free to meet you from 2pm to 5pm *je serai à Bruxelles le 2 février, et je pourrais vous voir entre 14.00 et 17.00*

Should you need to change the time/date of our meeting, please contact me/my secretary as soon as possible *au cas où vous devriez changer l'heure/la date de notre rendez-vous, veuillez me contacter/contacter mon/ma secrétaire dans les plus brefs délais*

The date/time of the meeting has been brought forward/put back to ... *la date/l'heure de la réunion a été avancée/reportée à ...*

I'd like to bring forward/postpone/cancel the meeting if possible *je voudrais avancer/reporter/annuler la réunion si possible*

INTRODUCTORY REMARKS

Pleased to meet you, Mr/Ms Foster *enchanté(e) (the person's name is not used in French)*

It's good to see you again *c'est un plaisir de vous revoir*

I'm very glad of this opportunity to speak to you in person *je suis très heureux(-euse) d'avoir l'occasion de vous parler en personne*

I'm afraid Mr Murdoch can't be with us today *malheureusement, M. Murdoch ne peut pas se joindre à nous aujourd'hui*

Allow me to introduce ... *permettez-moi de présenter ...*

CONDUCTING THE MEETING

First and foremost *avant tout*

I'd just like to say *j'aimerais juste dire*

May I point out that ...? *puis-je me permettre d'observer que ...?*

The way I see it *à mon avis*

That's an interesting question/comment *c'est une question*

intéressante/un commentaire intéressant
I think it might be better to discuss this issue later *je pense qu'il serait (peut-être) préférable de discuter cela plus tard*
The next item on the agenda is ... *l'article suivant de l'ordre du jour est ...*
Please stress that in the minutes *veuillez insister sur ce point dans le procès-verbal*
Could you/may I expand on that? *pourriez-vous/puis-je développer ce point?*
The problem is that ... *le problème est que ...*
Does anyone have any suggestions? *est-ce que quelqu'un aurait des suggestions?*
What do you think of ...? *que pensez-vous de ...?*
Would anyone object to .../if ...? *est-ce qu'il y a quelqu'un qui aurait des objections contre .../si ...?*
When shall we reconvene? *quand nous réunirons-nous à nouveau?*

AGREEING
I totally agree *je suis tout à fait d'accord*
I'm glad we agree *je suis heureux(-euse) que nous soyons d'accord*
We are all very enthusiastic about this *cela nous enthousiasme tous beaucoup*
We will give your idea our total backing *nous appuierons totalement votre idée*
We will make sure this gets top priority *nous veillerons à ce que ceci ait la priorité absolue*
I agree to a certain extent, but I think ... *je suis d'accord jusqu'à un certain point, mais je pense que ...*
I think we are in broad agreement on the fundamental issues *je crois que, dans l'ensemble, nous sommes d'accord sur les questions de base*
I take your point *je vois ce que vous voulez dire*

DISAGREEING
It is hard to agree with ... *il est difficile d'être d'accord avec ...*
We must agree to differ on this one, I'm afraid *malheureusement, nous devons rester sur nos positions sur ce point*
There is only one point I can't agree with *il y a juste un point sur lequel je ne suis pas d'accord*
It's not really feasible to do that at this stage *ceci n'est pas vraiment faisable à ce stade*
Are you sure that is correct? *êtes-vous sûr que c'est exact?*
In that case, I'm afraid we have to decline your offer *dans ce cas,*

je suis dans le regret de devoir refuser votre offre

NEGOTIATIONS

NEGOTIATING CONDITIONS
The following is a list of typical conditions you may wish to discuss during negotiations, along with related phrases.

cancellation clause *(clause f résolutoire):*
There will be a 50 per cent charge on orders cancelled less than 6 weeks before due delivery *50 pour cent du montant des commandes annulées à moins de 6 semaines de la date de livraison seront facturés*

commission *(commission f):*
3 per cent commission on sales up to 20,000F and 5 per cent on sales thereafter *une commission de 3 pour cent sur les ventes jusqu'à concurrence de 20.000F, et de 5 pour cent au-delà*
2 per cent commission on sales up to 15,000F and 5 per cent on total sales when sales exceed this figure *une commission de 2 pour cent sur les ventes jusqu'à concurrence de 15.000F, et 5 pour cent du total si les ventes dépassent ce montant*

credit period *(délai m de paiement):*
90 days after receipt of invoice *90 jours à compter de la réception de la facture*
60 days after invoice for standard orders, 6 months after invoice for goods on consignment *60 jours à compter de la date de facturation pour les commandes ordinaires, 6 mois pour les marchandises en dépôt chez les consignataires*

delivery *(livraison f):*
We require delivery by 31 July *nous voulons la livraison d'ici le 31 juillet*
Delivery will be 2 weeks from receipt of order *la livraison se fera 15 jours après la réception de la commande*

discount *(remise f):*
early settlement discount *une remise pour règlement rapide*
2 per cent discount for payment within 14 days *une remise de 2 pour cent pour règlement dans les 14 jours*

exclusivity *(exclusivité f):*
We must have exclusivity over the Paris region *nous voulons l'exclusivité sur la région parisienne*
You would have absolute exclusivity over the West Coast *vous auriez l'exclusivité absolue sur la Côte Ouest*

The exclusive agency agreement will be reviewed annually *l'accord d'exclusivité sera revu tous les ans*

minimum quantity/order *(quantité f/commande f minimum)*:
A minimum order of 5,000 units *une commande de 5.000 unités minimum*

payment method *(méthode f de paiement)*:
confirmed irrevocable letter of credit *lettre f de crédit irrévocable confirmée*
bill of exchange *lettre f de change*

penalty clause *(clause f pénale)*:
The penalty clause is 4 per cent for each month of delay *la clause pénale est de 4 pour cent pour chaque mois de retard*

quantity discount *(remise f sur quantité)*:
We can offer 3 per cent on orders over 100,000F/on orders of more than 600 units *nous offrons une remise de 3 pour cent sur les commandes de plus de 100.000F/sur les commandes de plus de 600 unités*

royalty on sales *(redevance f sur les ventes)*:
3 per cent of turnover on sales under licence *3 pour cent du chiffre d'affaires sur les ventes sous licence*

sales targets *(objectifs mpl de vente)*:
Sales targets will be reviewed on a monthly basis *les objectifs de vente seront revus tous les mois*

staff training *(formation f du personnel)*:
We would insist on/require an intensive staff training course for sales personnel/engineers *nous insistons pour que/exigeons que le personnel de ventes/les ingénieurs suive(nt) un stage de formation intensif*
Staff training would be ongoing for the first year of the contract *il y aura formation continue du personnel pendant la première année du contrat*

unit price *(prix m unitaire)*:
We propose a unit price of 500F *nous proposons un prix unitaire de 500F*
On orders up to 1,000 the unit price is 600F *pour les commandes allant jusqu'à 1.000 unités, le prix unitaire est de 600F*

warranty *(garantie f)*:
Our products will carry an 18 month warranty from date of sale/

installation *nos produits sont garantis 18 mois à compter de la date de vente/d'installation*
Warranty will be 12 months parts and labour followed by 6 months parts only *il y a 12 mois de garantie pièces de rechange et main-d'œuvre, puis 6 mois pièces de rechange uniquement*

PRESENTING YOUR POSITION

INTRODUCTORY
We have a lot to discuss *nous avons de nombreux points à débattre*
I'm sure our discussions will be mutually beneficial *je suis sûr(e) que nos discussions seront fructueuses pour tout le monde*
I think there's some room for negotiation *je pense qu'il y a lieu de négocier*
I'm confident we'll reach agreement *je suis sûr(e) que nous parviendrons à un accord*
I look forward to hearing your proposals *je me réjouis de voir vos propositions*
I think you'll be pleasantly surprised/interested by our proposals *je crois que nos propositions vous surprendront agréablement/ vous intéresseront*

OPENING THE DISCUSSION
Shall we begin? *êtes-vous prêt(e)s à commencer?*
Perhaps I could start by ... *je pourrais peut-être commencer par ...*
This is how we see it *voici notre position*
Our position on warranty/exclusivity is as follows *notre position sur la garantie/l'exclusivité est la suivante*
We believe it's reasonable/appropriate to ... *nous pensons qu'il serait raisonnable/approprié de ...*
If I could just outline our proposals *j'aimerais simplement exposer les grandes lignes de nos propositions*
What we propose is ... *ce que nous proposons, c'est ...*

CLOSING THE DISCUSSION
Does anyone have any further questions? *y a-t-il encore des questions?*
Let's take a break for lunch/some refreshments *faisons une pause pour le déjeuner/pour prendre quelque chose*
If no one wishes to add anything further, perhaps we can bring the meeting to a close? *s'il n'y a plus rien à ajouter, je propose de lever la séance*
It has been a very fruitful discussion *cette discussion a été très fructueuse*

I hope we have clarified our position *j'espère que nous avons clarifié notre position*
May I suggest we continue discussions at a later date? *je suggère que nous poursuivions nos discussions une autre fois*
Thank you (all) for coming *merci (à tous) d'être venu(s)*
When will we hear from you? *quand nous contacterez-vous?*
We will be in touch very soon *nous vous contacterons sous peu*

ADDITIONAL VOCABULARY

adjourn	*ajourner*
adjournment	*ajournement m*
agenda	*ordre m du jour*
AGM (annual general meeting)	*AG f (assemblée f générale annuelle)*
AOCB (any other competent business)	*autres matières fpl à l'ordre du jour*
attend	*assister à*
audio conferencing	*audioconférence f*
board (of directors)	*conseil m d'administration*
board meeting	*réunion f du conseil d'administration*
brainstorming (session)	*brainstorming m*
breakfast meeting	*petit déjeuner m d'affaires*
briefing	*briefing m*
business lunch	*déjeuner m d'affaires*
cancel	*annuler*
casting vote	*voix f prépondérante*
chairman	*président m*
chairwoman	*présidente f*
composite motion	*motion f composite*
concession	*concession f*
consensus	*consensus m*
deal	*accord m*
decide	*décider*
decision	*décision f*
delegate *n*	*participant(e) m(f)*
delegate *vb*	*déléguer*
delegation	*délégation f*
dialogue	*dialogue m*
discussion	*discussion f*
EGM (extraordinary general meeting)	*AGE f (assemblée f générale extraordinaire)*
feedback	*feed-back m*
flipchart	*tableau m à feuilles mobiles*

interpreter	*interprète m/f*
lunch meeting	*déjeuner m d'affaires*
meeting	*réunion f*
minute book	*registre m des procès-verbaux*
minutes	*procès-verbal m*
mover	*auteur m d'une proposition*
negotiate	*négocier*
negotiation	*négociation f*
overhead projector	*rétroprojecteur m*
point of order	*point m de procédure*
report *n*	*rapport m*
statutory meeting	*assemblée f statutaire*
subject to confirmation	*sous réserve de confirmation*
video conference	*vidéoconférence f*
working breakfast/lunch/dinner	*petit déjeuner m/déjeuner m/ dîner m de travail*

acknowledge	*accuser réception de*
acknowledgement (slip)	*accusé m de réception*
addressing machine	*machine f à adresser*
agenda	*ordre m du jour*
answering machine	*répondeur m automatique*
archive *n*	*archives fpl*
archive *vb*	*classer dans les archives*
audio-typing	*audiotypie f*
audio-typist	*audiotypiste m/f*
automatic document feeder	*dispositif m d'alimentation de documents*
azerty keyboard	*clavier m AZERTY*
box file	*carton m de classement*
business card	*carte f de visite (professionnelle)*
calculator	*calculatrice f*
carbon copy	*carbone m*
card index	*fichier m*
circular *n*	*circulaire f*
clerical staff	*personnel m administratif*
collate	*collationner*
compliments slip	*fiche f de transmission*
computer	*ordinateur m*
console	*console f*
continuous stationery	*papier m en continu*
copy holder	*porte-copie m*
copy paper	*papier m à photocopieur*
copy typist	*dactylo m/f*
correcting fluid	*liquide m correcteur*
correction ribbon/tape	*ruban m correcteur*
daisy wheel printer	*imprimante f à marguerite*
data processing (DP)	*traitement m de données, informatique f*
dead file	*fichier m mort*
desk	*bureau m*
desk diary	*agenda m de bureau*
desk light	*lampe f de bureau*
desk pad	*bloc-notes m, sous-main m*
desktop computer	*ordinateur m de bureau*
desktop copier	*copieur m de bureau*
Dictaphone ®	*Dictaphone m ®*

I need access to a fax machine/computer *il faut que j'aie accès à un télécopieur/un ordinateur*
I'd like three copies of this, please *je voudrais trois copies de ceci, s'il vous plaît*

dictate	*dicter*
dictionary	*dictionnaire m*
disk box	*boîte f à disques*
diskette	*disquette f*
duplicate *n*	*double m, duplicata m*
duplicate *vb*	*faire un double de*
electric typewriter	*machine f à écrire électrique*
electronic mail	*courrier m électronique*
enlarge	*agrandir*
enlargement	*agrandissement m*
eraser	*gomme f*
ergonomics	*ergonomie f*
extension	*poste m*
extension number	*numéro m de poste*
fax *n*	*télécopie f*
fax *vb*	*envoyer par télécopie*
fax *vb (somebody)*	*envoyer une télécopie à*
fax machine	*télécopieur m*
file *n*	*dossier m*
file *vb*	*classer*
file copy	*exemplaire m d'archive*
filing	*classement m*
filing cabinet	*classeur m*
filing system	*système m de classement*
floppy disk	*disquette f*
folder	*chemise f*
franking machine	*machine f à affranchir*
guillotine	*massicot m*
ink	*encre f*
intercom	*interphone m*
internal memo	*note f de service*
in-tray	*courrier m "arrivée"*
keyboard	*clavier m*
laser printer	*imprimante f à laser*
letterhead	*en-tête m*
lever arch file	*classeur m à levier*
memorandum	*note f de service*
memory typewriter	*machine f à écrire à mémoire*
microfiche	*microfiche f*
microfiche reader	*lecteur m de microfiches*
microfilm	*microfilm m*
microfilm reader	*lecteur m de microfilms*
mouse	*souris f*

to take dictation *écrire sous dictée*

office	*bureau m*
office building	*bureaux mpl*
office equipment	*matériel m de bureau*
office hours	*heures fpl de bureau*
office manager	*responsable m/f administra-tif(-ive), chef m de bureau*
office staff	*employés(-ées) mpl(fpl) de bureau*
office supplies	*fournitures fpl de bureau*
office worker	*employé(e) m(f) de bureau*
open-plan office	*bureau m paysager*
out-tray	*courrier m "départ"*
overhead projector	*rétroprojecteur m*
paper clip	*trombone m*
paper punch	*perforateur m*
paperwork	*travail m administratif*
pending tray	*courrier m en souffrance*
petty cash	*caisse f de dépenses courantes*
photocopier	*copieur m*
photocopy n	*photocopie f*
photocopy vb	*photocopier*
portable (computer)	*portable m*
printer	*imprimante f*
print-out	*listing m*
qwerty keyboard	*clavier m QWERTY*
reception area	*réception f*
ribbon	*ruban m*
ring binder	*classeur m à anneaux*
screen	*écran m*
secretary	*secrétaire m/f*
shredder	*destructeur m de documents*
single-line display	*affichage m uniligne*

is ... in the office today? *est-ce que ... est au bureau aujourd'hui?*
I will be in the office all day/from 9am/until 2pm *je serai au bureau toute la journée/à partir de 9H00/jusqu'à 14H00*
is there a photocopier/fax machine in the office? *est-ce qu'il y a un photocopieur/télécopieur dans le bureau?*
could you provide me with an office from 1 to 22 April? *pourriez-vous mettre un bureau à ma disposition du 1er au 22 avril?*
what are your office hours? *quelles sont vos heures de bureau?*
our normal office hours are from 9 to 5 *nos heures de bureau habituelles sont de 9H00 à 17H00*
I will need secretarial help *j'aurai besoin de l'assistance d'une secrétaire or de secrétaires*
you will be sharing an office with ... *vous partagerez un bureau avec ...*

single-sheet feed	*alimentation f feuille à feuille*
staple	*agrafe f*
stapler	*agrafeuse f*
stationery *(general)*	*fournitures fpl de bureau*
stationery *(letter paper)*	*papier m à lettres*
stationery cupboard	*armoire f à fournitures*
street map	*plan m de la ville*
suspension file	*dossier m suspendu*
telephone *n*	*téléphone m*
telephone *vb*	*téléphoner*
telephone *vb (somebody)*	*téléphoner à*
telephone directory	*annuaire m (téléphonique)*
telex *n*	*télex m*
telex *vb*	*envoyer par télex*
telex *vb (somebody)*	*envoyer un télex à*
telex (machine)	*télex m*
time clock	*pointeuse f*
toner	*encre f*
type *vb*	*taper (à la machine)*
typewriter	*machine f à écrire*
typist	*dactylo m/f*
VDU (visual display unit)	*console f de visualisation*
visitor's book	*livre m d'or*
window envelope	*enveloppe f à fenêtre*
word processor	*machine f de traitement de texte*
words per minute (wpm)	*mots/minute mpl*
work station	*poste m de travail*

who speaks English in the office? *qui parle anglais au bureau?*
to type up notes *taper des notes*

See also **JOB APPLICATIONS** *and* **COMPANY STRUCTURES**

absenteeism	*absentéisme m*
across-the-board wage increase	*augmentation f générale des salaires*
agreed procedure	*procédure f conventionnelle*
appeal *n*	*appel m*
appeal (against) *vb*	*faire appel (contre)*
appraisal interview	*entretien m d'évaluation*
appraisal method	*méthode f d'évaluation*
apprentice	*apprenti(e) m(f)*
apprenticeship	*apprentissage m*
aptitude test	*test m d'aptitude*
arbitrate	*arbitrer*
arbitration	*arbitrage m*
arbitrator	*arbitre m*
assess	*évaluer*
assessment	*évaluation f*
back pay	*rappel m de salaire*
back shift	*équipe f du soir*
basic wage	*salaire m de base*
benefit-in-kind	*avantages mpl en nature*
block release	*congé m de formation*
blue-collar worker	*travailleur(-euse) m(f) manuel(le)*
bonus	*prime f*
career development	*déroulement m de carrière*
casual worker	*travailleur(-euse) m(f) temporaire*
clock in/on	*pointer (à l'arrivée)*
clock off/out	*pointer (en départ)*
closed shop	*monopole m syndical*
code of practice	*déontologie f*
collective agreement	*convention f collective*
collective bargaining	*négociations fpl collectives*
company car	*voiture f de fonction*
complainant	*demandeur(-deresse) m(f)*
conciliation	*conciliation f*
conditions of employment	*conditions fpl de travail*
constructive dismissal	*démission f provoquée*
consultation	*consultation f*
contract of employment	*contrat m de travail*
contributory pension scheme	*régime m de retraite avec retenues sur le salaire*

to pay/receive a bonus payment *verser/recevoir une prime*

day release course	*cours m professionnel à temps partiel*
day shift	*équipe f de jour*
delegate *n*	*délégué(e) m(f)*
delegation	*délégation f*
demarcation	*démarcation f*
demote	*rétrograder*
demotion	*rétrogradation f*
derecognition	*désaveu m du pouvoir syndical*
direct labour	*main-d'œuvre f directe*
discrimination	*discrimination f*
dismiss	*licencier*
dismissal	*licenciement m*
dispute	*conflit m*
double time	*double paie f*
downgrade	*déclasser*
early retirement	*retraite f anticipée, préretraite f*
education *(general)*	*éducation f*
education *(teaching)*	*enseignement m*
education *(training)*	*formation f*
employ *vb*	*employer*
employee	*employé(e) m(f)*
employee benefit	*avantage m social or en nature*
employer	*employeur(-euse) m(f)*
employers' association	*organisation f patronale*
employer's contribution	*cotisation f patronale*
employer's liability	*responsabilité f patronale*
employment agency	*agence f de placement*
equality	*égalité f*
equal opportunities employer	*employeur m qui ne fait pas de discrimination*
equal pay	*égalité f des salaires*
evaluation	*évaluation f*
expenses	*frais mpl*
fixed term contract	*contrat m de durée déterminée*
flat rate	*taux m uniforme de salaire*
flexitime	*horaire m flexible*
foreman	*contremaître m*
forewoman	*contremaîtresse f*

to be on day release *faire un (or deux) jour(s) par semaine de stage (de formation)*

does French/Swiss employment law cover this? *est-ce que ceci est couvert par le droit français/suisse?*

we are expanding our staff *nous augmentons nos effectifs*

freelance (worker)	*travailleur(-euse) m(f) indépendant(e)*
freelance *vb*	*travailler à son compte*
fringe benefit	*avantage m social or en nature*
general strike	*grève f générale*
golden handcuffs	*contrat m très avantageux*
golden handshake	*prime f de départ*
golden hello	*indemnité f de transfert*
golden parachute	*indemnité f de départ*
graduate *n*	*diplomé(e) m(f) universitaire*
graduated pension	*retraite f proportionnelle*
grievance	*grief m*
grievance procedure	*procédure f d'arbitrage*
guaranteed wage	*salaire m garanti*
headhunter	*chasseur m de têtes*
health and safety	*hygiène f et sécurité f*
health insurance	*assurance f maladie*
homeworker	*travailleur(-euse) m(f) à domicile*
house style	*culture f de la société*
human relations	*relations fpl humaines*
human resources	*ressources fpl humaines*
human resources development (HRD)	*développement m des ressources humaines*
incentive	*prime f*
incentive scheme	*système m de primes*
increment	*augmentation f*
individual bargaining	*négociations fpl au niveau individuel*
induction	*accueil m du nouveau personnel, introduction f*
induction course	*stage m préparatoire*
industrial accident	*accident m du travail*
industrial action	*grève f*
industrial dispute	*conflit m du travail*
industrial relations	*relations fpl du travail*
industrial tribunal	*conseil m de prud'hommes*
industry-wide agreement	*convention f par secteur*
in-house training	*formation f en entreprise*
job description	*profil m du poste*
job losses	*suppressions fpl d'emplois*
job satisfaction	*satisfaction f professionnelle*
job security	*sécurité f de l'emploi*
job specification	*caractéristiques fpl du poste*
job title	*titre m*
labour market	*marché m du travail*

last in, first out (LIFO)	*dernier entré, premier sorti (DEPS)*
lay-off *n*	*licenciement m*
lay off *vb*	*licencier*
learning curve	*courbe f d'expérience*
length of service	*ancienneté f*
lock-out	*lock-out m, fermeture f*
luncheon voucher	*ticket m repas*
management consultant	*conseiller(-ère) m(f) de direction*
man management	*maniement m du personnel*
manpower forecast	*prévision f des besoins en main-d'œuvre*
maternity benefit	*allocation f de maternité*
maternity leave	*congé m de maternité*
medical insurance	*assurance f maladie*
merit pay	*salaire m au mérite*
minimum wage	*salaire m minimum*
mobility of labour	*mobilité f de la main-d'œuvre*
moonlighting	*travail m au noir*
National Insurance	*Sécurité f sociale*
natural wastage	*départs mpl naturels*
negotiate	*négocier*
negotiation	*négociation f*
net pay	*salaire m net*
night shift *(workers)*	*équipe f de nuit*
non-contributory pension scheme	*régime m de retraite sans retenues*
occupational accident	*accident m du travail*
occupational hazard	*risque m professionnel*
occupational pension scheme	*régime m de retraite professionnelle*
official strike	*grève f officielle*
off-the-job	*hors de l'entreprise*
on-the-job	*dans l'entreprise*
organizational culture	*culture f de la société*
overstaffed	*aux effectifs mpl excédentaires*
overtime	*heures fpl supplémentaires*
overtime ban	*refus m or grève f des heures supplémentaires*

to lay staff off *licencier des employés*
to achieve cuts by natural wastage *faire des économies en ne remplaçant pas les départs naturels*
the department is overstaffed *il y a un excédent de personnel dans ce service*

paid holidays	*congés* mpl *payés*
part-timer	*employé(e)* m(f) *à temps partiel*
paternity leave	*congé* m *de paternité*
payment-by-results system	*système* m *de rémunération au rendement*
payroll	*registre* m *des salaires*
pay slip	*bulletin* m *de paie*
pension scheme	*régime* m *de retraite*
performance-related pay	*salaire* m *au rendement*
performance review	*évaluation* f *des performances*
personnel department	*service* m *du personnel*
personnel management	*direction* f *du personnel*
personnel manager	*chef* m *du personnel*
picket n	*piquet* m *de grève*
picket vb	*organiser un piquet de grève*
placement	*stage* m
plant bargaining	*négociations* fpl *au niveau de l'usine*
probationary period	*période* f *probatoire*
proficiency test	*test* m *de compétence*
profit-sharing	*intéressement* m *aux bénéfices*
profit-sharing scheme	*système* m *d'intéressement (aux bénéfices)*
promote	*promouvoir*
promotion	*promotion* f
pro rata adj, adv	*au prorata*
rationalize	*rationnaliser*
recruit vb	*recruter*
recruitment	*recrutement* m
recruitment drive	*exercice* m *de recrutement*
redeployment	*réaffectation* f
redundancy	*licenciement* m
redundancy agreement	*accord* m *de licenciement*
redundancy payment	*indemnité* f *de licenciement*
redundant	*licencié(e)*
reinstate	*rétablir, réintégrer*
reinstatement	*réintégration* f

we have 2,000 employees on our payroll *nous avons un effectif de 2.000 employés*
to picket a factory *mettre un piquet de grève devant une usine*
to recruit from abroad *recruter à l'étranger*
we are recruiting 50 new employees this month *nous allons recruter 50 employés ce mois-ci*
the company has had to make 30 staff redundant *la société a dû mettre à pied 30 employés*

relocation	*déménagement m*
retire	*prendre sa retraite*
retirement	*retraite f*
salary	*salaire m*
salary increase	*augmentation f de salaire*
salary review	*révision f des salaires*
salary scale	*échelle f des salaires*
security of tenure	*stabilité f de l'emploi, titularisation f*
self-employed	*à son compte*
semi-skilled worker	*ouvrier(-ière) m(f) spécialisé(e)*
shiftwork	*travail m posté*
shiftworker	*travailleur(-euse) m(f) posté(e)*
shop steward	*délégué(e) m(f) syndical(e)*
short-staffed	*à court de personnel*
short time	*horaire m réduit*
shut-down	*fermeture f*
sick pay	*indemnité f de maladie*
single status	*statut m d'égalité*
sit-in	*sit-in m inv, occupation f de locaux*
skilled worker	*ouvrier(-ière) m(f) qualifié(e)*
staff *n*	*personnel m*
staff *vb*	*pourvoir en personnel*
statutory deduction	*prélèvement m obligatoire*
strike *n*	*grève f*
strike *vb*	*faire grève*
striker	*gréviste m/f*
take-home pay	*salaire m net*
teamwork	*travail m d'équipe*
termination date	*date f effective de démission or de licenciement*
termination of employment	*licenciement m*
threshold agreement	*accord m d'indexation des salaires*
time-and-a-half	*salaire m majoré de moitié*
time card	*carte f de pointage*
time clock	*pointeuse f*
time-sheet	*feuille f de présence*
trade dispute	*conflit m social*
trade union	*syndicat m*
trade union agreement	*convention f collective*

to get the sack *se faire licencier*
to go on strike *se mettre en grève*
to be on strike *faire grève*

trade union recognition	*reconnaissance f officielle du syndicat*
training	*formation f*
training course	*stage m de formation*
training officer	*responsable m/f de la formation*
understaffed	*à court de personnel*
unfair dismissal	*licenciement m abusif*
union dues	*cotisations fpl syndicales*
unskilled worker	*manœuvre m*
vacancy	*poste m vacant*
vocational guidance	*orientation f professionnelle*
vocational training	*formation f professionnelle*
voluntary deductions	*déductions fpl volontaires*
voluntary redundancy	*départ m volontaire*
wage differential	*éventail m des salaires*
wage freeze	*blocage m des salaires*
wage negotiations	*négociations fpl salariales*
wages	*salaire m*
wages policy	*politique f salariale*
white-collar worker	*employé(e) m(f) de bureau*
wildcat strike	*grève f sauvage*
workforce	*main-d'œuvre f*
work-in	*occupation f d'usine*
working conditions	*conditions fpl de travail*
working week	*semaine f de travail*
workload	*charge f de travail*
work measurement	*mesure f du travail*
work permit	*permis m de travail*
work placement	*stage m*
work-to-rule *n*	*grève f du zèle*
work to rule *vb*	*faire la grève du zèle*
wrongful dismissal	*licenciement m abusif*

action	action f
activity chart	graphique m des activités
agenda	ordre m du jour
allow for	tenir compte de
brief n	instructions fpl
brief vb	donner des instructions à
budget n	budget m
budget vb	établir un budget
contingency	événement m imprévu
contingency plan	plan m d'urgence
contingency planning	planification f pour urgences
corporate planning	planification f de l'entreprise
cost n	coût m
cost vb (have a price)	coûter
cost vb (calculate cost of)	établir le coût de
crisis management	gestion f de crise
critical path analysis	analyse f du chemin critique
deadline	date f or heure f limite
decision	décision f
decision-making	prise f de décision
delegate vb	déléguer
department manager	chef m de service
diversification	diversification f
early warning system	système m d'alarme
efficiency	efficacité f
ergonomics	ergonomie f
extrapolation	extrapolation f
financial management	gestion f financière
flow chart	graphique m d'évolution
forecast n	prévision f
forecast vb	prévoir
histogram	histogramme m
inefficiency	inefficacité f
inventory control	contrôle m des stocks
junior management	jeunes cadres mpl
long-term	à long terme

to allot time for sth réserver du temps à quelque chose
to keep to budget se tenir au budget
to go over budget dépasser le budget
we are budgeting for sales/losses of ... des ventes/pertes de ... sont prévues dans le budget
to chase someone up on something relancer quelqu'un pour quelque chose
to meet/miss a deadline respecter les délais/dépasser la date limite
to set an unrealistic deadline fixer une date limite peu réaliste

manage	*gérer*
(the) management	*(la) direction f*
management *(process)*	*gestion f*
management appraisal	*évaluation f de la gestion*
management audit	*contrôle m de gestion*
management by crisis	*direction f par crises*
management by exception	*direction f par exception*
management by objectives	*direction f par objectifs (DPO f)*
management committee	*comité m de direction*
management consultant	*conseiller(-ère) m(f) de direction*
management course	*stage m de gestion*
management development	*développement m des cadres*
management information system (MIS)	*système m intégré de gestion (SIG m)*
management style	*mode m de gestion*
management team	*équipe f de direction*
management training	*formation f des cadres*
manager(ess) *(of company, business)*	*directeur(-trice) m(f)*
manager(ess) *(of department)*	*chef m*
managerial level	*niveau m de la direction*
managerial staff	*cadres mpl*
man-hour	*heure f travaillée*
man management	*maniement m du personnel*
manpower planning	*planification f des effectifs*
middle management	*cadres mpl moyens*
motivate	*motiver*
motivation	*motivation f*
office manager	*responsable m/f administratif(-ive), chef m de bureau*
organization chart	*organigramme m*
overspend	*trop dépenser*
phase	*phase f*
plan *n*	*projet m*
plan (ahead) *vb*	*planifier*
plan (to do) *vb*	*projeter (de faire)*
procedure	*procédure f*

a well-/badly-managed project *un projet bien/mal géré*
efficient/inefficient management *gestion f efficace/inefficace*
the decision must be taken at managerial level *cette décision doit être prise au niveau de la direction*
the next phase is scheduled to begin this month *le début du prochain stade est prévu pour ce mois*
the project is entering its final phase *le projet arrive à son stade final*
to plan for all contingencies *prévoir toutes les éventualités*

programme	*programme m*
progress *n*	*progression f*
progress *vb*	*avancer*
progress chaser	*responsable m/f du suivi*
progress report	*rapport m d'activité*
project *n*	*projet m*
project *vb*	*projeter*
projected	*projeté(e)*
projection	*prévision f*
project manager	*chef m de projet*
rationalization	*rationalisation f*
redeployment	*réaffectation f*
reminder	*rappel m*
reschedule	*reprogrammer*
schedule *n*	*programme m*
scheduling	*ordonnancement m*
short-term	*à court terme*
status report	*état m*
strategy	*stratégie f*
think tank	*groupe m de réflexion*
timescale	*durée f d'exécution*
work measurement	*mesure f du travail*
work study	*étude f du travail*

to follow progress *suivre la progression*
everything is progressing smoothly *tout avance sans problème*
on schedule *dans les temps*
ahead of/behind schedule *en avance/en retard sur le programme*
to draw up a schedule *dresser un programme*
to stick to a schedule *se tenir à un programme*
to schedule something for next week/year *mettre quelque chose au programme pour la semaine/l'année prochaine*
please provide a status report on the project *veuillez nous donner un rapport d'avancement sur le projet*

See also **THE LAW AND CONTRACTS** *and* **BUYING AND SELLING**

access	*accès m*
acre	*acre f*
advertise	*passer une annonce*
advertisement	*annonce f*
agricultural land	*terrain m agricole*
air conditioning	*climatisation f*
apartment	*appartement m*
apartment building	*immeuble m*
architect	*architecte m*
attic	*grenier m*
attic room	*mansarde f*
balcony	*balcon m*
basement	*sous-sol m*
bathroom	*salle f de bain(s)*
bay window	*baie f vitrée*
bedroom	*chambre f (à coucher)*
brochure	*prospectus m, dépliant m*
builder	*entrepreneur(-euse) m(f)*
building *(offices, flats)*	*immeuble m*
building *(process)*	*construction f*
building land	*terrain m à bâtir*
building site	*chantier m (de construction)*
buy *vb*	*acheter*
buyer	*acheteur(-euse) m(f)*
buyer's market	*marché m à la baisse*

the property offers accommodation for four offices *la propriété abrite quatre bureaux*

to advertise a property for sale *passer une annonce pour une propriété à vendre*

I would like to place an advertisement in your "properties for sale"/"to let" section *je voudrais passer une annonce dans votre rubrique "propriétés à vendre"/"à louer"*

I saw your advertisement in Property Magazine of 1 July, and am interested in ... *j'ai vu votre annonce dans le Magazine des Propriétés du 1er juillet, et je m'intéresse à or au ...*

the airport is an hour away by car/train/bus *l'aéroport est à une heure en voiture/en train/en bus*

how far away is the airport/station/city centre? *à quelle distance se trouve l'aéroport/la gare/le centre-ville?*

three/four-bedroomed house *une maison de quatre/cinq pièces (NB the French measure in terms of rooms, not bedrooms)*

to the front/side/rear of the building *sur le devant/sur le côté/à l'arrière du bâtiment*

the house was built in 1981 *la maison date de 1981*

cable TV	télévision f par câble
car park	parking m
carpet	moquette f
ceiling	plafond m
cellar	cave f
central heating	chauffage m central
city centre	centre-ville m
commission n	commission f
completion (of sale)	signature f
completion (of work)	achèvement m
construction	construction f
contract	contrat m
conversion	aménagement m
convert	aménager
conveyancing	rédaction f des actes de cession de propriété
cottage	petite maison f (à la campagne), cottage m
decoration	décoration f intérieure
demolition	démolition f
detached house	pavillon m
details	détails mpl
dining room	salle f à manger
double glazing	double vitrage m
downstairs adj	du rez-de-chaussée, de l'étage inférieur
downstairs adv	en bas
electricity	électricité f
endowment mortgage	prêt-logement m avec assurance mixte
entrance	entrée f
entrance hall	vestibule m
entryphone	interphone m
estate (residential estate)	lotissement f
estate (around large house)	domaine m, propriété f
estate agency	agence f immobilière
estate agent	agent m immobilier
estate manager	régisseur m

the property comprises ... over a surface area of 200m² *la propriété comprend ... sur une surface de 200m²*
in poor/fair/good/excellent decorative order *décoration intérieure en mauvais/assez bon/bon/excellent état*
to develop a site *aménager un site*
to be equipped *or* fitted with ... *être équipé de ...*
to exchange contracts *échanger les contrats à la signature*

facade	*façade f*
fair rent	*loyer m raisonnable*
fees	*frais mpl, honoraires mpl*
fire escape	*escalier m de secours*
fire exit	*sortie f de secours*
fireplace	*cheminée f*
fixtures and fittings	*installations fpl*
flat	*appartement m*
floor *(of room)*	*sol m*
floor *(storey)*	*étage m*
floor-to-ceiling	*du sol au plafond*
forecourt	*avant-cour f*
foundations	*fondations fpl*
freehold *n*	*pleine propriété f*
freehold property	*propriété f foncière libre*
front *(of a building)*	*devant m*
fully-equipped	*entièrement équipé(e)*
furnished	*meublé(e)*
garden	*jardin m*
gas	*gaz m*
good-sized	*grand(e)*
ground floor	*rez-de-chaussée m*
ground rent	*redevance f foncière*
grounds	*parc m*
hotel	*hôtel m*
house	*maison f*
industrial building	*bâtiment m industriel*
industrial estate	*zone f industrielle*
insurance	*assurance f*
interior *n*	*intérieur m*
interior decoration	*décoration f (d'intérieurs)*
interior decorator	*décorateur(-trice) m(f) (d'intérieurs)*
kitchen	*cuisine f*

all fixtures and fittings are included in the sale/rental price *les installations et équipements sont compris dans le prix/le loyer*
what floor is it on? *c'est à quel étage?*
the flat is situated on the first/second floor *l'appartement est situé au premier/deuxième étage*
first/second-floor flat *un appartement situé au premier/deuxième étage*
how many rooms are there? *combien de pièces y a-t-il?*
how many square metres does the property cover? *combien de mètres carrés fait la propriété?*
what does the price include? *qu'est-ce qui est compris dans le prix?*
to get the keys to a property *obtenir les clefs d'une propriété*

land	terrain m
landing	palier m
landlady (of flat etc)	propriétaire f
landlord (of flat etc)	propriétaire m
lawyer	notaire m
lease n	bail m
lease vb	louer à bail
leasehold adj	loué(e) à bail
leasehold n (contract)	bail m
leasehold n (property)	propriéte f louée à bail
legal fees	frais mpl juridiques
let n	location f
let vb	louer
to let	à louer
lift	ascenseur m
loft	grenier m
lounge	salon m
mains sewage	égouts mpl de la ville
mains water	eau f de la ville
mortgage (home-buyer's loan)	emprunt-logement m
neighbour	voisin(e) m(f)
obtain	obtenir
occupied	occupé(e)
offer n	offre f
offer vb	offrir
office accommodation	bureaux mpl
office block	immeuble m de bureaux
office space	bureaux mpl
overpriced	excessivement cher(-ère)
owner	propriétaire m/f
parking facilities	parking m
partition wall	cloison f
penthouse	appartement m (de luxe) en attique
picture window	fenêtre f panoramique

---

to take out a long/short lease on a property louer une propriété avec un bail à long terme/à court terme

we are interested in a long/short let nous cherchons à louer pour une longue/courte période

to put a property on the market mettre une propriété en vente

the building has been on the market for two months l'immeuble est à vendre depuis deux mois

to take out a mortgage on ... prendre une hypothèque or un emprunt-logement sur ...

parking for four cars parking pour quatre voitures

planning permission	*permis m de construire*
plumbing	*tuyauterie f*
power point	*prise f de courant*
price	*prix m*
private	*privé(e)*
property	*propriété f*
property developer	*promoteur m immobilier*
property development	*promotion f immobilière*
property management	*gérance f*
property manager	*gérant(e) m(f), syndic m*
property market	*marché m immobilier*
radiator	*radiateur m*
real estate	*biens mpl immobiliers*
rear *(of a building)*	*arrière m*
rebuild	*reconstruire*
redecorated	*repeint(e)*
refurbished	*remis(e) à neuf*
refurbishment	*remise f à neuf*
relocate	*transférer*
rent *n*	*loyer m*
rent *vb*	*louer*
for rent	*à louer*
replumbed	*à la tuyauterie refaite à neuf*
request *vb*	*demander*
residential area	*quartier m résidentiel*
residential building	*bâtiment m d'habitation*
residential use	*vocation f résidentielle*
restored	*restauré(e)*
rewired	*à l'installation électrique refaite à neuf*
roof	*toit m*
room	*pièce f*
sale	*vente f*
for sale	*à vendre*
satellite dish	*antenne f parabolique*
security guard	*vigile m*
sell	*vendre*
seller	*vendeur(-euse) m(f)*
seller's market	*marché m à la hausse*
semidetached house	*maison f jumelée or jumelle*

when was the building refurbished? *quand est-ce que le bâtiment a été rénové?*

who is responsible for the cleaning/upkeep of ...? *qui est chargé du nettoyage/de l'entretien de ...?*

services	services mpl municipaux
shower (room)	salle f d'eau
sitting tenant	locataire m/f occupant(e)
skylight	lucarne f
solicitor	notaire m
spacious	spacieux(-euse)
speculation	spéculation f (immobilière)
stairs	escalier m
storey	étage m
structural engineer	ingénieur-constructeur m
structurally sound	d'une construction solide
structural repairs	réparations fpl de structure
structural report	rapport m de construction
sublet vb	sous-louer
subsidence	affaissement m
suburb	banlieue f
survey n	expertise f
survey vb	expertiser
survey fee	frais mpl d'expertise
surveyor	expert m
tenancy	location f
tenant	locataire m/f
terraced	attenant(e) aux maisons voisines
tinted window	fenêtre f teintée
toilet	toilettes fpl
town centre	centre-ville m
underground car park	parking m souterrain
underpriced	en vente à bas prix
unfurnished	non-meublé(e)
unoccupied	inoccupé(e)
unsold	non-vendu(e)
upstairs adj	du haut, de l'étage supérieur
upstairs adv	en haut
utility room	buanderie f
vacant	inoccupé(e), libre
vacant possession	jouissance f immédiate
valuation	évaluation f
video entry system	portier m électronique

the property is situated in the centre of/just outside/within easy reach of
... *la propriété est située au centre de/juste à l'extérieur de/à portée de* ...
to get a property surveyed *faire expertiser une propriété*
the property was valued at over/under £500,000 *la propriété a été évaluée à plus de/moins de 500.000 livres sterling*

villa	*villa* f
wall	*mur* m
wallpaper	*papier* m *peint*
wall-to-wall carpeting	*moquette* f
warehouse	*entrepôt* m
waste disposal unit	*broyeur* m *d'ordures*
window	*fenêtre* f
wiring	*installation* f *électrique*

AI (artificial intelligence)	IA f (intelligence f artificielle)
application	application f
application development	développement m d'applications
applied research	recherche f appliquée
breakthrough	percée f
CAD/CAM (computer-assisted design/manufacture)	CFAO f (conception f et fabrication f assistées par ordinateur)
computer	ordinateur m
computer model	modèle m informatique
concept	concept m
customer trial	essai m auprès de la clientèle
cybernetics	cybernétique f
design n (concept)	conception f
design n (drawing)	dessin m
design vb	concevoir
designer	concepteur(-trice) m(f), dessinateur(-trice) m(f)
design team	équipe f de conception, équipe f de dessinateurs
develop	développer
development	développement m
development costs	frais mpl de développement
devise	imaginer
ergonomics	ergonomie f
industrial design	esthétique f industrielle
industrial espionage	espionnage m industriel
innovation	innovation f
innovative	innovateur(-trice)
innovator	innovateur(-trice) m(f)
invent	inventer
invention	invention f
inventor	inventeur(-trice) m(f)
laboratory	laboratoire m
laboratory manager	directeur(-trice) m(f) du laboratoire
laboratory technician	laboratin(e) m(f), technicien(ne) m(f) de laboratoire
man-year costs	coût m des années de travail

we hope to recover all development costs within 5 years *nous espérons récupérer tous les frais de développement en 5 ans*

a forward-looking R & D policy *une politique de recherche et développement qui voit loin*

to invest money in research *investir de l'argent dans la recherche*

market trial	*essai m sur le marché*
mock-up	*maquette f*
modernize	*moderniser*
new technology	*nouvelles technologies fpl*
out-of-date	*dépassé(e)*
patent *n*	*brevet m (d'invention)*
patent *vb*	*faire breveter*
payback time	*délai m de récupération*
pilot plant	*usine f pilote*
pilot project	*projet m pilote*
preproduction	*préproduction f*
product	*produit m*
product development	*développement m de produits*
prototype	*prototype m*
pure research	*recherche f pure*
R & D (research and development)	*R-D f (recherche-développement f)*
research *n*	*recherche(s) f(pl)*
research (into) *vb*	*faire des recherches (sur)*
research and development (R & D)	*recherche-développement f (R-D f)*
research budget	*budget m de recherche*
research department	*service f de recherche*
researcher	*chercheur(-euse) m(f)*
research manager	*directeur(-trice) m(f) de la recherche*
research programme	*programme m de recherches*
research laboratory	*laboratoire m de recherche*
research worker	*chercheur(-euse) m(f)*
robotics	*robotique f*
technological	*technologique*
technology	*technologie f*
test *n*	*essai m*
test *vb*	*mettre à l'essai*
trial	*essai m*

to find a marketable application for an invention *trouver une application commercialisable à une invention*

to take out a patent on something *faire breveter quelque chose*

the prototype will be ready in September *le prototype sera prêt en septembre*

to undertake research in the field of ... *entreprendre des recherches dans le domaine de ...*

this research will pay for itself within 5 years *le coût des recherches se récupérera en 5 ans*

to carry out trials of a new product *mettre un nouveau produit à l'épreuve*

up-to-date *très récent(e)*
user-friendly *facile à utiliser, convivial(e)*

the new product will be unveiled at the trade fair in Paris/Berlin *le nouveau produit sera dévoilé à la foire-exposition de Paris/Berlin*

See also **IMPORT-EXPORT AND SHIPPING**

bin card	*bon m de prélèvement*
bin tag	*étiquette f de magasin*
buffer stocks	*stocks mpl régulateurs*
computerized stocktaking	*inventaire m informatisé*
demurrage	*surestarie f*
depository	*dépôt m*
inventory	*inventaire m*
inventory control	*contrôle m des stocks*
last in, first out (LIFO)	*dernier entré, premier sorti (DEPS)*
overstock	*stocker en surabondance*
procurement	*achat m, approvisionnement m*
stock *n*	*stock m*
stock *vb*	*stocker*
in stock	*en stock, en réserve*
out of stock	*en rupture de stock*
stock code	*numéro m de stock*
stock control	*gestion f des stocks*
stock controller	*responsable m/f de la gestion des stocks*
stock-in-trade	*marchandises fpl en magasin*
stock level	*niveau m des stocks*
stocklist	*inventaire m*
stock management	*gestion f des stocks*
stocktaking	*inventaire m*
stock turnover	*rotation f des stocks*
stock up	*faire des réserves*
take stock	*faire l'inventaire*
warehouse	*entrepôt m*
warehouse capacity	*capacité f d'entreposage*
warehousing costs	*frais mpl d'entreposage*

to buy in 500 units of ... *acheter 500 unités de ...*
to make an inventory *faire un inventaire*
what is the position regarding stocks of ...? *quelle est la situation des stocks de ...?*
we have 30,000 units in stock *nous avons 30.000 unités en stock*
this item is out of stock *cet article est épuisé or en rupture de stock*
the stock level is getting low *le niveau des stocks commence à être bas*
in order to maintain stock levels of ... *pour maintenir le niveau des stocks de ...*
to stock up on something *faire des réserves de quelque chose*
we regret that the following items are unavailable at the moment *malheureusement, les articles suivants ne sont pas disponibles pour le moment*

ad valorem tax	*taxe f proportionnelle*
after tax	*après l'impôt*
anti-dumping duty	*droits mpl anti-dumping*
back duty	*rappel m d'impôts*
basic rate	*première tranche f d'imposition*
before tax	*avant l'impôt*
Budget *(of government)*	*budget m*
capital gains tax (CGT)	*impôt m sur les plus-values*
capital transfer tax	*impôt m sur les mutations*
corporation tax	*impôt m sur les sociétés*
council tax	*impôts mpl municipaux*
death duty	*droits mpl de succession*
direct taxation	*imposition f directe*
double taxation agreement	*convention f relative aux doubles impositions*
double taxation relief	*dégrèvement m sur double imposition*
earned income	*revenu m du travail*
excise duties	*impôts mpl prélevés par la régie*
fiscal policy	*politique f fiscale*
fiscal year	*année f fiscale*
free of tax	*exonéré(e) d'impôt*
income	*revenu m*
income tax	*impôt m sur le revenu*
indirect taxation	*imposition f indirecte*
Inland Revenue (IR)	*fisc m britannique*
Internal Revenue Service (IRS)	*fisc m des États-Unis*
investment income	*revenu m de placement*
luxury tax	*taxe f sur les produits de luxe*
mortgage relief	*dégrèvement m hypothécaire*
non-taxable	*non-imposable*
non-taxable income	*revenu m non-imposable*
PAYE (pay as you earn)	*retenue f à la source de l'impôt sur le revenu*
personal allowance	*abattement m personnel*
pre-tax	*avant impôt(s)*
profits tax	*impôt m sur les bénéfices*
progressive taxation	*imposition f progressive*

profits before/after tax *bénéfices bruts/nets*
a favourable/an unfavourable Budget *un budget de l'État favorable/ défavorable*
to sell at pre-Budget prices *vendre aux prix d'avant le budget de l'État*
the increase/reduction will come into force as of 1 January *l'aug- mentation/la réduction entrera en vigueur le 1er janvier*
to buy something duty-free *acheter quelque chose hors-taxe*

property tax	*impôt m foncier*
stamp duty	*droit m de timbre*
standard rate	*taux m d'imposition ordinaire*
tax *n*	*impôt m, taxe f*
tax *vb*	*taxer*
taxable	*imposable*
tax accountant	*comptable m/f fiscal(e)*
tax allowance	*exonération f fiscale*
tax avoidance	*évasion f fiscale légale*
tax bill	*avertissement m*
tax bracket	*tranche f d'imposition*
tax code	*code m des impôts*
tax collection	*perception f des impôts*
tax collector	*percepteur m*
tax concession	*dégrèvement m d'impôts*
tax consultant	*conseiller(-ère) m(f) fiscal(e)*
tax credit	*crédit m d'impôt*
tax cut	*réduction f d'impôt*
tax-deductible	*sujet(-ette) à dégrèvements (d'impôts)*
tax evasion	*fraude f fiscale*
tax exemption	*exonération f d'impôts*
tax-free *adj*	*exempt(e) d'impôts*
tax-free *adv*	*hors taxe*
tax haven	*paradis m fiscal*
tax holiday	*période f d'exemption d'impôts*
tax increase	*majoration f de l'impôt*
tax loophole	*possibilité f légale d'échapper à l'impôt*
tax loss	*déficit m fiscal reportable*
tax rebate	*ristourne f d'impôts*
tax relief	*dégrèvement m fiscal*
tax reserve certificate	*certificat m de provisions pour impôts*
tax return	*déclaration f d'impôts*

to recover/reclaim VAT paid on something *récupérer/réclamer la TVA payée sur quelque chose*
these goods are taxed at 15% *ces marchandises sont taxées à 15%*
to have a tax bill of over ... *avoir une feuille d'impôts de plus de ...*
to benefit from tax concessions *bénéficier de dégrèvements d'impôts*
please advise us of the tax implications regarding this deal *veuillez nous aviser des conséquences fiscales de cet accord*
to exploit a tax loophole *exploiter un moyen légal d'échapper au fisc*
to do something for tax purposes *faire quelque chose pour des raisons fiscales*

tax schedules	*barèmes mpl fiscaux*
tax shelter	*échappatoire f fiscale*
tax tables	*barèmes mpl fiscaux*
tax year	*année f fiscale*
unearned income	*revenu m financier*
VAT (value-added tax)	*TVA f (taxe f à la valeur ajoutée)*
VAT-exempt	*exonéré(e) de TVA*
wealth tax	*impôt m sur la fortune*
zero-rated	*exonéré(e) de TVA*
zero-rating	*taux m de TVA nul*

GETTING INTO THE COUNTRY

EC citizens have free access to all EC countries for up to three months at a time; after that you should apply for a resident's permit. Non-EC citizens need a visa to enter an EC country and a work permit is compulsory for all non-EC citizens working in an EC country.

If you intend to spend more than eight days on business in Switzerland in any three month period, you must register with the local authorities.

EC-passport holders do not usually require a visa if entering Canada on a short business trip. If, however, you are intending to work in Canada, you must apply for a work permit. In either case, it is advisable to contact the Canadian High Commission for further details.

Commercial samples must always be declared and accompanied by the appropriate import documents.

TRAVELLING

Dates to avoid are around Easter, 1 May, the first and middle weekend of each of the school holiday months (July, August and September), and the Christmas/New Year period. Many people take a full month's holiday in summer.

On the express TGV (*train à grande vitesse*) lines in France, taking the train may be as fast as travelling by air once you take into account the time spent getting to and from the airport. A seat reservation is compulsory on the TGV.

If you are driving your own car, you are advised to have a Green Card for full insurance cover overseas and, if you are driving a vehicle which was hired or leased in the UK, you will need a VE103 certificate. It is compulsory to display a country of origin sticker and to carry spare bulbs for headlights and indicators and a warning triangle for use in case of a breakdown. If you have a British vehicle, you must also convert your headlights for driving on the right and tint them yellow. The motoring organizations will be able to give you advice on any other requirements.

The EC driving licence is recognized in all EC countries and in Switzerland but non-EC licence-holders require an international driving licence.

There are no tolls on Belgian motorways (*autoroutes*), nor in Luxembourg, but there are tolls on French motorways — it costs about £20–£25 for a 500-mile journey. Many toll booths accept international credit cards, most of which are known by the same name in French. Access, however, may be better known as

Mastercard. Tolls are payable on some roads in Quebec and for Swiss motorways you will need to buy an annual disc (*vignette*), costing about £12.50, and display it on your windscreen. It can be bought at border crossings or tourist offices.

See also **AT THE HOTEL**

ARRANGING THE BUSINESS TRIP

Please meet me at the airport/at my hotel *pourriez-vous venir à ma rencontre à l'aéroport/à l'hôtel?*

I will be on flight BA007, arriving at 8.45pm *je prendrai le vol BA007 qui arrive à 20H45*

I will make my own way to my hotel/the meeting *j'irai à l'hôtel/à la réunion par mes propres moyens*

I have never been to Brussels before *c'est la première fois que je vais à Bruxelles*

I know Luxembourg quite well already *je connais déjà assez bien Luxembourg*

BOOKING A PLANE/TRAIN TICKET

How much is a single/return to London? *combien coûte un aller simple/un aller (et) retour pour Londres?*

When is the next/last plane/train to London? *à quelle heure est le prochain/dernier avion/train pour Londres?*

What time does the train leave/arrive? *à quelle heure part/arrive le train?*

What time does the plane take off/land? *quelle est l'heure de départ/d'arrivée du vol?*

What is the latest check-in time? *quelle est l'heure-limite d'enregistrement?*

I'd like a non-smoking window seat *je voudrais une place non-fumeur près du hublot*

Not over the wing *pas sur l'aile*

I'd like a seat facing the engine/with my back to the engine *je voudrais être dans le sens de la marche/tourner le dos au sens de la marche*

I'd like to book two seats *je voudrais réserver deux places*

I'd like to confirm my booking *je voudrais confirmer ma réservation*

Is there a direct flight? *y a-t-il un vol direct?*

How long is the stopover? *quelle est la durée de l'escale?*

Can I go via Brussels? *est-il possible de passer par Bruxelles?*

I'd like to change my reservation *je voudrais changer ma réserva-*

tion

I'd like to upgrade my ticket *je voudrais échanger mon billet pour un billet de la classe au-dessus*

Is there any room left in first class/smoking? *reste-t-il des places en première classe/fumeurs?*

Is there an earlier/later flight/train? *y a-t-il un vol/train plus tôt/ plus tard?*

If I go on stand-by, what chance is there that I'll get a seat? *si je pars en stand-by, quelles sont les chances d'avoir une place?*

I'd like a vegetarian/salt-free meal *je voudrais un repas végétarien/sans sel*

I am diabetic, can I get a special meal? *je suis diabétique, puis-je avoir un repas spécial?*

Are meals served on that train/plane? *sert-on des repas dans ce train/vol?*

AT THE AIRPORT/RAILWAY STATION

Where can I hire a car? *où puis-je louer une voiture?*

Where can I change money? *où puis-je changer de l'argent?*

Where can I buy magazines/a newspaper? *où puis-je acheter des magazines/un journal?*

Is the 18.30 to Geneva due to leave on time? *est-ce que le train/ vol de 18H30 pour Genève partira à l'heure?*

I am due to meet a Ms Greig here. Could you page her? *je dois rencontrer Mme Greig ici. Pourriez-vous faire une annonce?*

Do you have facilities for the disabled? *avez-vous des installations pour personnes handicapées?*

AIRPORT

Where is the British Airways desk, please? *où est le comptoir de British Airways, s'il vous plaît?*

I have only one piece of hand luggage *j'ai seulement un bagage à main*

Can I book my luggage straight through? *puis-je enregistrer mes bagages directement jusqu'à la destination finale?*

My luggage hasn't arrived *mes bagages ne sont pas arrivés*

Can I check in for the 14.30 to London (yet)? *puis-je (déjà) passer à l'enregistrement pour le vol de 14H30 à destination de Londres?*

Is the Air France flight to Edinburgh boarding yet? *est-ce que l'embarquement du vol Air France pour Édimbourg est (déjà) commencé?*

Has the 12.20 to New York been called yet? *est-ce qu'on a (déjà) annoncé le vol de 12H20 à destination de New York?*

I am in transit *je suis en transit*

How often do shuttles leave for the city centre? *quelle est la fréquence des navettes pour le centre-ville?*

Does this shuttle go to terminal two? *est-ce que cette navette va au terminal deux?*

I would prefer not to put these diskettes through the X-ray machine *j'aimerais mieux ne pas faire passer ces disquettes par l'appareil à rayons X*

RAILWAY STATION

Where is platform 14, please? *où est le quai numéro 14, s'il vous plaît?*

Is this the right platform for Brussels? *c'est bien le quai pour Bruxelles?*

Which platform does the London train leave from? *de quel quai part le train pour Londres?*

Which window sells international tickets? *quel est le guichet pour les billets internationaux?*

Can I buy a ticket on the train? *peut-on acheter les billets dans le train?*

PHRASES YOU ARE LIKELY TO HEAR AT THE AIRPORT OR RAILWAY STATION

Fumeur ou non-fumeur? *smoking or non-smoking?*

Avez-vous des bagages? *do you have any luggage?*

Ce vol/train est complet *that flight/train is fully booked*

Voulez-vous partir en stand-by? *would you like to go on stand-by?*

L'embarquement se fera à la Porte 35 *please go straight to Gate 35*

Allez directement à la Porte 35 *you will be boarding at Gate 35*

Votre vol sera annoncé à 9 heures *your flight will be called at 9am*

Votre vol/train a du retard *your flight/train has been delayed*

Le décollage/départ est maintenant prévu pour 21H00 *take-off/departure is now scheduled for 9pm*

Comment réglez-vous? *how will you be paying?*

ON THE PLANE OR TRAIN

Could I change seats? *pourrais-je changer de place?*

I'd prefer to be by the window/in an aisle seat *j'aimerais mieux être près du hublot/près de l'allée*

What time will breakfast/lunch/dinner be served? *à quelle heure sert-on le petit déjeuner/le déjeuner/le dîner?*

What time is it, local time? *quelle heure est-il selon l'heure*

locale?
What time will we arrive in Paris? *à quelle heure arriverons-nous à Paris?*
I'm sorry, but you're sitting in my seat *je suis désolé(e), mais vous êtes assis(e) à ma place*
Excuse me, this is a non-smoking compartment/section *excusez-moi, mais nous sommes dans un compartiment/une section non-fumeurs*

PLANE
Please do not wake me up *pourriez-vous ne pas me réveiller?*
I ordered a special meal *j'ai commandé un repas spécial*
All the lockers are full. Where can I put my bag? *tous les casiers sont pleins. Où puis-je mettre mon sac?*
Could I have a washing kit, please? *puis-je avoir une trousse de voyage?*
I'm feeling airsick *j'ai le mal de l'air*

TRAIN
Is it all right if I open/close the window? *cela vous dérange-t-il si j'ouvre/je ferme la fenêtre?*
Where should I change for Amsterdam? *où faut-il changer pour Amsterdam?*
I was told that I could buy a ticket on the train *on m'a dit que je pouvais acheter le billet dans le train*
Is there a telephone on the train? *y a-t-il un téléphone dans le train?*

AT CUSTOMS

I am here on business *je viens pour affaires*
I represent Clarke & Co *je représente Clarke & Cie*
I will be spending three days here *je vais rester trois jours ici*
I have nothing to declare *je n'ai rien à déclarer*
I have the usual allowance of cigarettes and alcohol *j'ai la quantité autorisée d'alcool et de cigarettes*
I will be re-exporting these samples *je vais ré-exporter ces échantillons*
Could I have a receipt? *puis-je avoir un reçu?*

PHRASES YOU ARE LIKELY TO HEAR AT CUSTOMS
Quel est le but de votre visite? *what is the purpose of your visit?*
Combien de temps resterez-vous en France? *how long will you be staying in France?*
Veuillez ouvrir votre sac *open your bag, please*

Avez-vous quelque chose à déclarer? *have you anything to declare?*

Il y a des droits à payer sur ces articles *you will have to pay duty on these items*

TAKING A TAXI

Could you order me a taxi, please? *pourriez-vous m'appeler un taxi (s'il vous plaît)?*

Where can I get a taxi? *où puis-je prendre un taxi?*

Take me to this address, please *emmenez-moi à cette adresse, s'il vous plaît*

How much to the airport/railway station? *c'est combien pour l'aéroport/la gare?*

I'm in a hurry *je suis pressé(e)*

Please wait here *veuillez attendre ici*

Stop here, please *arrêtez-vous ici s'il vous plaît*

How much is that? *je vous dois combien?*

Can I pay you in sterling? *est-ce que vous prenez les livres sterling?*

Keep the change *gardez la monnaie*

Can I have a receipt? *pourriez-vous me donner un reçu?*

Please pick me up here at 4 o'clock *pourriez-vous venir me chercher ici à 16H00?*

But the meter says only ... *mais le compteur indique seulement ...*

This is the third time we've been down this street *c'est la troisième fois que nous passons par cette rue*

HIRING AND DRIVING A CAR

Where can I hire a car? *où puis-je louer une voiture?*

I reserved a car. My name is Fraser *j'ai réservé une voiture au nom de Fraser*

I'd like a two-door/four-door model *je voudrais un modèle à deux/quatre portières*

I'd like a Renault 21 for 3 days *je voudrais une Renault 21 pour 3 jours*

Have you got a larger/smaller car? *avez-vous une plus grande/plus petite voiture?*

What does the hire price include? *qu'est-ce qui est compris dans le prix (de location)?*

Is mileage/insurance included? *est-ce que le kilométrage est compris/l'assurance est comprise?*

Can I return the car outside office hours? *est-il possible de rendre la voiture en dehors des heures de bureau?*

Can you show me the controls? *pourriez-vous me montrer les commandes?*

Can you tell me the way to ...? *pourriez-vous m'indiquer le chemin pour ...?*

How far is the next service station? *à quelle distance se trouve la prochaine station-service?*

Can I park here? *puis-je me garer ici?*

I'd like to put some air in the tyres *je voudrais gonfler les pneus*

Fifty litres, please *cinquante litres s'il vous plaît*

Fill her up, please *le plein s'il vous plaît*

Would you check the oil/water/tyre pressure? *pourriez-vous vérifier l'huile/l'eau/la pression des pneus?*

Could you clean the windscreen? *pourriez-vous nettoyer le pare-brise?*

Can you take me to the nearest garage? *pourriez-vous m'emmener au garage le plus proche?*

Can you give me a tow? *pouvez-vous me remorquer?*

How long will it take to repair? *combien de temps durera la réparation?*

PHRASES YOU ARE LIKELY TO HEAR WHEN HIRING A CAR

Montrez-moi votre permis de conduire *could I see your driving licence?*

C'est la première fois que vous conduisez en France? *have you driven in France before?*

L'assurance n'est pas comprise *insurance costs extra*

Le kilométrage est limité à ... *the mileage limit is ...*

Avez-vous d'autres pièces d'identité? *have you any other form of identification?*

ILLNESS AND EMERGENCIES

In EC countries, EC citizens can have medical treatment and medication partially refunded by filling in an E111 form (available in the UK from Post Offices), which will generally ensure that you receive a 70–75% refund on medical expenses paid to chemists and doctors or hospitals working within the state health service. This covers most hospitals in France (private hospitals are usually called *cliniques*) and all doctors or dentists who are *conventionnés* (i.e. linked to the state health scheme). You must get the form filled in at the time of treatment.

If you want to call an ambulance in France, you should ask for the *pompiers* (firemen), or *Police Secours*. If you need a doctor, you can ask in any chemist which local doctor is on duty (*de service*). If the chemist is closed, there will be a notice in the window telling you where the nearest open one is.

Belgian hospitals charge an extra non-refundable daily rate and ambulance services are private.

Non-EC citizens should have private medical insurance, as should EC citizens travelling to Quebec and Switzerland.

I feel ill *je me sens mal*
I feel sick *j'ai des nausées*
I feel faint *j'ai un malaise*
My ... hurts *j'ai mal au/à la/aux ...*
I have a pain in the ... *j'ai une douleur dans le/la/les ...*
I am allergic to penicillin/milk products *je suis allergique à la pénicilline/aux produits laitiers*
I have a headache *j'ai mal à la tête*
I have a high temperature *j'ai beaucoup de température*
I think I have broken my ... *je crois que je me suis cassé le/la/les ...*
I have been bitten/stung by a bee/wasp/mosquito/snake *j'ai été piqué(e)/mordu(e) par une abeille/une guêpe/un moustique/un serpent*
My companion is ill *mon compagnon/ma compagne est malade*
He/she is unconscious *il/elle est inconscient(e)*
I'd like to see a doctor/dentist immediately *je voudrais voir un médecin/dentiste immédiatement*
Can you give me a prescription for ...? *pouvez-vous me donner une ordonnance pour ...?*
This is an emergency *c'est une urgence*
Please call an ambulance/the fire brigade/the police *appelez une ambulance/les pompiers/la police*
There is a fire *il y a un incendie*
There has been an accident *il y a eu un accident*
I have been attacked/robbed *j'ai été attaqué(e)/volé(e)*
I have lost my ... *j'ai perdu mon/ma/mes ...*
Help! *au secours!*

ADDITIONAL VOCABULARY

accident	*accident m*
aeroplane	*avion m*
airport	*aéroport m*
airport police	*police f de l'air*
airport tax	*taxes fpl d'aéroport*
airsickness	*mal m de l'air*
aisle seat	*place f près de l'allée*
ambulance	*ambulance f*

APEX ticket	*billet m APEX*
arrivals (area)	*arrivées fpl*
arrivals board	*tableau m des arrivées*
aspirin	*aspirine f*
baggage allowance	*poids m (de bagages) autorisé*
baggage reclaim	*livraison f des bagages*
bank	*banque f*
bar	*bar m*
blood group	*groupe m sanguin*
boarding card	*carte f d'embarquement*
boat train	*train-paquebot m*
breakdown	*panne f*
breakdown van	*dépanneuse f*
buffet car	*buffet m*
business class	*classe f affaires*
business trip	*voyage m d'affaires*
cafeteria	*cafétéria f*
cancellation	*annulation f*
cancelled	*annulé(e)*
car	*voiture f*
car hire	*location f de voitures*
car hire firm	*entreprise f de location de voitures*
car park (*long-term*)	*parking m de long séjour*
(*short-term*)	*parking m de court séjour*
car phone	*téléphone m de voiture*
cash dispenser	*distributeur m de billets*
charter flight	*vol m charter*
check in *vb*	*passer à l'enregistrement*
check-in desk	*enregistrement m*
club class	*classe f club*
coach	*car m*
compartment	*compartiment m*
confirm	*confirmer*
confirmation	*confirmation f*
couchette	*couchette f*
customs	*douane f*
customs declaration	*déclaration f de douane*
customs officer	*douanier(-ière) m(f)*
delayed	*retardé(e)*
dentist	*dentiste m/f*
departure lounge	*salle f d'embarquement*
departures (area)	*départs mpl*
departures board	*tableau m des départs*
diabetic	*diabétique m/f*

diarrhoea	*diarrhée f*
diesel (fuel)	*gas-oil m*
dining car	*wagon-restaurant m*
doctor	*médecin m*
domestic arrivals	*arrivées fpl des vols intérieurs*
domestic departures	*départs mpl des vols intérieurs*
domestic flight	*vol m intérieur*
driver	*chauffeur m*
driving licence	*permis m de conduire*
duty	*droits mpl de douane*
duty-free goods	*articles mpl hors-taxe*
duty-free shop	*boutique f hors-taxe*
economy class	*classe f touriste*
emergency exit	*issue f de secours*
emergency telephone	*téléphone m de secours*
excess baggage	*excédent m de bagages*
executive class	*classe f affaires*
exit *(on motorway)*	*sortie f*
express train	*rapide m*
ferry	*ferry m*
filling *(in tooth)*	*plombage m*
fire brigade	*pompiers mpl*
firm booking	*réservation f ferme*
first aid post	*poste m de secours*
first class	*première classe f*
first class lounge	*salon m de première classe*
flat tyre	*pneu m plat*
flight	*vol m*
flying time	*durée f de vol*
food poisoning	*intoxication f alimentaire*
fully booked	*complet(-ète)*
gate	*porte f*
guard *(on train)*	*chef m de train*
hand luggage	*bagages mpl à main*
headphones	*casque m*
hire *vb*	*louer*
hire price	*prix m de (la) location*
hospital	*hôpital m*
hovercraft	*aéroglisseur m*
hydrofoil	*hydrofoil m*
immigration (counter)	*immigration f*
information desk	*bureau m de renseignements*
injection	*injection m*
insulin	*insuline f*
insurance	*assurance f*

international arrivals	*arrivées fpl des vols internationaux*
international departures	*départs mpl des vols internationaux*
international flight	*vol m international*
itinerary	*itinéraire m*
land *vb*	*atterrir*
landing	*atterrissage m*
left-luggage locker	*casier m à consigne automatique*
left-luggage office/counter	*consigne f*
lost property office	*bureau m des objets trouvés*
luggage locker *(on plane)*	*casier m*
map *(of country)*	*carte f*
(of town, underground etc)	*plan m*
medical insurance	*assurance f maladie*
meter *(in taxi)*	*compteur m*
mileage	*kilométrage m*
motorway	*autoroute f*
non-smoking compartment/ section	*compartiment m/section f non-fumeurs*
no-show	*passager(-ère) m(f) qui ne se présente pas*
oil	*huile f*
one-way ticket	*aller m simple*
open return	*aller (et) retour m open*
overbook	*faire du surbooking*
overbooked	*surréservé(e)*
passport	*passeport m*
passport control	*contrôle m des passeports*
petrol	*essence f*
platform	*quai m*
police	*police f; gendarmes mpl (French police and gendarmes are two separate organizations)*
policeman/woman	*policier m/femme f policier; gendarme m*
police station	*commissariat m de police; gendarmerie f*
porter	*porteur m*
post office	*poste f*
pregnant	*enceinte*
prescription	*ordonnance f*
punctured tyre	*pneu m crevé*
railway police	*police f des chemins de fer*
reservation	*réservation f*

reserve	*réserver*
restaurant car	*wagon-restaurant m*
return ticket	*aller (et) retour m*
safety belt	*ceinture f de sécurité*
sample	*échantillon m*
scheduled flight	*vol m régulier*
seasickness	*mal m de mer*
seatbelt	*ceinture f de sécurité*
second class	*deuxième classe f*
service station	*station-service f*
shuttle	*navette f*
single ticket	*aller m (simple)*
sleeping compartment	*voiture-lit f*
smoking compartment	*(compartiment m) fumeurs mpl*
speed limit	*limitation f de vitesse*
stand-by ticket	*stand-by m*
station	*gare f*
stationmaster	*chef m de gare*
steward	*steward m*
stewardess	*hôtesse f*
stopover	*escale f*
supplement	*supplément m*
take off	*décoller*
take-off	*décollage m*
taxi	*taxi m*
taxi driver	*chauffeur m de taxi*
taxi rank	*station f de taxi*
terminal *(air)*	*terminal m, aérogare f*
(rail, bus)	*terminus m*
through train	*direct m*
ticket office	*guichet m*
toilet	*toilettes fpl*
toothache	*mal m de dents*
(very bad)	*rage f de dents*
train	*train m*
transit lounge	*salle f de transit*
transit stop	*escale f de transit*
travel agency	*agence f de voyages*
travel agent	*agent m de voyages*
traveller's cheque	*traveller m, chèque m de voyage*
travel sickness *(car)*	*mal m de la route*
(air)	*mal m de l'air*
(sea)	*mal m de mer*
underground	*métro m*
unleaded petrol	*essence f sans plomb*

unlimited mileage	*kilométrage m illimité*
vaccination	*vaccination f*
vaccination certificate	*certificat m de vaccination*
visa	*visa m*
waiting room	*salle f d'attente*
wheelchair	*fauteuil m roulant*
window *(aeroplane)*	*hublot m*
(train, bus)	*fenêtre f*
(car)	*vitre f*
window seat *(aeroplane)*	*place f côté hublot*
(train, bus)	*place f côté fenêtre*

To help you translate business material from French, this glossary contains all the French words given as translations in the first section of the book and their translations in a business context. In addition, for the most common words, translations of basic meanings are also provided.

abandonner *to abort*

abattement *m allowance*

abattement *m* **personnel** *personal allowance*

absentéisme *m absenteeism*

absorption *f absorption*

accéder à *to access; to grant; to get to*

acceptation *f acceptance*

accepteur(-euse) *m(f) acceptor*

accès *m access*

accès *m* **aléatoire** *random access*

accès *m* **direct** *direct access*

accès *m* **sélectif** *random access*

accident *m accident*

accident *m* **du travail** *industrial accident; occupational accident*

accidentel(le) *accidental*

accord *m agreement; deal*

accord *m* **bilatéral** *bilateral agreement*

accord *m* **d'agence exclusive** *exclusive agency agreement*

accord *m* **de cession-bail** *leaseback arrangement*

accord *m* **de libre échange réciproque** *fair-trade agreement*

accord *m* **de licence** *licensing agreement*

accord *m* **de licenciement** *redundancy agreement*

accord *m* **de vente sous réserve** *conditional sale agreement*

accord *m* **d'indexation des salaires** *threshold agreement*

accord *m* **entre le fournisseur-créditeur et le débiteur** *debtor-creditor-supplier agreement*

accorder *to award; to grant; to allow*

accords *mpl* **de maintien des prix** *price maintenance agreement*

accoster *to dock*

accueil *m* **du nouveau personnel** *induction*

accueil *m* **réservé à une marque** *brand acceptance*

accumulation *f accrual; accumulation*

accusation *f charge*

accusé *m* **de réception** *acknowledgement (slip)*

accuser réception de *to acknowledge*

achat *m purchase; buying; procurement*

achat *m* **à crédit** *hire purchase*

achat *m* **d'impulsion** *impulse purchase*

achat *m* **en gros** *bulk buying*

achats *mpl* **de soutien** *support buying*

achat *m* **spontané** *impulse purchase; impulse buying*

acheter *to buy*

acheteur(-euse) *m(f) buyer*

acheteur(-euse) *m(f)* **d'espace média** *media buyer*

achèvement *m completion*

aciérie *f steelworks*

acompte *m deposit; instalment; down payment; part payment; earnest money*

acquisition *f acquisition*

acquisition *f* **d'argent** *money-making*

acre *f acre*

acte *m* **de donation** *deed of covenant*

acte *m* **délictuel** *tort*

acte *m* **judiciaire** *writ*

acte *m* **notarié** *deed*

acteur(-trice) *m(f) actor*

actif *m asset(s); credit*

actif(-ive) *buoyant*

actif *m* **circulant** *current assets*

actif *m* **incorporel** *invisible assets*

actif *m* **net** *net assets*

actifs *mpl* **gelés** *frozen assets*
action *f action; share*
action *f* **entièrement libérée** *fully-paid share*
action *f* **gratuite** *bonus share*
actionnaire *m/f shareholder; stockholder*
actionnaire *m/f* **majoritaire** *majority shareholder*
actionnaire *m/f* **minoritaire** *minority shareholder*
action *f* **ordinaire** *ordinary share; common stock*
action *f* **ordinaire à droit de vote limité** *B shares*
action *f* **partiellement libérée** *partly-paid share*
actions *fpl shares; stock*
actions *fpl* **ordinaires** *ordinary shares; equities*
actions *fpl* **ordinaires privilégiées** *preferred ordinary shares*
actions *fpl* **ordinaires (sans droit de vote)** *A shares*
actions *fpl* **privilégiées** *preference shares*
actions *fpl* **sans droit de vote** *non-voting shares*
actuaire *m/f actuary*
actuariel(le) *actuarial*
adaptateur *m* **de graphique amélioré** *EGA (enhanced graphics adaptor)*
adaptateur *m* **de graphique couleur** *CGA (colour graphics adaptor)*
additif *m additive*
administrateur(-trice) *m(f) administrator; director; company director; non-executive director*
administrateur *m* **judiciaire** *(official) receiver*
administration *f administration; directorate*
adresse *f address*
adresse *f* **au bureau** *business address*
adresse *f* **du siège social** *business address; address of the head office*
aérogare *f airport terminal*

aéroglisseur *m hovercraft*
aéroport *m airport*
aérosol *m aerosol spray*
affacturage *m factoring*
affaire *f bargain; deal; matter; case*
affaire *f* **prospère** *going concern*
affaire *f* **recevable** *prima facie case*
affaires *fpl business*
affaissement *m subsidence*
affectation *f appropriation; appointment; assignment*
affichage *m billing; display*
affichage *m* **uniligne** *single-line display*
affiche *f poster*
affiche *f* **cartonnée** *showcard*
afficheur *m* **à cristaux liquides** *LCD (liquid crystal display)*
affirmation *f affirmation*
agence *f agency; branch; office*
agence *f* **(de courtage) louche** *bucket shop*
agence *f* **de notation de solvabilité** *credit agency*
agence *f* **de placement** *employment agency*
agence *f* **de publicité** *advertising agency*
agence *f* **de recouvrement** *debt collection agency*
agence *f* **de relations publiques** *public relations firm*
agence *f* **de voyages** *travel agency*
agence *f* **immobilière** *estate agency*
Agence *f* **internationale de l'énergie atomique (AIEA** *f)* *International Atomic Energy Agency (IAEA)*
Agence *f* **spatiale européenne (ASE** *f)* *European Space Agency (ESA)*
agenda *m* **de bureau** *desk diary*
agent *m agent; policeman*
agent *m* **accrédité** *accredited agent*
agent *m* **d'art** *actor's agent*
agent *m* **d'assurances** *insurance agent or broker*
agent *m* **de change** *stockbroker; broker*
agent *m* **de publicité** *press agent*
agent *m* **de voyages** *travel agent*

agent *m* **en douane** *customs broker*

agent *m* **exclusif** *sole agent*

agent *m* **fiduciaire** *fiduciary*

agent *m* **immobilier** *estate agent*

agent *m* **littéraire** *literary agent*

agent *m* **maritime** *shipping agent*

agios *mpl handling charge*

agrafe *f staple*

agrafeuse *f stapler*

agrandir *to enlarge; to expand; to extend*

agrandissement *m enlargement; expansion; extension*

agro-industries *fpl agribusiness*

aide *f* **financière** *accommodation; financial aid*

aire *f* **de chargement** *loading bay*

air *m* **pur** *clean air*

ajournement *m adjournment*

ajourner *to adjourn*

ajuster *to adjust*

alimentation *f* **feuille à feuille** *single-sheet feed*

aller (et) retour *m return ticket*

aller (et) retour *m* **open** *open return*

aller *m* **(simple)** *single ticket; one-way ticket*

allocation *f* **de maternité** *maternity benefit*

alphanumérique *alphanumeric*

altération *f corruption*

altéré(e) *corrupt*

altérer *to corrupt*

ambulance *f ambulance*

aménagement *m conversion; fitting; development*

aménager *to convert; to fit out*

amorcer *to boot (up); to begin*

amortir *to write off; to pay off; to depreciate; to amortize*

amortissement *m paying off; depreciation; amortization*

analogique *m analog(ue)*

analyse *f* **des médias** *media analysis*

analyse *f* **des ventes** *sales analysis*

analyse *f* **du chemin critique** *critical path analysis*

analyse *f* **du marché** *market analysis*

analyse *f* **fonctionnelle** *systems analysis*

analyste *m/f* **de coûts** *cost accountant*

analyste *m/f* **fonctionnel(le)** *systems analyst*

ancienneté *f length of service*

année *f* **fiscale** *tax year; fiscal year*

annonce *f advertisement; announcement*

passer une annonce *to advertise*

annonce *f* **isolée** *solus*

annonce *f* **mystère** *teaser*

annonceur *m advertiser*

annuaire *m* **des télex** *telex directory*

annuaire *m* **(téléphonique)** *telephone directory*

annulation *f cancellation*

annulé(e) *cancelled*

annuler *to cancel*

antenne *f* **parabolique** *satellite dish*

antidater *to backdate*

appareil *m* **monté en armoire** *rack-mounted unit*

appareil-photo *m (pl ~s-~) camera*

appartement *m flat; apartment; suite*

appartement *m* **de réunion** *function suite*

appel *m appeal*

faire appel *m* **(contre)** *to appeal (against)*

appelant(e) *m(f) appellant*

appel *m* **de presse** *press call*

appel *m* **de relance** *follow-up call*

appeler *to call*

appel *m* **impromptu** *cold call*

appel *m* **par Réunion-Téléphone ®** *conference call*

appel *m* **payé par carte de crédit** *credit card call*

application *f application*

apprenti(e) *m(f) apprentice*

apprentissage *m apprenticeship*

approvisionnement *m procurement; supplying*

apurement *m audit*

arbitrage *m* arbitration
arbitre *m* arbitrator
arbitrer to arbitrate
architecte *m* architect
archives *fpl* archive(s); records
argent *m* money
argent *m* **bon marché** cheap money
argent *m* **cher** dear money
argent *m* **facile** easy money
argent *m* **improductif** idle money
argent *m* **qui dort** idle money
armateur *m* shipowner; ship's manager
armement *m* arms trade; armament(s)
armoire *f* **à fournitures** stationery cupboard
arrêt *m* stoppage; stop
arrêt *m* **de travail** stoppage; sick leave; sick note
arrhes *fpl* deposit; earnest money
arriéré *m* arrears
arrière *m* rear
arrivage *m* consignment
arrivée *f* arrival
arrivées *fpl* **des vols intérieurs** domestic arrivals
arrivées *fpl* **des vols internationaux** international arrivals
art *m* **de la vente** salesmanship
article *m* article; record
article *m* **sacrifié** loss leader
articles *mpl* **de marque** proprietary goods
articles *mpl* **dépareillés** broken lot
articles *mpl* **hors-taxe** duty-free goods
ascenseur *m* lift
aspirine *f* aspirin
assemblée *f* **générale annuelle (AG** *f***)** annual general meeting (AGM)
assemblée *f* **générale extraordinaire (AGE** *f***)** extraordinary general meeting (EGM)
assemblée *f* **statutaire** statutory meeting
assigner to assign
assistant(e) *m(f)* assistant
assister à to attend
association *f* partnership; associa-

tion
Association *f* **des nations de l'Asie du Sud-Est (ASEAN** *f***)** Association of South-East Asian Nations (ASEAN)
Association *f* **européenne de libre échange (AELE** *f***)** European Free Trade Association (EFTA)
Association *f* **internationale pour le développement (AID** *f***)** International Development Association (IDA)
associé(e) *m(f)* partner
assurance *f* insurance (policy); insurance (company); assurance
assurance *f* **à capital différé** endowment assurance; endowment policy
assurance *f* **à capital différé avec bénéfice** with-profits endowment assurance
assurance *f* **à terme** term insurance
assurance *f* **au tiers** third-party insurance
assurance-automobile *f* (*pl* ~s-~) car insurance; motor insurance
assurance *f* **contre les accidents** accident insurance
assurance *f* **contre les détournements** fidelity bond
assurance *f* **de compensation** indemnity insurance
assurance *f* **en cas de décès** whole-life insurance
assurance-incendie *f* (*pl* ~s-~) fire insurance
assurance *f* **maladie** health insurance; medical insurance
assurance *f* **maritime** marine insurance
assurance *f* **mobilier-habitation** (home) contents insurance
assurance *f* **responsabilité civile** liability insurance
assurance *f* **responsabilité produit** product liability insurance
assurance *f* **sur fret** freight insurance
assurance *f* **sur l'immeuble** build-

ings insurance

assurance *f* **tempête** *storm insurance*

assurance *f* **tous risques** *comprehensive insurance; all-risks policy; blanket policy*

assurance *f* **transport** *transport insurance*

assurance-vie *f* (*pl* ~**s**-~) *life insurance*

assurance *f* **vol et incendie** *fire and theft (insurance) policy*

assurance-voyage *f* (*pl* ~**s**-~) *travel insurance*

assuré(e) *m(f)* *insured (person); policy-holder*

assurer *to insure; to ensure; to secure*

(s')assurer *to insure (oneself)*

assurer la liaison (avec) *to liaise (with)*

assureur *m* *insurer; underwriter*

astuce *f* **promotionnelle** *gimmick*

astuce *f* **publicitaire** *gimmick*

atelier *m* *workshop*

atelier *m* **de réparation** *service centre*

atelier *m* **d'usinage** *machine shop*

ateliers *mpl* *shop floor*

atmosphère *f* *atmosphere*

attaché(e) *m(f)* **de presse** *press officer*

atteindre *to reach*

atteintes *fpl* **à l'environnement** *environmental damage*

atterrir *to land*

atterrissage *m* *landing*

attestation *f* **d'assurance** *insurance certificate*

attestation *f* **provisoire d'assurance** *cover note*

attrait *m* *appeal*

attribution *f* *allotment; allocation*

au-dessous du pair *below par*

au-dessus du pair *above par*

audience *f* **cumulée** *reach*

audioconférence *f* *audio conferencing*

audiotypie *f* *audio-typing*

audiotypiste *m/f* *audio-typist*

audit *m* **environnement** *environmental audit*

auditoire *m* *audience*

augmentation *f* *increment*

augmentation *f* **de salaire** *salary increase*

augmentation *f* **générale des salaires** *across-the-board wage increase*

augmenter la puissance *to upgrade*

auteur *m* *author*

auteur *m* **à succès** *bestselling author*

auteur *m* **d'une proposition** *mover*

auteur *m* **principal (du délit)** *principal (offender)*

autofinancement *m* *self-financing*

automatisation *f* *automation*

automatisé(e) *automated*

autonome *autonomous; stand-alone*

(en mode) autonome *off-line*

autoroute *f* *motorway*

autres matières *fpl* **à l'ordre du jour** *any other competent business (AOCB)*

avaliseur *m* *accommodation party*

avancer *to progress*

avantage *m* **concurrentiel** *competitive advantage; competitive edge*

avantages *mpl* **en nature** *benefit-in-kind; fringe benefits*

avantage *m* **social** *employee benefit; fringe benefit*

avant-cour *f* (*pl* ~-~**s**) *forecourt*

avant-première *f* (*pl* ~-~**s**) *preview*

avant-première *f* **exclusive** (*pl* ~-~**s**) *sneak preview*

avarie *f* *average*

avec avarie particulière *with particular average (WPA)*

avenant *m* *codicil*

avertissement *m* *warning; tax bill*

avertisseur *m* **de poche** *pager*

avion *m* *aeroplane*

par avion *by air; airmail*

avis *m* *notification*

avis *m* **d'exécution** *contract note*

avis *m* **d'expédition** *advice note*

avis *m* **d'indemnisation** *letter of indemnity*

avocat(e) *m(f)* *solicitor; lawyer; advocate; attorney*

avocat(e) *m(f)* **de la défense** *counsel for the defence*

avocat(e) *m(f)* **(plaidant(e))** *barrister*

avoir *m credit note*

bagages *mpl luggage*

bagages *mpl* **à main** *hand luggage*

baguette *f pointer*

baie *f* **vitrée** *bay window*

bail *m lease; leasehold*

louée à bail *leasehold*

bailleur *m* **de fonds** *backer; sponsor; sleeping partner; silent partner*

bain *m bath*

baisse *f fall; drop*

à la baisse *bearish; falling*

balance *f* **commerciale** *balance of trade*

balance *f* **commerciale déficitaire** *adverse trade balance*

balance *f* **des paiements** *balance of payments*

balancer *to balance*

balcon *m balcony*

bande *f* **magnétique** *magnetic tape*

banlieue *f suburb*

banque *f bank; banking*

banque *f* **d'affaires** *merchant bank*

Banque *f* **d'Angleterre** *Bank of England*

banque *f* **de dépôt** *clearing bank; commercial bank*

banque *f* **de données** *databank*

banque *f* **d'émission** *central bank*

banque *f* **de placement** *investment bank*

Banque *f* **des règlements internationaux (BRI** *f)* *Bank for International Settlements (BIS)*

Banque *f* **européenne de la reconstruction et du développement (BERD** *f)* *European Bank for Reconstruction and Development (EBRD)*

Banque *f* **européenne d'investisse-**

ment (BEI *f)* *European Investment Bank (EIB)*

Banque *f* **internationale pour la reconstruction et le développement (BIRD** *f)* *International Bank for Reconstruction and Development (IBRD)*

Banque *f* **mondiale** *World Bank*

banque *f* **présentatrice** *collecting bank*

banquier *m* *banker; merchant banker*

bar *m bar*

baraterie *f barratry*

barèmes *mpl* **fiscaux** *tax tables; tax schedules*

barre *f* **d'espacement** *space bar*

barrière *f* **douanière** *tariff barrier; trade barrier*

en bas *adv downstairs*

bas de gamme *adj down-market*

base *f* **de données** *database*

bassin(s) *m(pl)* *dock(s)*

bâtiment *m building; construction industry*

bâtiment *m* **d'habitation** *residential building*

bâtiment *m* **industriel** *industrial building*

bénéfice *m profit*

bénéfice *m* **brut** *gross profit*

bénéfice *m* **d'exploitation** *operating profit*

bénéfice *m* **escompté** *anticipated profit*

bénéfice *m* **net** *net profit*

bénéfice *m* **par action** *earnings per share*

bénéficiaire *m/f beneficiary; payee*

besoins *mpl* **du marché** *market demand*

best-seller *m* (*pl* ~-~**s**) *bestseller*

biens *mpl goods; property; estate*

biens *mpl* **de consommation** *consumer goods*

biens *mpl* **de consommation à débit rapide** *fast-moving consumer goods (FMCG)*

biens *mpl* **de consommation durables** *consumer durables*

biens *mpl* **d'équipement** *capital goods; industrial goods*

biens *mpl* **et effets** *mpl goods and chattels*

biens *mpl* **immobiliers** *real estate*

bière *f beer*

bière *f* **blonde** *lager*

bière *f* **brune** *stout*

bilan *m balance sheet; assessment*

bilan *m* **consolidé** *consolidated balance sheet*

billet *m ticket; banknote*

billet *m* **à ordre** *promissory note*

billet *m* **de banque** *banknote*

billet *m* **de complaisance** *accommodation bill*

bimensuel(le) *bi-monthly; twice a month*

bimensuellement *twice a month*

bimestriel(le) *every two months*

biodégradable *biodegradable*

biosphère *f biosphere*

bits *mpl* **par pouce** *bpi (bits per inch)*

bits *mpl* **par seconde** *bps (bits per second)*

blanchisserie *f laundry service*

blocage *m arrestment*

blocage *m* **des salaires** *wage freeze*

bloc-notes *m* *(pl inv)* *desk pad; clipboard*

boisson *f drink*

boisson *f* **non-alcoolisée** *soft drink*

boîte *f* **à disques** *disk box*

boîte *f* **aux lettres** *mailbox*

boîte *f* **de nuit** *nightclub*

boîte *f* **postale (BP** *f)* *PO Box*

boîtier *m* **de sécurité** *dongle*

bon *m coupon; bond; voucher*

bon *m* **de commande** *order form*

bon *m* **de livraison** *delivery note*

bon *m* **de prélèvement** *bin card*

bon *m* **de réception des marchandises** *goods received note*

bon *m* **du Trésor** *treasury bill*

bonus *m no-claims bonus*

boom *m boom*

bordereau *m docket*

bordereau *m* **de versement** *deposit slip*

bordereau *m* **d'expédition** *consignment note*

bourse *f* **(des valeurs)** *stock exchange*

bourse *f* **de marchandises** *commodity exchange*

boutique *f* **hors-taxe** *duty-free shop*

brainstorming *m* *brainstorming (session)*

brasserie *f brewery; brasserie*

brevet *m* **(d'invention)** *(letters) patent*

faire breveter *to patent*

briefing *m briefing*

brochure *f brochure; leaflet*

brouillard *m daybook*

brouillon *m draft*

faire le brouillon de *to draft*

broyeur *m* **d'ordures** *waste disposal unit*

buanderie *f laundry; utility room*

budget *m budget; account*

Budget *m* **communautaire** *Common Budget*

budget *m* **de recherche** *research budget*

budget *m* **d'investissement** *capital budget*

budget *m* **publicitaire** *advertising budget*

buffet *m buffet (car)*

bulletin *m* **de paie** *pay slip*

bureau *m office; desk*

bureau *m* **automatisé** *paperless office*

bureau *m* **de photocopie** *copy shop*

bureau *m* **de poste** *post office*

bureau *m* **de renseignements** *information desk or office*

bureau *m* **des brevets** *patent office*

bureau *m* **des objets trouvés** *lost property office*

bureau *m* **de traduction** *translation agency*

bureau *m* **d'informatique** *computer agency*

bureaux *mpl offices; office build-*

ing; office accommodation; office space

à but lucratif profit-making

à but non-lucratif non-profit-making

cabinet m office; surgery

cabinet-conseil m (pl ~s-~s) consultancy

cabine f **téléphonique** telephone box

câble m **à fibre optique** fibre-optic cable

cachet m **de la poste** postmark

cadeau m gift; freebie

cadeau m **publicitaire** give-away; freebie

cadres mpl managerial staff

cadres mpl **moyens** middle management

CAF (coût, assurance, fret) CIF (cost, insurance and freight)

CAF & C (coût, assurance, fret et commission) CIF & C (cost, insurance, freight and commission)

café m coffee; café

cafétéria f cafeteria

cageot m (fruit) crate

caisse f check-out (desk); cashdesk; crate

caisse f **de dépenses courantes** petty cash

caisse f **d'épargne** savings bank

caisse f **d'épargne et de financement immobilier** building society

caisse f **de retraite** pension fund

caissier(-ière) m(f) cashier; teller

calculatrice f calculator

calcul m **du prix de revient** costing

calculer le prix de revient de to cost

cambiste m/f foreign exchange broker

"camembert" m pie chart

caméra f film camera

caméraman m cameraman

caméscope ® m video camera; camcorder

camion m lorry; truck

camionette f van

campagne f **de nettoyage** clean-up campaign

campagne f **de promotion des ventes** sales drive

campagne f **de publicité** advertising campaign

campagne f **de ventes** sales campaign

campagne f **d'exportations** export drive

canaux mpl **de communication** channels of communication

candidat(e) m(f) candidate; applicant

candidature f candidacy; application

CAO f **(conception** f **assistée par ordinateur)** CAD (computer-assisted design)

capacité f **d'entreposage** warehouse capacity

capacité f **de traitement** throughput

capacité f **du disque** disk capacity

capacité f **excédentaire** excess capacity

capacité f **industrielle** industrial capacity

capital m capital; asset(s)

capital m **appelé** called-up capital

capital m **émis** issued capital

capital m **investi** capital employed

capital m **non-émis** unissued capital

capital-obligations m (pl ~aux-~) loan capital; debenture capital

capital-risque m sing venture capital; risk capital

capital m **social** share capital; authorized capital

capitaux mpl **circulants** circulating capital

capitaux mpl **propres** equity capital

car m coach

caractère m character

caractère m **de remplacement** wildcard

caractères mpl **gras** bold type

caractères mpl **par pouce (CCPP**

mpl) *characters per inch (cpi)*

caractères/seconde *cps (characters per second)*

caractéristique *f feature*

caractéristiques *fpl* **du marché** *market profile*

caractéristiques *fpl* **du poste** *job specification*

carbone *m carbon copy*

cargaison *f cargo; shipment*

cargaison *f* **en vrac** *bulk cargo*

carnet *m* **de commandes** *order book*

carte *f map; chart; card; menu*

carte *f* **de crédit** *credit card*

carte *f* **d'embarquement** *boarding card*

carte *f* **de pointage** *time card*

carte *f* **de retrait** *cash card*

carte *f* **de visite (professionnelle)** *business card*

carte *f* **d'identité bancaire** *cheque (guarantee) card; banker's card*

carte *f* **eurochèque** *Eurocheque card*

cartel *m cartel*

carte-réponse *f (pl ~s-~s)* *reply-paid postcard*

carte *f* **téléphonique** *phonecard*

carte *f* **verte internationale** *green card*

carton *m carton; cardboard box; cardboard*

carton *m* **de classement** *box file*

carton *m* **sur palette** *palletized carton*

cartouche *f cartridge*

cas *m* **de force majeure** *act of God; force majeure*

cash-flow *m (pl ~~s)* *cash flow*

cash-flow *m* **actualisé** *(pl ~-~s)* *discounted cash flow*

casier *m luggage locker (on plane); pigeon-hole*

casier *m* **à consigne automatique** *left-luggage locker*

casque *m helmet; headphones*

casse *f breakage*

cassette *f cassette*

catalogue *m catalogue*

catégorie *f* **socio-professionnelle** *socioeconomic group*

causalité *f causation*

caution *f bail*

cautionnement *m indemnity; surety*

cave *f cellar*

CCPP *mpl* **(caractères** *mpl* **par pouce)** *cpi (characters per inch)*

CD *m* **(disque** *m* **compact)** *CD (compact disc)*

cédant(e) *m(f) assignor*

ceinture *f* **de sécurité** *safety belt; seatbelt*

centre *m centre*

centre *m* **de conférences** *conference centre*

centre *m* **de distribution** *distribution centre*

centre *m* **de profit** *profit centre*

centrer *to centre*

centre-ville *m (pl ~s-~s)* *city or town centre*

CERN *m* **(Conseil européen pour la recherche nucléaire)** *CERN*

certificat *m* **de douane** *clearance certificate*

certificat *m* **de provisions pour impôts** *tax reserve certificate*

certificat *m* **de vaccination** *vaccination certificate*

certificat *m* **de valeur** *certificate of value*

certificat *m* **d'expédition** *certificate of shipment*

certificat *m* **d'origine** *certificate of origin*

cessation *f* **du risque** *cessation of risk*

cession *f assignment; transfer*

cession-bail *f (pl ~s-baux)* *leaseback; sale and lease back*

cessionnaire *m/f assignee*

C et F (coût et fret) *c & f (cost and freight)*

CFAO *f* **(conception** *f* **et fabrication** *f* **assistées par ordinateur)** *CAD/CAM (computer-assisted design/manufacture)*

chaîne *f chain; (TV) channel; string*

chaîne *f* **(de fabrication)** *production line*

chaîne *f* **de montage** *assembly line*

chaîne *f* **de télévision** *TV channel*

chambre *f* **(à coucher)** *bedroom*

chambre *f* **à un lit** *single room*

Chambre *f* **de commerce** *Chamber of Commerce*

Chambre *f* **de commerce internationale (CCI** *f***)** *International Chamber of Commerce (ICC)*

chambre *f* **de compensation** *clearing house*

chambre *f* **de grand standing** *executive room*

chambre *f* **pour deux personnes** *double room*

chambre *f* **pour non-fumeurs** *non-smoking room*

chambres *fpl* **attenantes** *connecting rooms*

chambres *fpl* **voisines** *adjacent rooms*

change *m* *foreign exchange*

changement *m* **de ligne** *line feed*

chantier *m* **(de construction)** *building site*

charge *f* **de travail** *workload*

chargement *m* *load; loading*

charger *to load*

charges *fpl* **d'exploitation** *operating costs*

chargeur *m* *shipper; cartridge*

charge *f* **utile (CU** *f***)** *payload*

charte-partie *f* **(***pl* **~s-~s)** *charter party*

chasseur *m* **de têtes** *headhunter*

chauffage *m* **central** *central heating*

chauffeur *m* *driver; chauffeur*

chauffeur *m* **de taxi** *taxi driver*

chef *m* *manager(ess)*

chef *m* **de bureau** *office manager*

chef *m* **de gare** *stationmaster*

chef *m* **de produit** *product manager*

chef *m* **de projet** *project manager*

chef *m* **d'équipe** *chargehand; foreman*

chef *m* **de service** *department manager; head of department*

chef *m* **de train** *guard*

chef *m* **du développement des marchés** *market development manager*

chef *m* **du marketing** *marketing director; marketing manager*

chef *m* **du personnel** *personnel manager*

chef *m* **hiérarchique** *line manager*

cheminée *f* *fireplace; chimney; funnel*

chemise *f* *folder; shirt* .

chèque *m* *cheque*

chèque *m* **barré** *crossed cheque*

chèque *m* **cadeau** *gift voucher*

chèque *m* **de voyage** *traveller's cheque*

chèque *m* **non-barré** *open cheque; uncrossed cheque*

chèque *m* **postdaté** *post-dated cheque*

cher(-ère) *dear; expensive*

chercheur(-euse) *m(f)* *researcher; research worker*

chiffre *m* *digit; figure*

chiffre *m* **d'affaires** *turnover; sales figures*

chiffres *mpl* **corrigés des variations saisonnières** *seasonally-adjusted figures*

chiffres *mpl* **de ventes** *sales figures*

choix *m* **de cible** *targeting*

chômage *m* *unemployment; unemployment benefit*

au chômage *unemployed*

chronique *f* **économique** *business news summary*

cibler *to target*

CIF & I (coût, assurance, fret et intérêts) *CIF & C (cost, insurance, freight and interest)*

cinéma *m* *cinema*

circuits *mpl* **de distribution** *channels of distribution*

circulaire *f* *circular*

classe *f* **affaires** *business class; executive class*

classe *f* **club** *club class*

classement *m* *filing*
classer *to file*
classer dans les archives *to archive*
classe *f* **touriste** *economy class*
classeur *m* *filing cabinet*
classeur *m* **à anneaux** *ring binder*
classeur *m* **à levier** *lever arch file*
clause *f* *clause*
clause *f* **additionnelle** *rider*
clause *f* **compromissoire** *arbitration clause*
clause *f* **d'avaries** *average clause*
clause *f* **de dédommagement** *indemnity clause*
clause *f* **de force majeure** *force majeure clause*
clause *f* **de non-concurrence** *restrictive trading agreement*
clause *f* **dérogatoire** *escape clause*
clause *f* **d'exclusion** *exclusion clause*
clause *f* **d'exonération** *exemption clause*
clause *f* **pénale** *penalty clause*
clause *f* **résolutoire** *cancellation clause*
clavier *m* *keyboard; keypad*
clavier *m* **AZERTY** *azerty keyboard*
clavier *m* **numérique** *numeric keypad*
clavier *m* **QWERTY** *qwerty keyboard*
clef *f* *key*
client(e) *m(f)* *customer; client*
client(e) *m(f)* **potentiel(le)** *potential customer*
climatisation *f* *air conditioning*
cloison *f* *partition wall*
code *m* *code*
code *m* **barres** *bar code*
code *m* **binaire** *binary code*
code *m* **des impôts** *tax code*
code *m* **postal** *post code*
coffre *m* **de nuit** *night safe*
coffre-fort *m* *(pl ~s-~s)* *safe*
cognac *m* *brandy*
coiffeur(-euse) *m(f)* *hairdresser*
colis *m* *parcel*
collage *m* *collage; paste-up*

collationner *to collate*
collecte *f* **de données** *data collection*
colloque *m* *seminar*
colonne *f* **entière** *single-column spread*
colorant *m* *colouring*
combustible *m* **fossile** *fossil fuel*
comédie *f* *comedy*
comité *m* **de direction** *management committee*
comité *m* **d'entreprise** *works council*
commande *f* *command; order; job*
fait(e) sur commande *custom-built*
commande *f* **de réapprovisionnement** *repeat order*
commander *to order*
commanditaire *m/f* *sponsor; silent partner; sleeping partner*
commandité(e) *m(f)* *active partner*
commanditer *to sponsor*
commencement *m* **de preuve** *prima facie evidence*
commencement *m* **du risque** *commencement of risk*
commencer en retrait *to indent*
commerçant(e) *m(f)* **indépendant(e)** *sole trader*
commerce *m* *commerce*
commerce *m* **bilatéral** *bilateral trade*
commerce *m* **compensé** *countertrading*
commerce *m* **intracommunautaire** *intra-community trade*
commercial(e) *commercial*
commercialisation *f* *marketing; merchandising*
commercialiser *to market; to merchandise*
commis *m* **de bureau** *office junior*
commissaire *m* **aux comptes** *auditor*
commissariat *m* **de police** *police station*
commission *f* *commission*
commission *f* **de l'agent** *agent's commission*
Commission *f* **des CE** *European*

Commission

commissionnaire *m confirming house; commission agent*

commissionnaire-exportateur (-trice) *m(f) (pl ~s-~s) export agent*

Communauté *f* **économique européenne (CEE** *f*) *European Economic Community (EEC)*

Communauté *f* **européenne (CE** *f*) *European Community (EC)*

Communauté *f* **européenne de l'énergie atomique (CEEA** *f*) *EURATOM*

Communauté *f* **européenne du charbon et de l'acier (CECA** *f*) *European Coal and Steel Community (ECSC)*

communication *f* **en PCV** *transfer charge call*

communication *f* **interurbaine** *long-distance call; trunk call*

communication *f* **personnelle** *personal call*

communication *f* **urbaine** *local call*

communiqué *m* **de presse** *press release*

compagnie *f* **d'assurance** *insurance company*

compagnie *f* **d'assurance mutuelle** *mutual insurance company*

compagnie *f* **d'assurance-vie** *assurance company; life insurance company*

compagnie *f* **de navigation** *shipping company*

compartiment *m compartment*

compatible *compatible*

compatible binaire *binary compatible*

complet(-ète) *complete; full; fully booked*

comportement *m* **des acheteurs** *buying behaviour*

comportement *m* **des consommateurs** *consumer behaviour*

composant *m component*

composer le numéro *to dial*

compromis *m compromise*

faire un compromis *to compro-*

mise

compromis *m* **de vente** *agreement to sell*

comptabilité *f accountancy; accounts; accounts department; accounting; book-keeping*

comptabilité *f* **analytique** *cost accounting*

comptabilité *f* **de gestion** *management accounting*

comptabilité *f* **en coûts réels** *current cost accounting*

comptabilité *f* **en partie simple** *single-entry book-keeping*

comptable *m/f accountant*

comptable *m/f* **fiscal(e)** *tax accountant*

compte *m account*

à son compte *self-employed*

en compte *on account*

compte *m* **à intérêts élevés** *high-interest account*

compte *m* **bloqué** *frozen account*

compte *m* **clients** *accounts receivable*

compte *m* **courant** *current account*

compte *m* **d'affectation** *appropriation account*

compte *m* **de caisse** *cash account*

compte *m* **de capital** *capital account*

compte *m* **d'épargne** *savings account*

compte *m* **de pertes et profits** *profit and loss account*

compte *m* **de prêt** *loan account*

compte *m* **de produits** *revenue account*

compte *m* **de recettes et de dépenses** *income and expenditure account*

compte *m* **d'exploitation** *trading account; operating statement*

compte *m* **du client** *credit account*

compte *m* **en banque** *bank account*

compte *m* **inactif** *dead account*

compte *m* **joint** *joint account*

compte *m* **numéroté** *numbered account*

compte *m* **rémunéré** *interest-*

earning account

compte-rendu m (pl ~-s-~s) report; review

compte-rendu m **de visite** call report

comptes mpl **consolidés** consolidated accounts

comptes mpl **fournisseurs** accounts payable

comptes mpl **préliminaires** draft accounts

comptes mpl **semestriels** interim accounts

comptes mpl **trimestriels** interim accounts

compte m **sur livret** deposit account

compteur m meter

concept m concept

concept m **de commercialisation** marketing concept

concepteur(-trice) m(f) designer

conception f design

conception f **du produit** product design

concession f concession

concessionnaire m/f concessionaire; distributor

concevoir to design

conciliation f conciliation

concurrence f competition

concurrence f **acharnée** cut-throat competition

conditionnel(le) conditional

conditionnement m packaging

conditions fpl **de paiement** terms of payment

conditions fpl **de travail** conditions of employment; working conditions

conditions fpl **de vente** conditions of sale

sans conditions unconditional

conférence f conference; lecture

conférence f **de presse** press conference

Conférence f **des Nations Unies pour le commerce et le développement (CNUCED** f) UN Conference on Trade and Development

(UNCTAD)

"confidentiel" "private and confidential"

configuration f **multiposte** multiuser system

confirmation f confirmation

confirmer to confirm

confisquer to impound

conflit m dispute

conflit m **du travail** industrial dispute

conflit m **social** trade dispute

congé m **de formation** block release

congé m **de maternité** maternity leave

congé m **de paternité** paternity leave

congés mpl **payés** paid holidays

conglomérat m conglomerate

conjoncture f **économique** economic climate; economic trend

connaissement m bill of lading

connaissement m **sans réserves** clean bill of lading

faire connaître to publicize

conseil m **d'administration** board of directors; directorate

Conseil m **de l'Europe** Council of Europe

conseil m **de prud'hommes** industrial tribunal

Conseil m **des Ministres** Council of Ministers

conseiller(-ère) m(f) consultant

conseiller(-ère) m(f) **de direction** management consultant

conseiller(-ère) m(f) **en relations publiques** public relations consultant

conseiller(-ère) m(f) **fiscal(e)** tax consultant

consensus m consensus

consentir une aide financière to accommodate

conserverie f cannery

consigne f left-luggage office/counter

console f console

console f **de visualisation** VDU

(visual display unit)
consolidation *f consolidation*
consommateur(-trice) *m(f)* consumer; end user
consortium *m consortium*
consortium *m* **de réassurance** reinsurance pool
construction *f construction; building*
construction *f* **navale** shipbuilding
consultation *f consultation*
contamination *f contamination*
contaminer *to contaminate*
conteneur *m container*
conteneurisation *f containerization*
conteneuriser *to containerize*
continental(e) *continental*
contingent *m* **d'importation** import quota
contrat *m contract; covenant*
sous contrat *under contract*
contrat *m* **à prix ferme** fixed-price contract
contrat *m* **à terme** forward contract
contrat *m* **de crédit** hire-purchase agreement
contrat *m* **de durée déterminée** fixed term contract
contrat *m* **de franchise** franchise agreement
contrat *m* **de louage** contract of hire
contrat *m* **de sous-traitance** sub-contract
contrat *m* **de travail** contract of employment
contrat *m* **de vente** bill of sale; contract of sale
contrat *m* **résiliable** voidable contract
contremaître *m foreman*
contremaîtresse *f forewoman*
contre-offre *f* (*pl* ~-~s) counter-offer
faire une contre-offre *to make a counter-offer*
contrepartie *f quid pro quo*
contresigner *to countersign*

contrôle *m* **antipollution intégré** Integrated Pollution Control (IPC)
contrôle *m* **budgétaire** budgetary control
contrôle *m* **de gestion** management audit
contrôle *m* **de (la) production** production control
contrôle *m* **de qualité** quality control
contrôle *m* **des changes** exchange control
contrôle *m* **des coûts** cost control
contrôle *m* **des passeports** passport control
contrôle *m* **des prix** price control
contrôle *m* **des salaires** wage restraint
contrôle *m* **des stocks** inventory control
contrôle *m* **du crédit** credit control
contrôle *m* **orthographique** spellchecker
contrôleur(-euse) *m(f)* assessor; auditor; inspector; regulator
contrôleur(-euse) *m(f)* **de la qualité** quality controller
contrôleur(-euse) *m(f)* **financier(-ière)** financial controller
convention *f convention*
convention *f* **collective** trade union agreement; collective agreement
convention *f* **par secteur** industry-wide agreement
convention *f* **relative aux doubles impositions** double taxation agreement
convertisseur *m* **analogique-numérique** A/D converter
convertisseur *m* **numérique-analogique** D/A converter
convivial(e) *user-friendly*
coopérative *f cooperative*
copie *f copy*
copie *f* **de sauvegarde** back-up (copy)
copie *f* **pirate** pirate copy
copier *to copy*
copieur *m photocopier*

copieur *m* **de bureau** *desktop copier*

copropriété *f* *co-ownership*

corbeille *f* **de devises** *basket of currencies*

cotisation *f* **patronale** *employer's contribution*

cotisations *fpl* **à la sécurité sociale** *national insurance contributions*

cotisations *fpl* **syndicales** *union dues*

couchette *f* *couchette*

coupable *m/f* *guilty party*

coup *m* **de téléphone** *phone call*

coupe *f* **et insertion** *f* *cut and paste*

couper-coller *to cut and paste*

coupon-réponse *m* **international** (*pl* ~**s**-~) *international reply coupon*

coupure *f* *note; denomination*

courbe *f* **d'expérience** *learning curve*

cour *f* **d'appel** *Court of Appeal; appeal court*

cour *f* **de justice** *law court*

Cour *f* **de Justice des communautés européennes (CJCE** *f*) *European Court of Justice (ECJ)*

Cour *f* **des Comptes (des communautés européennes)** *European Court of Auditors*

Cour *f* **internationale de justice (CIJ** *f*) *International Court of Justice (ICJ)*

courrier *m* **"arrivée"** *in-tray*

courrier *m* **(à tarif) normal** *first-class post*

courrier *m* **à tarif réduit** *second-class post*

courrier *m* **"départ"** *out-tray*

courrier *m* **électronique** *electronic mail*

courrier *m* **en souffrance** *pending tray*

cours *m* *rate; price; currency; class; course*

en cours *in progress*

cours *m* **de clôture** *closing price*

cours *m* **de l'action** *share price*

cours *m* **d'ouverture** *opening price*

coursier *m* *courier*

courtage *m* *brokerage*

à court de personnel *short-staffed; understaffed*

courtier *m* *broker*

courtier(-ière) *m(f)* *dealer*

courtier *m* **d'escompte** *bill-broker*

courtier(-ière) *m(f)* **en devises** *foreign exchange dealer*

court métrage *m* *short film*

à court terme *short-term*

coût *m* *cost*

coût *m* **de distribution** *distribution cost*

coût *m* **de la main-d'œuvre** *labour cost(s)*

coût *m* **de remplacement** *replacement cost*

coût *m* **des années de travail** *man-year costs*

coûter *to cost*

coût *m* **fixe moyen** *average fixed cost*

coût *m* **marginal** *marginal cost*

coût *m* **moyen** *average cost*

coûts *mpl* **complets** *absorption costing*

coût *m* **unitaire** *unit cost*

coût *m* **variable** *variable cost; direct cost*

coût *m* **variable moyen** *average variable cost*

couverture *f* *cover; blanket*

couverture *f* **intensive** *blanket coverage*

couverture *f* **provisoire** *temporary cover*

couvrir *to cover*

crayon *m* **optique** *light pen*

créance *f* **douteuse** *bad debt*

créance *f* **irrécouvrable** *bad debt*

créancier(-ière) *m(f)* *creditor*

créancier(-ière) *m(f)* **différé(e)** *deferred creditor*

créancier(-ière) *m(f)* **garanti(e)** *secured creditor*

créancier(-ière) *m(f)* **hypothécaire** *mortgagee*

créancier(-ière) *m(f)* **sans garantie** *unsecured creditor*

créatif(-ive) *m(f) designer*
crédit *m credit; loan*
crédit *m* **à bon marché** *easy money*
crédit *m* **à la consommation** *consumer credit; customer credit*
crédit *m* **à renouvellement automatique** *revolving credit*
crédit *m* **d'impôt** *tax credit*
crédit *m* **en eurodevises** *Eurocurrency credit*
créditer *to credit*
crédit *m* **gratuit** *interest-free credit; interest-free loan*
créer *to create*
créneau *m niche*
crise *f depression; slump*
critique *f review*
faire la critique de *to review*
croissance *f* **économique** *economic growth*
cuisine *f kitchen*
culture *f* **de la société** *organizational culture; house style*
curseur *m cursor*
cybernétique *f cybernetics*
cycle *m* **de fabrication** *manufacturing cycle*
cycle *m* **des visites** *calling cycle*
cycles *mpl* **par seconde** *cps (cycles per second)*
dactylo *m/f (copy) typist*
dactylographié(e) *typewritten*
date *f* **d'échéance** *due date; maturity date; settlement date*
date *f* **d'effet** *effective date*
date *f* **d'entrée en vigueur** *starting date; effective date*
date *f* **de parution** *publication date*
date *f* **d'expiration** *expiry date*
date *f* **effective de démission** *termination date*
date *f* **effective de licenciement** *termination date*
date *f* **limite** *deadline*
date *f* **limite de vente** *sell-by date*
débat *m debate*
débit *m debit*
débiteur(-trice) *m(f) debtor*
débiteur(-trice) *m(f)* **hypothécaire** *mortgagor*

débouché *m outlet*
débouché *m* **marginal** *fringe market*
débouchés *mpl* **disponibles** *available market(s)*
décaféiné *m decaffeinated coffee*
décharge *f dump; landfill site*
déchet *m waste product*
déchets *mpl waste; rubbish*
déchets *mpl* **nucléaires** *nuclear waste*
décider *to decide*
décision *f decision; ruling*
déclaration *f clearance*
déclaration *f* **de douane** *customs declaration; bill of entry*
déclaration *f* **de sinistre** *(insurance) claim*
faire une déclaration de sinistre *to claim*
déclaration *f* **d'impôts** *tax return*
déclaration *f* **frauduleuse** *fraudulent claim*
déclaration *f* **(sous serment)** *affidavit*
déclasser *to downgrade*
décollage *m take-off*
décoller *to take off*
décomposition *f breakdown*
décontaminer *to decontaminate*
décorateur(-trice) **(d'intérieurs)** *m(f) interior decorator*
décoration *f* **(d'intérieurs)** *interior decoration*
décoration *f* **intérieure** *decoration*
découvert *m overdraft*
dédouanement *m clearance*
déduction *f* **(fiscale) pour investissement** *capital allowance*
déductions *fpl* **volontaires** *voluntary deductions*
défaut *m defect; flaw*
défaut *m* **de livraison** *non-delivery*
défectueux(-euse) *defective*
défendeur(-deresse) *m(f) defendant*
défendre *to defend*
défense *f* **de l'environnement** *conservation*
défense *f* **du consommateur** *consumerism*

déficit m deficit

déficit m **fiscal reportable** tax loss

déflation f deflation

déflationniste deflationary

dégâts mpl damage

dégâts mpl **causés par le feu** fire damage

dégâts mpl **causés par une tempête** storm damage

dégradation f degradation

dégrèvement m tax relief

dégrèvement m **(d'impôts)** tax relief; tax concession

dégrèvement m **fiscal** tax relief

dégrèvement m **hypothécaire** mortgage relief

dégrèvement m **sur double imposition** double taxation relief

déjeuner m lunch

déjeuner m **d'affaires** business lunch; lunch meeting

déjeuner m **de travail** working lunch

délai m **de livraison** delivery time; lead time

délai m **de paiement** credit period

délai m **de récupération** payback time

délai m **de réflexion** cooling-off period

délai m **d'exécution** lead time

délai m **fixé** time limit

délégation f delegation

délégué(e) m(f) delegate

déléguer to delegate

délégué(e) m(f) **syndical(e)** shop steward

délit m **d'initié(s)** insider dealing

demande f demand; request; application

demande f **indirecte** indirect demand

demande f **induite** derived demand

demander to ask (for); to request; to demand

demande f **reconventionnelle** counter-claim

faire une demande reconventionnelle to counter-claim

demandeur(-deresse) m(f) complainant

démarcation f demarcation

démarchage m canvassing

démarcher to canvass

démarcheur(-euse) m(f) door-to-door salesman/woman; canvasser

déménagement m relocation; removal

demi-pension f (pl ~-~s) half board

demi-sec (pl ~-~s) medium dry

démission f resignation

démission f **provoquée** constructive dismissal

démolition f demolition

démonstration f demonstration

dénationalisation f denationalization

dénationaliser to denationalize

denrées fpl **périssables** perishable goods

dentiste m/f dentist

déontologie f code of practice

dépanneuse f breakdown van

départ m departure

départ usine ex factory; ex works

départs mpl **des vols intérieurs** domestic departures

départs mpl **des vols internationaux** international departures

départs mpl **naturels** natural wastage

départ m **volontaire** voluntary redundancy

dépassé(e) out-of-date

dépasser to exceed

dépense(s) f(pl) expenditure; spending

dépense f **en publicité-média** above-the-line advertising expenditure

dépenses fpl **de fonctionnement** revenue expenditure

dépenses fpl **d'équipement** capital expenditure

dépenses fpl **d'investissement** capital investment; capital expenditure

déplacement m trip; travelling

déplacement m **de la demande** shift in demand

dépliant m brochure

déposant(e) m(f) bailor

déposer to deposit; to copyright; to file

dépositaire m/f bailee

dépôt m depot; deposit; depository; bailment

dépôt m **bancaire** bank deposit

dépréciation f depreciation

(se) déprécier to depreciate

dépression f depression

député m **européen** Euro MP

dernier entré, premier sorti (DEPS) last in, first out (LIFO)

dernier rappel m final demand

dérobade f **fiscale** tax evasion

déroulement m **de carrière** career development

désaveu m **du pouvoir syndical** derecognition

description f **du poste** job description

déséconomies fpl **d'échelle** diseconomies of scale

désinflation f disinflation

désinvestir to disinvest

désinvestissement m disinvestment

dessert m dessert

dessin m design; drawing

dessinateur(-trice) m(f) designer

destinataire m/f consignee

destination f destination

destructeur m **de documents** shredder

détail m detail; retail trade

détergent m detergent

détournement m **de fonds** embezzlement

détourner des fonds to embezzle

dette f debt

dette f **non-acquittée** undischarged debt

dettes fpl **éventuelles** contingent liabilities

deuxième classe f second class

dévaluation f devaluation

dévaluer to devalue

devant m front

développement m development

développement m **d'applications** application development

développement m **de produits** product development

développement m **des cadres** management development

développement m **des ressources humaines** human resources development (HRD)

développement m **soutenable** sustainable development

développer to develop

déversement m dumping

déverser to dump

déviation f deviation

devis m estimate; quote; quotation

devise f **à convertibilité limitée** restricted currency

devise f **convertible** free currency

devise f **forte** hard currency

devise f **non-convertible** non-convertible currency

devises fpl foreign exchange

diabétique m/f diabetic

diagramme m diagram

diagramme m **en tuyaux d'orgue** bar chart

dialogue m dialogue

diapositive f slide

dicter to dictate

dictionnaire m dictionary

différé(e) deferred

diffuser to broadcast

dîner m dinner

dîner m **de travail** working dinner

diplôme m diploma

diplomé(e) m(f) **universitaire** graduate

direct m through train

direct(e) direct

directeur(-trice) m(f) director; executive director; manager(ess)

directeur(-trice) m(f) **adjoint(e)** associate director

directeur(-trice) m(f) **commercial(e)** sales manager

directeur(-trice) m(f) **d'agence** branch manager

directeur(-trice) m(f) **d'agence ban-**

caire *bank manager*

directeur(-trice) *m(f)* **de compagnie d'assurances** *insurance manager*

directeur(-trice) *m(f)* **de la production** *production manager*

directeur(-trice) *m(f)* **de la publicité** *advertising manager*

directeur(-trice) *m(f)* **de la recherche** *research manager*

directeur(-trice) *m(f)* **de produit** *brand manager*

directeur(-trice) *m(f)* **des nouveaux contrats** *new business manager*

directeur(-trice) *m(f)* **de succursale** *branch manager*

directeur(-trice) *m(f)* **du laboratoire** *laboratory manager*

directeur(-trice) *m(f)* **du marketing** *marketing director*

directeur(-trice) *m(f)* **du service d'exportations** *export manager*

directeur(-trice) *m(f)* **financier(-ière)** *finance director*

directeur(-trice) *m(f)* **général(e) (DG** *m/f)* *managing director (MD); chief executive; general manager*

directeur(-trice) *m(f)* **général(e) adjoint(e)** *deputy chief executive*

directeur(-trice) *m(f)* **intérimaire** *acting manager*

directeur(-trice) *m(f)* **régional(e)** *area manager*

(la) direction *f (the) management*

direction *f* **du personnel** *personnel management*

Direction *f* **Générale (DG** *f)* *Directorate General (DG)*

direction *f* **par crises** *management by crisis*

direction *f* **par exception** *management by exception*

direction *f* **par objectifs (DPO** *f)* *management by objectives*

directive *f directive; guideline*

directive *f* **de la CEE** *EEC directive*

directive *f* **européenne** *European directive*

diriger *to direct; to edit*

dirigisme *m interventionism*

discours *m speech*

discours-programme *m (pl ~-~s) keynote speech*

discrimination *f discrimination*

discussion *f discussion*

dispositif *m device*

dispositif *m* **d'alimentation de documents** *automatic document feeder*

dispositif *m* **de changement de page** *form feeder*

dispositif *m* **d'économie d'énergie** *energy-saving device*

dispositif *m* **d'entraînement** *drive*

disque *m disk; record*

disque *m* **compact** *compact disc*

disque *m* **compact-ROM** *CD ROM*

disque *m* **de sauvegarde** *back-up disk*

disque *m* **de travail** *working disk*

disque *m* **dur** *hard disk*

disque *m* **laser** *laser disk*

disque *m* **magnétique** *magnetic disk*

disquette *f diskette; floppy disk*

disquette *f* **double densité** *double-density diskette*

disquette *f* **haute densité** *high-density diskette*

distillerie *f distillery*

distribuer *to distribute*

distributeur *m dispenser*

distributeur(-trice) *m(f) distributor*

distributeur *m* **automatique** *vending machine*

distributeur *m* **(automatique) de billets** *cash dispenser*

distributeur *m* **(automatique) de timbres** *stamp machine*

distribution *f distribution*

diversification *f diversification*

diversifier *to diversify*

divertissement *m entertainment*

dividende *m dividend*

division *f* **du travail** *division of labour*

docudrame *m docudrama*

document *m document*

documentaire *m documentary*

documentation *f documentation;*

literature; handout

documentation *f* **publicitaire** *sales literature*

document *m* **d'offre** *offer document*

documents *mpl* **contre acceptation (DA** *mpl***)** *documents against acceptance (D/A)*

documents *mpl* **contre paiement (DP** *mpl***)** *documents against payment (D/P)*

documents *mpl* **d'expédition** *shipping documents*

domaine *m estate*

dommages *mpl* **aggravés** *aggravated damages*

dommages-intérêts *mpl* **damages**

dommages-intérêts *mpl* **accessoires** *incidental damages*

données *fpl data*

données *fpl* **de sortie** *output (data)*

données *fpl* **d'essai** *test data*

données *fpl* **en entrée** *input (data)*

données *fpl* **invalides** *garbage*

dossier *m file*

dossier *m* **suspendu** *suspension file*

douane *f customs*

douanier(-ière) *m(f) customs officer*

double *m duplicate*

faire un double de *to duplicate*

double indemnité *f double indemnity*

double paie *f double time*

double vitrage *m double glazing*

douche *f shower*

drap *m sheet*

droit *m duty; tax; fee; right; law*

droit *m* **civil** *civil law*

droit *m* **commercial** *commercial law*

droit *m* **communautaire** *community law*

droit *m* **contractuel** *contract law*

droit *m* **coutumier et jurisprudentiel** *common law*

droit *m* **des affaires** *company law*

droit *m* **d'occupation du logement** *security of tenure*

droit *m* **du travail** *employment law*

droit *m* **international** *international law*

droit *m* **maritime** *maritime law*

droit *m* **pénal** *criminal law*

droits *mpl rights; duty; dues*

droits *mpl* **anti-dumping** *anti-dumping duty*

droits *mpl* **d'adaptation (cinématographique)** *film rights*

droits *mpl* **d'auteur** *royalties; copyright*

droits *mpl* **de bassin** *dock dues*

droits *mpl* **de douane** *customs duty*

droits *mpl* **de douane à l'importation** *import tariff*

droits *mpl* **d'entrée** *import duty*

droits *mpl* **de port** *harbour dues*

droits *mpl* **de publication** *book rights*

droits *mpl* **de succession** *death duty*

droits *mpl* **de télévision** *television rights*

droits *mpl* **de timbre** *stamp duty*

droits *mpl* **de tirage spéciaux (DTS** *mpl***)** *special drawing rights (SDR)*

duplicata *m duplicate*

durée *f* **de vol** *flying time*

durée *f* **d'exécution** *lead time; length of a job; timescale*

durée *f* **d'exploitation** *run time*

EAO *m* **(enseignement** *m* **assisté par ordinateur)** *CAL (computer-assisted learning)*

eau *f* **de la ville** *mains water*

eau *f* **minérale** *mineral water*

ébauche *f draft*

ébaucher *to draft*

écart *m variance*

échantillon *m sample*

échappatoire *f* **fiscale** *tax shelter*

échappement *m escape*

échéance *f maturity (date); settlement date; deadline*

échelle *f* **des salaires** *salary scale*

écologie *f ecology*

écologique *environmentally friendly; ecological; green*

écologiste m/f ecologist; environmentalist

économie f economy; economics

économie f **centralisée** centralized economy

économie f **de marché** market economy

économie f **dirigée** controlled economy

économie f **mixte** mixed economy

économie f **planifiée** planned economy

économies fpl savings

économies fpl **d'échelle** economies of scale

économies fpl **d'énergie** energy conservation

économie f **souterraine** black economy

économiser to economize

économiste m/f economist

écran m screen

écu m ECU (European Currency Unit)

écu m **fort** hard ECU

éditer to edit

éditeur(-trice) m(f) publisher

éditeur(-trice) m(f) **de texte(s)** text editor

édition f publishing; edition

édition f **de créneau** niche publishing

édredon m quilt

éducation f education

effacer to delete; to erase

effectif m staff; workforce

aux effectifs mpl **excédentaires** overstaffed

effet m effect; bill

effet m **au porteur** bearer bill

effet m **de la bonne image de marque** halo effect

effet m **de serre** greenhouse effect

effets mpl **à payer** bills payable

effets mpl **à recevoir** bills receivable

efficacité f efficiency

à effleurement touch-sensitive

efflux m outflow

effondrement m slump

s'effondrer to slump

effraction f **informatique** hacking

égalité f equality

égalité f **des salaires** equal pay

égouts mpl **de la ville** mains sewage

électricité f electricity

électroménager m household appliances; white goods

électronique f electronics

élément m element; component

élimination f **des déchets** waste disposal

emballage m packaging; wrapper

emballage m **plastique** shrink-wrapping

sous emballage plastique shrink-wrapped

emballer sous film plastique to shrink-wrap

emballé(e) sous vide vacuum-packed

embargo m embargo

émettre to emit; to issue; to transmit

émission f programme; emission; issue; flotation; broadcast

émission f **d'actions** share issue

émission f **d'actions gratuites** bonus issue

émission f **d'euro-obligations** Eurobond issue

émission f **préférentielle** rights issue

employé(e) m(f) employee

employé(e) m(f) **à temps partiel** part-timer

employé(e) m(f) **de bureau** office worker; white-collar worker; clerk

employer to employ; to use

employeur(-euse) m(f) employer

emprunt m loan; borrowing

emprunter to borrow

emprunteur(-euse) m(f) borrower

emprunt-logement m (pl ~s-~) mortgage

encadrement m **du crédit** credit squeeze

encaisse f cash-in-hand

encaisser to cash

enchères *fpl* **à la baisse** *Dutch auction*

encre *f ink; toner*

endommagé(e) *damaged*

endommager *to damage*

endossataire *m/f endorsee*

endosser *to endorse*

endosseur *m endorser*

engagement *m engagement; obligation; covenant*

engagement *m* **contractuel** *contractual obligation*

engagement *m* **de responsabilité absolue** *absolute undertaking*

enlèvement *m collection*

enlever *to collect; to take off*

enregistrement *m recording; registration; check-in desk*

passer à l'enregistrement *to check in*

enregistrer *to record; to log*

enseignement *m education*

entente *f* **sur les prix** *price-fixing*

en-tête *m* (*pl* ~-~**s**) *letterhead*

entrée *f entrance; way in; entry; input; starter*

entrée *f* **en ordinateur par microfilm** *CIM (computer input from microfilm)*

entreposer *to store; to bond*

entrepôt *m warehouse*

entrepôt *m* **des douanes** *bonded warehouse*

en entrepôt des douanes *in bond*

entrepreneur(-euse) *m(f) entrepreneur; contractor; builder*

entrepreneur(-euse) *m(f)* **de transport routier** *haulage contractor*

entreprise *f company; firm; business*

entreprise *f* **de location de voitures** *car hire firm*

entreprise *f* **de transport (routier)** *trucking company*

entreprise *f* **de transport routier** *haulage contractor*

entreprise *f* **d'exportation** *export house*

entreprise *f* **du tertiaire** *tertiary industry*

entreprise *f* **en participation** *joint venture*

entreprise *f* **en tête du marché** *market leader*

entrer *to enter; to input*

entrer (dans le système) *to log in/on*

entretien *m* **d'évaluation** *appraisal interview*

enveloppe *f envelope; wrapper*

enveloppe *f* **à fenêtre** *window envelope*

enveloppe *f* **affranchie** *prepaid envelope*

enveloppe *f* **affranchie avec adresse** *sae (stamped addressed envelope)*

environnement *m environment*

envoi *m sending; parcel; consignment; dispatching*

envoi *m* **recommandé** *recorded delivery; registered post*

envoyer *to send*

envoyer par télécopie *to fax*

envoyer par télex *to telex*

éponge *f sponge; eraser*

épuisé(e) *out of stock; out of print*

équilibrer *to balance*

équilibrer le budget *to break even*

équipe *f* **de conception** *design team*

équipe *f* **de dactylos** *typing pool*

équipe *f* **de dessinateurs** *design team*

équipe *f* **de direction** *management team*

équipe *f* **de jour** *day shift*

équipe *f* **de maintenance** *maintenance shift*

équipe *f* **de nuit** *night shift*

équipe *f* **de tournage** *film crew*

équipe *f* **de vente** *sales force*

équipe *f* **du soir** *back shift*

équitable *equitable*

équité *f equity*

ergonomie *f ergonomics*

erreur *f mistake; error; bug*

erreur *f* **commune** *common mistake*

erreur *f* **de syntaxe** *syntax error*

erreur f **unilatérale** unilateral mistake

E/S (entrée/sortie) I/O (input/output)

escale f stopover

escale f **de transit** transit stop

escalier m stairs

escalier m **de secours** fire escape

escompte m **de caisse** cash discount

espace m **publicitaire** advertising space

espèces fpl cash

espérance f **de vie** life expectancy

espionnage m **industriel** industrial espionage

essai m test; trial

essai m **auprès de la clientèle** customer trial

essai m **sur le marché** market trial

essence f petrol

essence f **sans plomb** unleaded petrol

estampille f **de qualité** kite mark

estaries fpl lay days

esthétique f **industrielle** industrial design

estimation f estimate

estimation f **au jugé** guesstimate

estimer to estimate

établir le coût de to cost

établir un budget to budget; to prepare a budget

étage m storey; floor

de l'étage m **inférieur** downstairs

de l'étage m **supérieur** upstairs

étalage m display

étalon-or m (pl inv) gold standard

état m state; condition; status report

état m **de trésorerie** cash-flow statement

état m **financier** financial statement

état m **livrable** deliverable state

états mpl **associés** associated states

États mpl **membres** Member States

étendue f **de la couverture** extent of cover

étiquette f **de magasin** bin tag

étiquette f **porte-prix** price tag

étude f **de cas** case study

étude f **de comportement** attitude survey

étude f **de départ** baseline study

étude f **de faisabilité** feasibility study

étude f **de marché** market research

étude f **de marché par courrier** postal survey

étude f **des médias** media research

étude f **d'opinion** opinion research; opinion poll; audience research

étude f **du rapport coûts-bénéfices** cost-benefit analysis

étude f **du travail** work study

étudiant(e) m(f) student

EURATOM f EURATOM

EUREKA f EUREKA (European Research & Coordination Agency)

eurochèque m Eurocheque

eurocrate m/f Eurocrat

eurodépôt m Eurodeposit

eurodevise f Eurocurrency

eurodollar m eurodollar

euromarché m Euromarket

euro-obligation f (pl ~-~s) Eurobond

europalette f Europallet

Europe f Europe

européaniser to Europeanize

Europe f **continentale** continental Europe

Européen(ne) m(f) European

européen(ne) adj European

europhile m/f Europhile

Europort m Europort

euro-sterling m Eurosterling

eurotunnel m Eurotunnel

évaluation f evaluation; valuation; assessment

évaluation f **de la gestion** management appraisal

évaluation f **des performances** performance review

évaluation f **des tâches** job evaluation

évaluation *f* **environnementale** *environmental assessment*
évaluer *to assess; to evaluate*
événement *m* **imprévu** *contingency*
éventail *m* **des salaires** *wage differential*
excédent *m* **de bagages** *excess baggage*
exclusivité *f exclusivity*
ex-dividende *ex dividend*
ex-droits *ex rights*
exécution *f performance*
exemplaire *m copy*
exemplaire *m* **d'archive** *file copy*
exemplaire *m* **de service de presse** *review copy*
exempt(e) d'impôts *tax-free*
exercice *m financial year*
exercice *m* **(budgétaire)** *financial year*
exercice *m* **de recrutement** *recruitment drive*
exercice *m* **financier** *accounting period*
ex navire *ex ship*
exonération *f* **d'impôts** *tax exemption; tax allowance*
exonéré(e) de TVA *VAT-exempt; zero-rated*
exonéré(e) d'impôt *free of tax*
expédier *to ship; to dispatch; to consign*
expédier par la poste *to post*
expéditeur(-trice) *m(f)* *shipper; consignor*
expédition *f shipping*
expert *m estimator; surveyor*
expert-comptable *m/f* (*pl* ~**s**-~**s**) *chartered accountant (CA); certified accountant*
expert *m* **en assurances** *adjuster*
expert *m* **(évaluateur)** *estimator; surveyor*
expertise *f valuation; survey*
expertise *f* **d'avarie** *damage survey*
expertise *f* **maritime** *marine survey*
expertiser *to value; to survey*
exploitable sur machine *machine-readable*

exploitation *f* **des ressources** *resource utilization*
exploitation *f* **minière** *mining*
exploiter *to exploit; to run; to operate*
exportateur(-trice) *m(f)* *exporter*
exportation *f export trade; export*
exportations *fpl* **invisibles** *invisible exports*
exportations *fpl* **visibles** *visible exports*
exporter *to export*
exposant(e) *m(f)* *exhibitor*
exposé *m presentation*
exposer *to exhibit; to display*
exprès *m express delivery*
extensible *upgradeable*
extrapolation *f extrapolation*
fabricant *m manufacturer*
fabrication *f* *manufacture; manufacturing*
fabrication *f* **en série** *mass production*
fabrication *f* **"juste-à-temps"** *just-in-time manufacturing*
fabriqué(e) **en** **série** *mass-produced*
fabriquer *to manufacture*
façade *f facade*
facile à utiliser *user-friendly*
facilités *fpl* **de paiement** *credit facilities*
facture *f invoice; bill*
facture *f* **à l'exportation** *export invoice*
facture *f* **consulaire** *consular invoice*
facture *f* **pro forma** *pro-forma invoice*
facturer *to invoice; to bill*
failli(e) *m(f)* *bankrupt*
failli(e) *m(f)* **non-réhabilité(e)** *undischarged bankrupt*
faillite *f bankruptcy*
en faillite *adj bankrupt*
faire faillite *to go bankrupt*
FAO *f* **(fabrication** *f* **assistée par ordinateur)** *CAM (computer-assisted manufacture)*
fausse déclaration *f misrepresenta-*

tion

faux frais *mpl incidental expenses*

fax *m fax*

fédéral(e) *federal*

fédéralisme *m federalism*

fédération *f federation*

feed-back *m (pl inv) feedback*

femme *f* **d'affaires** *businesswoman*

femme *f* **de chambre** *chambermaid*

femme *f* **policier** *policewoman*

fenêtre *f window*

fenêtre *f* **panoramique** *picture window*

fenêtre *f* **teintée** *tinted window*

fermer *to close; to shut (down)*

fermeture *f closure; shut-down; lock-out*

feuille *f* **(de papier)** *sheet (of paper)*

feuille *f* **de calcul (électronique)** *spreadsheet*

feuille *f* **de présence** *time-sheet*

feuille *f* **de style** *style sheet*

feuilleton *m serial*

feutre *m felt pen*

fibre *f* **optique** *fibre optics*

fiche *f* **de commande** *job card*

fiche *f* **de transit communautaire** *community transit form*

fiche *f* **de transmission** *compliments slip*

fichier *m file; card index*

fichier *m* **de travail** *scratch file*

fichier *m* **mort** *dead file*

fidéicommis *m trust*

fidéicommissaire *m/f trustee*

fidélité *f* **à la marque** *brand loyalty*

filiale *f affiliated company; subsidiary (company)*

filière *f* **bois** *timber industry*

film *m film*

filmer *to film*

filtre *m filter*

finance(s) *f(pl) finance*

financement *m finance; financing; backing*

financier *m financier*

FIO *f* **(fabrication** *f* **intégrée par ordinateur)** *CIM (computer-integrated manufacturing)*

fisc *m Inland Revenue; Internal Revenue Service*

FLB (franco long du bord) *FAS (free alongside ship)*

FLQ (franco long du quai) *FAQ (free alongside quay)*

fluctuation *f fluctuation*

fluctuer *to fluctuate*

fluide *m* **pulseur** *propellant*

FOB (franco à bord) *FOB (free on board)*

bonne foi *f good faith*

mauvaise foi *f bad faith*

foire(-exposition) *f* **commerciale** *(pl ~s(-~s)) trade fair*

fonctionnement *m operation*

fondations *fpl foundations*

fonderie *f foundry*

Fonds *m* **commun pour les produits de base** *Common Fund for Commodities (CFC)*

fonds *m* **d'amortissement** *sinking fund*

fonds *m* **de roulement** *working capital; floating capital*

Fonds *m* **européen de coopération monétaire (FECOM** *m***)** *European Monetary Cooperation Fund (EMCF)*

Fonds *m* **européen de développement (FED** *m***)** *European Development Fund (EDF)*

Fonds *m* **européen de développement régional (FEDER** *m***)** *European Regional Development Fund (ERDF)*

Fonds *m* **international de développement agricole (FIDA** *m***)** *International Fund for Agricultural Development (IFAD)*

Fonds *m* **monétaire international (FMI** *m***)** *International Monetary Fund (IMF)*

Fonds *m* **social européen** *European Social Fund*

force *f* **de vente** *sales force*

formalité *f formality*

formatage *m formatting*

formater *to format*

formation *f training; education*

formation *f* **de capital** *capital formation*

formation *f* **des cadres** *management training*

formation *f* **du personnel** *staff training*

formation *f* **en entreprise** *in-house training*

formation *f* **professionnelle** *vocational training*

formulaire *m* *form*

formulaire *m* **de candidature** *application form*

formulaire *m* **de déclaration en douane** *customs form*

formulaire *m* **de proposition d'assurance** *proposal form*

à forte proportion de capitaux *capital-intensive*

fourneau *m* *furnace*

fournisseur(-euse) *m(f)* *supplier*

fournitures *fpl* **de bureau** *stationery; office supplies*

frais *mpl* *expenses; fees; charges; costs*

frais *mpl* **d'administration** *administrative expenses*

frais *mpl* **de banque** *bank charges*

frais *mpl* **de déménagement** *relocation expenses*

frais *mpl* **de développement** *development costs*

frais *mpl* **de fonctionnement** *running costs*

frais *mpl* **de manutention** *handling charge*

frais *mpl* **d'entreposage** *warehousing costs*

frais *mpl* **de port et d'emballage** *postage and packing*

frais *mpl* **d'équipement** *plant cost*

frais *mpl* **de récupération** *salvage costs*

frais *mpl* **de transport** *haulage (cost)*

frais *mpl* **d'expertise** *survey fee*

frais *mpl* **d'instance et dépens** *costs*

frais *mpl* **fixes** *fixed charge*

frais *mpl* **flottants** *floating charge*

frais *mpl* **généraux** *overheads*

frais *mpl* **juridiques** *legal fees*

frais *mpl* **non-échus** *accrued charges*

franc(franche) d'avarie particulière *free of particular average (FPA)*

franchise *f* *franchise; excess clause*

franchisé *m* *franchisee*

franchise *f* **postale** *Freepost* ®

franchiser *to franchise*

franchiseur *m* *franchiser*

franco (de port) *post-free*

franco de port *carriage free*

franco gare de réception *free to receiving station*

franco long du bord (FLB) *free alongside ship (FAS)*

franco wagon (FOR) *free on rail (FOR)*

frappant(e) *hard-hitting*

frappe *f* *keystroke; typing*

fraude *f* *fraud*

fraude *f* **fiscale** *tax evasion*

frauder *to defraud*

freinte *f* *loss in transit*

fréquence *f* **des visites** *call frequency*

fret *m* *freight*

fret *m* **aérien** *air freight; air cargo*

fuite *f* *leakage*

fumée *f* *smoke*

fusion *f* *merge; merger; amalgamation*

fusionner *to merge; to amalgamate*

gâcher *to spoil*

gage *m* *pledge*

gamme *f* *range; line*

gamme *f* **de prix** *price range*

gamme *f* **de produits** *product range*

garant(e) *m(f)* *guarantor*

garantie *f* *guarantee; warranty; warrant; security*

sous garantie *under guarantee; under warranty*

garantir *to guarantee; to underwrite*

gardien *m* **de nuit** *night porter; night watchman*

gare *f station*
gas-oil *m diesel (fuel)*
gaspillage *m* **des ressources** *waste of resources*
gaspiller *to waste*
gaz *m gas*
gendarme *m policeman*
gendarmerie *f police station*
génération *f* **de parole** *speech generation*
génie *m* **civil** *civil engineering*
gérance *f property management*
gérant(e) *m(f) manager(ess); property manager*
géré(e) par ordinateur *computer-controlled*
gérer *to manage*
gestion *f management*
gestion *f* **de bases de données** *database management*
gestion *f* **de crise** *crisis management*
gestion *f* **de l'environnement** *environmental management*
gestion *f* **des déchets** *waste management*
gestion *f* **(des disques)** *housekeeping*
gestion *f* **des stocks** *stock management; stock control*
gestion *f* **financière** *financial management*
gigaoctet *m gigabyte*
gomme *f eraser*
goulot *m* **d'étranglement** *bottleneck*
grand livre *m ledger*
grand marché *m* **(européen)** *single (European) market*
grand public *adj inv mass-market*
grand réseau *m WAN (wide area network)*
les sept grands *mpl Group of 7 (G7)*
graphique *m chart; graph*
graphique *m* **circulaire** *pie chart*
graphique *m* **de rentabilité** *break-even chart*
graphique *m* **des activités** *activity chart*
graphique *m* **d'évolution** *flow chart*

graphique *m* **en tuyaux d'orgue** *bar chart*
gratification *f ex gratia payment*
grenier *m attic; loft*
grève *f strike; industrial action*
faire grève *to strike*
grève *f* **des heures supplémentaires** *overtime ban*
grève *f* **du zèle** *work-to-rule*
faire la grève du zèle *to work to rule*
grève *f* **générale** *general strike*
grève *f* **officielle** *official strike*
grève *f* **sauvage** *wildcat strike*
gréviste *m/f striker*
grief *m grievance*
groupe *m* **de pression écologiste** *environmental pressure group; environmental lobby*
groupe *m* **de réflexion** *think tank*
Groupe *m* **des trois** *Group of 3 (G3)*
Groupe *m* **des cinq** *Group of 5 (G5)*
Groupe *m* **des dix** *Group of 10 (G10)*
groupe *m* **de travail** *working group*
groupe *m* **témoin** *control group*
guerre *f* **des prix** *price war*
guerre *f* **économique** *economic warfare*
guichet *m counter; ticket office*
guichet *m* **automatique de banque (GAB** *m) automated telling machine (ATM)*
guichetiers(-ières) *mpl(fpl) counter staff*
hall *m foyer; lobby*
hall *m* **d'exposition** *exhibition centre*
hardware *m hardware*
à la hausse *bullish*
du haut *adj upstairs*
en haut *adv upstairs*
haut de gamme *adj up-market*
(à) haute définition *f high resolution*
hebdomadaire *weekly*
herbicide *m herbicide*

heure(s) *f(pl)* **de grande écoute** *prime time*

heure *f* **estimée d'arrivée** *estimated time of arrival (ETA)*

heure *f* **limite** *deadline*

heure *f* **limite d'occupation** *checkout time*

heures *fpl* **de bureau** *office hours*

heures *fpl* **supplémentaires** *overtime*

heure *f* **travaillée** *man-hour*

histogramme *m* *histogram*

holding *m* *holding company*

homme *m* **d'affaires** *businessman*

honoraires *mpl* *fee(s)*

hôpital *m* *hospital*

hoquet *m* *hiccup*

horaire *m* **flexible** *flexitime*

horaire *m* **réduit** *short time*

hors de l'entreprise *off-the-job*

hors taxe *adv* *duty-free; tax-free*

hôtel *m* *hotel*

hôtesse *f* *stewardess*

hublot *m* *porthole; window*

huile *f* *oil*

hygiène *f* **et sécurité** *f* *health and safety*

hyperinflation *f* *hyperinflation*

hypothèque *f* *mortgage*

hypothéquer *to mortgage*

icône *f* *icon*

illégal(e) *illegal*

illégalement *illegally*

illégalité *f* *illegality*

illustration *f* *illustration*

image *f* **de l'entreprise** *corporate identity*

image *f* **de marque** *image; brand image*

image *f* **de marque de l'entreprise** *corporate image* or *identity*

imaginer *to imagine; to devise*

immeuble *m* *building; apartment building*

immeuble *m* **de bureaux** *office block*

immigration *f* *immigration (counter)*

immobilisations *fpl* *fixed assets; capital assets*

impact *m* *impact*

avoir un impact (sur) *to impact (on)*

impact *m* **sur l'environnement** *environmental impact*

imparfait(e) *imperfect; flawed*

impayé(e) *unpaid*

imperméable *waterproof*

implicite *adj* *default*

importateur(-trice) *m(f)* *importer*

importation *f* *importing; import*

importations *fpl* **invisibles** *invisible imports*

importations *fpl* **visibles** *visible imports*

importer *to import*

import-export *m* *(pl ~s-~s) import-export*

imposable *taxable*

imposition *f* **directe** *direct taxation*

imposition *f* **indirecte** *indirect taxation*

imposition *f* **progressive** *progressive taxation*

impôt(s) *m(pl)* *tax*

après l'impôt *after tax*

avant impôt(s) *pre-tax; before tax*

avant l'impôt *pre-tax; before tax*

impôt *m* **foncier** *property tax*

impôts *mpl* **municipaux** *council tax*

impôts *mpl* **prélevés par la régie** *excise duties*

impôt *m* **sur la fortune** *wealth tax*

impôt *m* **sur le revenu** *income tax*

impôt *m* **sur les bénéfices** *profits tax*

impôt *m* **sur les mutations** *capital transfer tax*

impôt *m* **sur les plus-values** *capital gains tax (CGT)*

impôt *m* **sur les sociétés** *corporation tax*

imprimante *f* *printer*

imprimante *f* **à jet d'encre** *ink jet printer*

imprimante *f* **à laser** *laser printer*

imprimante *f* **à marguerite** *daisy wheel printer*

imprimante *f* **par points** *dot matrix printer*

imprimer *to print*
imprimerie *f printing works; printing industry*
imprimés *mpl* **publicitaires** *junk mail*
incompatible *incompatible*
indemnisation *f* **par versement unique** *lump sum settlement*
indemniser *to compensate*
indemnité *f compensation*
indemnité *f* **de départ** *golden parachute*
indemnité *f* **de licenciement** *redundancy payment*
indemnité *f* **de maladie** *sick pay*
indemnité *f* **de transfert** *golden hello*
indicatif *m code; answer-back code*
indice(s) *m(pl)* **d'écoute** *ratings*
indice *m* **de la Bourse** *share index*
indice *m* **de liquidité** *liquidity ratio*
indice *m* **des prix de détail** *retail price index*
indice *m* **du coût de la vie** *cost of living index*
indiquer *to indicate; to point out; to quote*
industrie *f industry*
industrie *f* **aéronautique** *aeronautical industry*
industrie *f* **alimentaire** *food processing; food industry*
industrie *f* **automobile** *car industry*
industrie *f* **chimique** *chemical industry*
industrie *f* **de la musique** *music industry*
industrie *f* **du bâtiment** *construction industry*
industrie *f* **du film** *film industry*
industrie *f* **du spectacle** *entertainment industry*
industrie *f* **en pleine expansion** *growth industry*
industriel *m industrialist*
industrie *f* **légère** *light industry*
industrie *f* **lourde** *heavy industry*
industrie *f* **nationalisée** *nationalized industry*
industrie *f* **pharmaceutique** *pharmaceutical industry; pharmaceuticals*
industrie *f* **textile** *textile industry; textiles*
inefficacité *f inefficiency*
inflation *f inflation*
inflation *f* **galopante** *galloping inflation*
inflation *f* **par la demande** *demand-pull inflation*
inflation *f* **par les coûts** *cost-push inflation*
informaticien(ne) *m(f)* *computer scientist*
informations *fpl* **commerciales** *marketing intelligence*
informatique *f computing; information technology (IT); data processing (DP); computer science*
infraction *f* **simple** *nuisance*
infrastructure *f infrastructure*
ingénierie *f engineering*
ingénierie *f* **du logiciel** *software engineering*
ingénieur-constructeur *m* (*pl* ~s- ~s) *structural engineer*
ingénieur *m* **du son** *sound engineer*
ingénieur *m* **en logiciel** *software engineer*
initialiser *to boot (up)*
initié(e) à l'informatique *computer literate*
injection *m injection*
injonction *f injunction*
innocent(e) *m(f) innocent party*
innovateur(-trice) *adj innovative*
innovateur(-trice) *m(f) innovator*
innovation *f innovation*
inoccupé(e) *vacant; unoccupied*
s'inscrire *to register; to check in*
insecticide *m insecticide*
insensible aux défaillances *fault-tolerant*
insérer *to insert*
insertion *f insertion; insert*
insolvabilité *f insolvency*
insolvable *insolvent*
installation *f installation(s); fitting (out); setting up*

installation *f* **commune** *shared facility*

installation *f* **électrique** *wiring*

installations *fpl* *fixtures and fittings; plant; facilities*

installer *to install; to set up*

instruction *f* *education; instruction; directive; (preliminary) investigation*

instructions *fpl* *instructions; directions; brief*

donner des instructions à *to brief*

intégration *f* **en amont** *backward integration*

intégration *f* **en aval** *forward integration*

intégration *f* **horizontale** *horizontal integration*

intégration *f* **verticale** *vertical integration*

intelligence *f* **artificielle (IA** *f***)** *artificial intelligence (AI)*

intensif(-ive) en main-d'œuvre *labour-intensive*

interconnecter *to network*

interdiction *f* *ban; banning*

interdiction *f* **d'importer** *import ban*

intéressement *m* **aux bénéfices** *profit-sharing*

intérêt *m* *interest; importance*

intérêt *m* **des capitaux** *capital charges*

intérêt *m* **des médias** *media interest*

intérêts *mpl* *interest*

intérêts *mpl* **composés** *compound interest*

intérêts *mpl* **courus** *accrued interest*

interface *f* *interface*

intérieur *m* *interior*

interjeter appel *to appeal*

interligne *m* *line spacing*

interphone *m* *intercom; entryphone*

interprète *m/f* *interpreter*

interrompre *to interrupt; to stop*

intervalle *m* *lapse of time*

intervenant(e) *m(f)* *speaker*

intervention *f* *intervention; talk; paper*

intervention *f* **de l'État** *government intervention*

intoxication *f* **alimentaire** *food poisoning*

introduction *f* *introduction; induction*

introduire *to introduce; to enter; to input*

introduire au clavier *to key in*

inventaire *m* *inventory; stocklist; stocktaking*

faire l'inventaire *to take stock*

inventaire *m* **informatisé** *computerized stocktaking*

inventer *to invent*

inventeur(-trice) *m(f)* *inventor*

invention *f* *invention*

investir (dans) *to invest (in)*

investissement *m* *investment*

investissement *m* **à l'étranger** *foreign investment*

investissement *m* **de premier ordre** *blue-chip investment*

investisseur(-euse) *m(f)* *investor*

irremboursable *irredeemable*

issue *f* **de secours** *emergency exit; fire exit*

italique *m* *italics*

itinéraire *m* *itinerary*

jaquette *f* *wrapper*

jardin *m* *garden*

jeu *m* **électronique** *computer game*

jeunes cadres *mpl* *junior management*

jeu *m* **vidéo** (*pl* ~**x** ~) *video game*

jouissance *f* **immédiate** *vacant possession*

jour *m* **férié** *bank holiday*

journal *m* *newspaper*

journal *m* **du dimanche** *Sunday newspaper*

journal *m* **gratuit** *freesheet*

journaliste *m/f* *journalist*

journal *m* **plein format** *broadsheet*

journée *f* **portes ouvertes** *open day*

juge *m* *judge*

jugement *m* *judgement; adjudication*

juger *to judge; to adjudicate*
juridiction *f jurisdiction*
juridiquement contraignant(e) *legally binding*
juriste *m/f lawyer*
juriste *m/f* **de droit maritime** *maritime lawyer*
justification *f justification*
justifier à gauche/à droite *to justify left/right*
kilométrage *m mileage*
kilométrage *m* **illimité** *unlimited mileage*
kilo-octet *m (pl ~-~s) kilobyte*
krach *m crash*
laboratin(e) *m(f) laboratory technician*
laboratoire *m laboratory*
laboratoire *m* **de recherche** *research laboratory*
lampe *f* **de bureau** *desk light*
lancement *m launch; flotation*
lancement *m* **(en Bourse)** *flotation*
lancer *to launch; to bring out; to float*
langage *m* **de programmation** *programming language*
langage *m* **machine** *computer language*
laps *m* **de temps** *lapse of time*
largeur *f* **de bande** *bandwidth*
lavabo *m washbasin*
leader *m* **du marché** *market leader*
lecteur *m* **de code barres** *bar-code reader*
lecteur *m* **de disques** *disk drive*
lecteur *m* **de microfiches** *microfiche reader*
lecteur *m* **de microfilms** *microfilm reader*
lecteur *m* **optique** *optical character reader (OCR)*
lecture *f* **optique** *optical character recognition (OCR)*
légal(e) *legal; lawful; statutory*
légalité *f legality*
légataire *m/f legatee*
légende *f caption*
législation *f legislation*
législation *f* **de la protection des données** *data protection law*
lettre *f letter*
lettre *f* **de candidature** *letter of application*
lettre *f* **de change** *bill of exchange*
lettre *f* **de change documentaire** *documentary bill of exchange*
lettre *f* **de change sans réserves** *clean bill of exchange*
lettre *f* **de crédit** *letter of credit*
lettre *f* **de crédit irrévocable confirmé** *confirmed irrevocable letter of credit*
lettre *f* **de garantie** *letter of guarantee*
lettre *f* **de mer** *clearance certificate*
lettre *f* **de transport aérien (LTA** *f***)** *air waybill; air consignment note*
lettre *f* **d'intention** *letter of intent*
liaison *f* **par fibre optique** *fibre-optic link*
libre *vacant; free*
libre-échange *m (pl ~s-~s) free trade*
libre entreprise *f free enterprise*
licence *f* **d'exportation** *export licence*
licence *f* **d'importation** *import licence*
licencié(e) *redundant*
licenciement *m redundancy; dismissal; termination of employment; lay-off*
licenciement *m* **abusif** *unfair dismissal; wrongful dismissal*
licencier *to dismiss; to lay off*
lieu *m* **de vente** *point of sale (POS)*
en ligne *on-line*
limitation *f* **de vitesse** *speed limit*
limite *f* **de crédit** *credit limit*
limite *f* **de découvert** *overdraft limit*
liquidateur(-trice) *m(f) liquidator*
liquidation *f liquidation; winding up; clearance sale*
liquidation *f* **volontaire** *voluntary liquidation*
liquide *m* **correcteur** *correcting fluid*
liquider *to liquidate; to wind up*

liquidité *f liquidity*
liquidités *fpl cash reserves*
liste *f* **d'adresses** *mailing list*
liste *f* **noire** *blacklist*
listing *m print-out*
lit *m bed*
litige *m litigation*
lits *mpl* **jumeaux** *twin beds*
livraison *f delivery*
livraison *f* **contre remboursement (CR)** *cash on delivery (COD)*
livraison *f* **des bagages** *baggage reclaim*
livraison *f* **directe** *drop shipment*
livraison *f* **exprès** *express delivery*
livraison *f* **franco à quai** *FD (free delivered at dock)*
livre *m* **de caisse** *cash book*
livre *m* **de petite caisse** *petty cash book*
livre *m* **d'or** *visitor's book*
livrer *to deliver*
livret *m* **de banque** *bankbook*
livre *f* **verte** *green pound*
locataire *m/f tenant*
locataire *m/f* **occupant(e)** *sitting tenant*
location *f let; tenancy; hire; rental*
location *f* **de voitures** *car hire*
lock-out *m (pl inv) lock-out*
logiciel *m software*
logiciel *m* **d'application** *application software*
logiciel *m* **intégré de comptabilité** *integrated accounting package*
logiciel *m* **sur mesure** *bespoke software*
logiciel *m* **utilitaire** *utility software*
logique *f logic*
logo *m logo*
logo *m* **de l'entreprise** *corporate logo*
loi *f law*
loi *f* **anti-trust** *anti-trust legislation*
long métrage *adj feature-length*
long métrage *m feature film*
à long terme *long-term*
lot *m batch; bundle*
lotissement *m estate*
louer *to rent; to let; to hire*

à louer *to let; for rent; for hire*
louer à bail *to lease*
loyer *m rent*
lucarne *f skylight*
lucratif(-ive) *moneymaking; profit-making*
lumière *f light*
lutrin *m lectern*
de luxe *up-market; de luxe*
machine *f machine*
machine *f* **à adresser** *addressing machine*
machine *f* **à affranchir** *franking machine*
machine *f* **à couper** *cutting machine*
machine *f* **à écrire** *typewriter*
machine *f* **à écrire à mémoire** *memory typewriter*
machine *f* **à écrire électrique** *electric typewriter*
machine *f* **à ficelage** *packet tying machine*
machine *f* **d'enroulement et d'empaquetage** *rolling and wrapping machine*
machine *f* **de traitement de texte** *word processor*
machine-outil *f (pl ~s-~s) machine tool*
machiniste *m/f machinist; driver*
macroéconomie *f macroeconomics*
magasin *m* **à succursales multiples** *chain store*
magasin *m* **de demi-gros** *discount store; discount house*
magasin *m* **de détail** *retail outlet*
magasin *m* **d'exposition** *showroom*
magistrat *m magistrate*
magnétophone *m cassette player*
magnétoscope *m video recorder*
mailing *m mailshot*
main-d'œuvre *f (pl ~s-~) work-force*
main-d'œuvre *f* **directe** *(pl ~s-~) direct labour*
maison *f house*
maison *f* **d'édition** *publishing house*
maison *f* **jumelée** *or* **jumelle** *semi-*

detached house

majoration *f* **de l'impôt** *tax increase*

majoration *f* **de prime** *loading*

majoration *f* **de prix** *mark-up*

majuscule *f* *capital (letter)*

manche *m* **à balai** *joystick*

mandat *m* *mandate; warrant*

mandataire *adj* *mandatory*

mandataire *m/f* *attorney; proxy; representative*

mandataire-liquidateur *m* (*pl* ~s-~s) *official receiver*

mandat *m* **d'exécution** *enforcement order*

mandat(-poste) *m* (*pl* ~s(-~)) *postal order*

maniement *m* **du personnel** *man management*

manifeste *m* *manifest; ship's manifest*

manifeste *m* **d'insolvabilité** *act of bankruptcy*

manipulation *f* **des prix** *market rigging*

manœuvre *m* *unskilled worker; manoeuvre*

manque *m* **de main-d'œuvre** *undermanning*

manque *m* **de personnel** *undermanning*

manquer à ses engagements *to default*

mansarde *f* *attic room*

manuscrit(e) *handwritten*

maquette *f* *artwork; mock-up*

marchand(e) *m(f)* *dealer; merchant*

marchandisage *m* *merchandising*

marchandise *f* *merchandise; commodity*

marchandises *fpl* *merchandise; goods*

marchandises *fpl* **à l'essai** *goods on approval*

marchandises *fpl* **déterminées** *ascertained goods*

marchandises *fpl* **en consignation** *goods on consignment*

marchandises *fpl* **en douane** *bonded goods*

marchandises *fpl* **en magasin** *stock-in-trade*

marchandises *fpl* **en transit** *goods in transit*

marchandises *fpl* **non-déterminées** *unascertained goods*

marchandises *fpl* **renvoyées** *returns*

marchandiseur *m* *merchandiser*

marché *m* *market; deal*

marchéage *m* *marketing mix*

marché *m* **à la baisse** *buyer's market; falling market; bear(ish) market*

marché *m* **à la hausse** *seller's market; bull(ish) market*

marché *m* **baissier** *bear(ish) market*

marché *m* **captif** *captive market*

marché *m* **cible** *target market*

Marché *m* **commun** *Common Market*

marché *m* **des consommateurs** *consumer market*

marché *m* **des devises** *foreign exchange market*

marché *m* **des eurodevises** *Eurocurrency market*

marché *m* **du travail** *labour market*

marché *m* **financier** *money market*

marché *m* **haussier** *bull(ish) market*

marché *m* **immobilier** *property market*

marché *m* **monétaire** *money market*

marché *m* **noir** *black market*

marché *m* **parallèle** *unofficial market*

marché *m* **stagnant** *static market*

marché *m* **unique** *single (European) market*

marge *f* *margin*

marge *f* **bénéficiaire** *profit margin; mark-up*

marketing *m* *marketing; marketing department*

marketing *m* **de créneau** *niche marketing*

marketing *m* **direct** *direct marketing*

marketing mix *m* marketing mix

marketing *m* **orienté** target marketing

marque *f* brand

marque *f* **de fabrique** trademark

marque *f* **déposée** registered trademark; proprietary brand

marque *f* **du distributeur** own brand

masse *f* **monétaire** money supply

massicot *m* guillotine

matériaux *mpl* materials

matériel *m* hardware; equipment; material

matériel *m* **de bureau** office equipment

matériel *m* **de publicité sur le lieu de vente** point-of-sale material

matériel *m* **PLV** point-of-sale material

matériel *m* **sauvé** salvage

matières *fpl* **premières** raw materials

matraquage *m* **publicitaire** hype

faire du matraquage publicitaire (pour) to hype

mécanicien(-ienne) *m(f)* mechanic; plant engineer

mécanisme *m* **de change** Exchange Rate Mechanism (ERM)

médecin *m* doctor

média *mpl* media

média-planneur *m* (*pl* ~-~s) media planner

méga-octet *m* **(Mo** *m***)** (*pl* ~-~s) megabyte (Mb)

membre *m* **du Parlement européen** MEP (Member of the European Parliament)

mémoire *f* memory

mémoire *f* **à bulles** bubble memory

mémoire *f* **centrale (MC** *f***)** main memory

mémoire *f* **fixe** ROM (read-only memory)

mémoire *f* **tampon** buffer

mémoire *f* **vive** RAM (random access memory)

ménagement *m* conversion

mensualité *f* monthly instalment

mentionné(e) ci-dessous under-mentioned

mentionné(e) ci-dessus above-mentioned

menu *m* menu

menu *m* **d'assistance** help menu

mer *f* sea

par mer by sea; surface mail

merchandising *m* merchandising

message *m* message

message *m* **(de guidage)** prompt

message *m* **d'erreur** error message

message *m* **enregistré** recorded message

messagerie *f* courier service

message *m* **publicitaire** commercial

mesure *f* **antipollution** antipollution measure

mesure *f* **du travail** work measurement

mesures *fpl* **fiscales** fiscal measures

métallurgie *f* metallurgy

méthode *f* method

méthode *f* **d'évaluation** appraisal method

méthode *f* **du chemin critique** CPM (critical path method)

métro *m* underground

metteur *m* **en scène** producer

mettre à jour to update

mettre à l'essai to test

mettre à l'étalage to display

mettre au point to develop; to settle; to debug

mettre en scène to produce

meublé(e) furnished

microéconomie *f* microeconomics

microfiche *f* microfiche

microfilm *m* microfilm

micromètre *m* micrometer

micro-ordinateur *m* (*pl* ~-~s) microcomputer

microphone *m* microphone

microprocesseur *m* microprocessor

microseconde *f* microsecond

millions *mpl* **d'instructions par seconde** mips (millions of instructions per second)

milliseconde *f milliseconde*

mini-bar *m (pl ~-~s) mini-bar*

minimisation *f* **des déchets** *waste minimization*

minimiser *to minimize*

ministère *f government; ministry; department*

mise *f* **à jour** *update*

mis(e) en carton *cartonned*

mise *f* **en garde de l'acheteur** *caveat emptor*

mise *f* **en mémoire** *storage*

mise *f* **sous séquestre** *sequestration*

mission *f* **commerciale** *trade mission*

Mo *Mb*

mobilité *f* **de la main-d'œuvre** *mobility of labour*

mode *f fashion; fashion industry; mode*

mode *m* **de gestion** *management style*

modèle *m model*

modèle *m* **de démonstration** *demonstration model*

modèle *m* **informatique** *computer model*

modem *m modem*

moderniser *to modernize*

module *m module*

monétarisme *m monetarism*

monétariste *m/f monetarist*

moniteur *m monitor*

moniteur *m* **de TV** *TV monitor*

monnaie *f* **convertible** *convertible currency*

monnaie *f* **de papier** *paper money*

monnaie *f* **de réserve** *reserve currency*

monnaie *f* **non-convertible** *blocked currency*

monopole *m monopoly*

monopole *m* **absolu** *absolute monopoly*

monopole *m* **syndical** *closed shop*

monopsone *m monopsony*

montage *m* **préparatoire** *subassembly*

monter *to go up; to assemble; to set up; to produce; to edit*

monteur(-euse) *m(f) fitter; (film) editor; paste-up artist*

moquette *f carpet; wall-to-wall carpeting*

moratoire *m moratorium*

mot *m* **de passe** *password*

motel *m motel*

motion *f* **composite** *composite motion*

motivation *f motivation*

motiver *to motivate*

mots/minute *mpl words per minute (wpm)*

mouvements *mpl* **de capitaux** *capital movement*

multiplet *m byte*

mur *m wall*

mutuelle *f mutual insurance company; friendly society*

nanoseconde *f nanosecond*

nantissement *m collateral*

nationalisation *f nationalization*

nationalisé(e) *nationalized; state-owned*

nationaliser *to nationalize*

navette *f shuttle*

navigabilité *f airworthiness; seaworthiness*

navire *m ship; vessel*

navire *m* **marchand** *merchantman*

négligence *f negligence*

négligent(e) *negligent*

négociable *negotiable*

négociant(e) *m(f)* **en titres** *jobber*

négociation *f negotiation*

négociations *fpl* **au niveau de l'usine** *plant bargaining*

négociations *fpl* **au niveau individuel** *individual bargaining*

négociations *fpl* **collectives** *collective bargaining*

négociations *fpl* **salariales** *wage negotiations*

négocier *to negotiate*

nettoyer *to clean (up)*

neuf(neuve) *new*

niveau *m level; standard*

de niveau moyen *mid-market*

niveau m **de la direction** *managerial level*

niveau m **de qualité acceptable** *acceptable quality level*

niveau m **des stocks** *stock level*

niveau m **de vie** *standard of living*

nombre m **de mots** *wordcount*

nom m **de fichier** *filename*

nom m **de l'utilisateur** *user-name*

non-acceptation f (pl ~-~s) *non-acceptance*

non-alcoolisé(e) *alcohol-free*

non-exécution f *non-performance*

non-imposable *non-taxable*

non-lucratif(-ive) *non-profit-making*

non-meublé(e) *unfurnished*

non-paiement m (pl ~-~s) *non-payment*

non-polluant(e) *pollution-free*

non-vendu(e) *unsold*

normes fpl *standards*

normes fpl **comptables** *accounting standards*

normes fpl **de sécurité** *safety standards*

normes fpl **publicitaires** *advertising standards*

notaire m *lawyer; solicitor*

notation f **de solvabilité** *credit rating*

note f *note; mark; bill*

note f **d'avoir** *credit note*

note f **de chargement** *shipping note*

note f **de débit** *debit note*

note f **de frais** *expense account*

note f **de service** *internal memo; memorandum*

notification f *notification*

notification f **de défaut** *default notice*

notoriété f **de la marque** *brand awareness; brand image*

nouveau (nouvelle) *new*

nouveau débouché m *spin-off; new outlet*

nouvelles technologies fpl *new technology*

nuisible *harmful; damaging*

nul(le) *void*

nul(le) et non avenu(e) *null and void*

numérique *digital*

numéro m **d'agence** *sort code*

numéro m **de commande** *order number; job number*

numéro m **de compte** *account number*

numéro m **de poste** *extension number*

numéro m **de stock** *stock code*

numéro m **de télécopieur** *fax number*

numéro m **d'immatriculation douanière** *customs registered number*

numéro m **SH** *HS number*

numéro m **sur la liste rouge** *ex-directory number*

numéro m **vert** *Freefone* ®

obligation f *debenture; bond; obligation*

obligation f **légale** *legal requirement*

obligations fpl **au porteur** *bearer bonds*

obligatoire *mandatory*

obsolescence f **planifiée** *built-in obsolescence*

obtenir *to obtain*

d'occasion *second-hand*

occupation f **de locaux** *sit-in*

occupation f **d'usine** *work-in*

occupé(e) *occupied; engaged; busy*

octet m *byte*

offre f *offer; bid*

faire une offre *to bid*

offre f **de lancement** *introductory offer*

l'offre f **et la demande** f *supply and demand*

offre f **promotionnelle** *promotional offer; bonus pack*

offre f **publique d'achat (OPA** f**)** *takeover bid*

offrir *to offer; to give*

oligopole m *oligopoly*

opérateur(-trice) m(f) **de saisie** *keyboarder*

opérateur m **du système** *system*

operator

opération *f operation; transaction*

opération *f* **de change à terme** *forward exchange*

opération *f* **de relations publiques** *public relations exercise; public relations event*

opération *f* **portes ouvertes** *open house*

opération *f* **publicitaire** *publicity event*

opérations *fpl operations*

opérations *fpl* **à terme** *futures*

opérations *fpl* **de transit** *freight forwarding*

opération *f* **spéculative** *venture*

opération *f* **témoin** *market test*

faire opposition (à) *to stop payment*

optimum *m optimum*

option *f option*

option *f* **d'achat** *call option*

option *f* **de vente** *put option*

ordinateur *m computer*

ordinateur *m* **de bureau** *desktop computer*

ordinateur *m* **type "tour"** *deskside computer*

ordonnance *f prescription; order*

ordonnancement *m scheduling*

ordre *m order; injunction*

à l'ordre de *payable to*

ordre *m* **d'achat** *purchase order*

ordre *m* **de renvoi** *return order*

ordre *m* **du jour** *agenda*

oreiller *m pillow*

organigramme *m organization chart*

Organisation *f* **de coopération et de développement économiques (OCDE** *f) Organization for Economic Cooperation and Development (OECD)*

Organisation *f* **des Nations Unies pour l'alimentation et l'agriculture (FAO** *f) Food and Agriculture Organization of the United Nations (FAO)*

Organisation *f* **des Nations Unies pour le développement industriel**

(ONUDI *f) UN Industrial Development Organization (UNIDO)*

Organisation *f* **des normes internationales (ISO** *f) International Standards Organization (ISO)*

Organisation *f* **des pays arabes exportateurs de pétrole (OPAEP** *f) Organization of Arab Petroleum Exporting Countries (OAPEC)*

Organisation *f* **des pays exportateurs de pétrole (OPEP** *f) Organization of Petroleum Exporting Countries (OPEC)*

Organisation *f* **internationale du commerce (OIC** *f) International Trade Organization (ITO)*

Organisation *f* **internationale du travail (OIT** *f) International Labour Organization (ILO)*

organisation *f* **patronale** *employers' association*

organisme *m* **législateur** *regulator*

orientation *f* **écologique** *greening*

orientation *f* **professionnelle** *vocational guidance*

outil *m tool*

ouvrier(-ière) *m(f) factory worker*

ouvrier(-ière) *m(f)* **qualifié(e)** *skilled worker*

ouvrier(-ière) *m(f)* **spécialisé(e)** *semi-skilled worker*

pages *fpl* **jaunes** *Yellow Pages* ®

pagination *f pagination*

paiement *m* **à la commande** *cash with order (CWO)*

paiement *m* **intégral** *payment in full*

paiement *m* **sur réception de facture** *payment on invoice*

palette *f pallet*

palettisation *f palletization*

palettiser *to palletize*

palier *m landing*

palmer *m micrometer*

paneuropéen(ne) *pan-European*

panne *f breakdown*

en panne *down; broken down*

tomber en panne *to break down; to crash*

panneau *m* **d'affichage** *billboard;*

hoarding

PAO f **(publication** f **assistée par ordinateur)** DTP (desktop publishing)

papier m paper; notepaper

papier m **à lettres** writing paper; notepaper; stationery

papier m **à photocopieur** copy paper

papier m **en continu** continuous stationery

papier m **peint** wallpaper

paquet m pack; packet; parcel

paradis m **fiscal** tax haven

paramètre m parameter

parc m park; grounds

parking m car park; parking facilities

parking m **de long séjour/court séjour** long-term/short-term car park

parking m **souterrain** underground car park

Parlement m **européen (PE** m**)** European Parliament (EP)

parler to speak

part f **du marché** market share

participant(e) m(f) participant; delegate

participation f **majoritaire** majority shareholding

participation f **minoritaire** minority shareholding

participation f **publicitaire** advertising allowance

partie f **adverse** opposing party; other party

partir to leave; to sail

pas en service off line; not in use

passage m **en douane** customs clearance; customs entry

passation f **d'écriture** entry

passeport m passport

passeport m **de la CEE** EEC passport

passer aux profits et pertes to write off

passible de poursuites actionable

passif m liabilities

passif m **exigible** current liabilities

patron m template; stencil; pattern

patron(ne) m(f) boss

pavillon m detached house

payable à l'avance payable in advance

payable à vue payable at sight

payable sur présentation payable on demand

payer to pay

pays m country; region

pays m **d'origine** country of origin

pénétration f **du marché** market penetration

pension f **complète** full board

percée f breakthrough

percepteur m tax collector

perception f **des impôts** tax collection

percer to drill

perceuse f drill

perforateur m paper punch

période f **budgétaire** budget period

période f **creuse** slack period

période f **d'exemption d'impôts** tax holiday

période f **probatoire** probationary period

périodique m periodical

périphérique m, adj peripheral

permis m **de conduire** driving licence

permis m **de construire** planning permission

permis m **de séjour** residence permit

permis m **de travail** work permit

personnel m staff; personnel

"personnel" "private"

pourvoir en personnel to staff

personnel m **administratif** clerical staff

personnel m **temporaire** temporary staff

perte f **d'avarie particulière** particular average loss

perte f **d'avaries communes** general average loss

perte f **nette** net loss

perte f **sèche** write-off

pesticide m pesticide

petit déjeuner *m* breakfast

petit déjeuner *m* d'affaires breakfast meeting

petit déjeuner *m* de travail working breakfast

petites annonces *fpl* classified advertisements

petits caractères *mpl* small print

pétrodollar *m* petrodollar

peu alcoolisé(e) low-alcohol

phase *f* phase

phosphates *mpl* phosphates

photo-call *m* (pl ~-~s) photo call

photocopie *f* photocopy

photocopier to photocopy

photographe *m/f* photographer

photo(graphie) *f* photograph

photographier to photograph

pièce *f* room

piquet *m* de grève picket

organiser un piquet de grève to picket

pirater to pirate

piscine *f* swimming pool

pistes *fpl* par pouce tpi (tracks per inch)

pixel *m* pixel

place *f* place; space; seat; job

place *f* boursière stock market

place *f* côté fenêtre window seat

place *f* côté hublot window seat

place *f* financière money market

placement *m* investment

place *f* près de l'allée aisle seat

plafond *m* ceiling

plage *f* beach; time slot

plagiat *m* plagiarism

plaignant(e) *m(f)* plaintiff

plan *m* plan; map

plan *m* de commercialisation marketing plan

plan *m* de la ville street map

plan *m* d'épargne-capitalisation personnel personal equity plan (PEP)

plan *m* directeur blueprint

plan *m* d'urgence contingency plan

planification *f* de la production production planning

planification *f* de l'entreprise corporate planning

planification *f* des effectifs manpower planning

planification *f* des ventes sales planning

planification *f* pour urgences contingency planning

planifier to plan (ahead)

planning *m* programme; schedule

plat *m* de résistance main course

plat *m* du jour dish of the day

plein emploi *m* full employment

pleine propriété *f* freehold

plombage *m* filling

plus-value *f* (pl ~-~s) capital gains; appreciation

pneu *m* crevé punctured tyre

pneu *m* plat flat tyre

podium *m* podium

poids *m* (de bagages) autorisé baggage allowance

poids-limite *m* (pl ~-~s) weight limit

point *m* d'accès port

point *m* de procédure point of order

point *m* de vente point of sale (POS); (retail) outlet

pointer (à l'arrivée) to clock in/on

pointer (en départ) to clock off/out

pointeuse *f* time clock

point *m* faible loophole

police *f* police; policy; font; typeface

police *f* (de caractères) font; typeface

police *f* de l'air airport police

police *f* des chemins de fer railway police

policier *m* policeman

Politique *f* agricole commune (PAC *f*) Common Agricultural Policy (CAP)

politique *f* de commercialisation advertising strategy

politique *f* d'économie d'énergie energy-saving policy

politique *f* de distribution distributor policy

politique *f* des prix pricing policy

politique *f* **des prix et des revenus** *prices and incomes policy*

politique *f* **des revenus** *incomes policy*

politique *f* **du laissez-faire** *laissez-faire policy*

politique *f* **fiscale** *fiscal policy*

politique *f* **monétaire** *monetary policy*

politique *f* **salariale** *wages policy*

polluant *m* *pollutant*

pollué(e) *polluted*

polluer *to pollute*

pollution *f* *pollution*

pollution *f* **de l'air** *air pollution*

pollution *f* **des eaux** *water pollution*

pollution *f* **par le bruit** *noise pollution*

pompe *f* *pump*

pompiers *mpl* *fire brigade; firemen*

pontée *f* *deck cargo*

portable *m* *portable (computer)*

port *m* **à la charge de l'acheteur** *carriage inwards*

port *m* **à la charge du vendeur** *carriage outwards*

portatif(-ive) *adj* *portable*

portatif *m* *laptop (computer)*

port *m* **d'entrée** *port of entry*

(en) port dû *postage due; carriage forward; freight forward*

porte *f* *door; gate*

porte-conteneurs *m* *(pl inv)* *container ship*

porte-copie *m* *(pl ~-~(s))* *copy holder*

portefeuille *m* *portfolio; wallet*

portefeuille *m* **de titres** *investment portfolio*

portefeuille *m* **d'investissements** *investment portfolio*

porte-parole *m* *inv* *spokesman/woman*

porteur(-euse) *m(f)* *bearer; holder; porter*

portier *m* *doorman*

portier *m* **électronique** *video entry system*

(en) port payé *post-paid; post-free;*

carriage paid

port *m* **payé par le destinataire** *freight inward*

poser sa candidature (pour) *to apply (for)*

possibilité *f* **légale d'echapper à l'impôt** *tax loophole*

poste *m* *job; extension; item*

poste *f* *post office*

poste *m* **de secours** *first aid post*

poste *m* **de travail** *work station*

poste *f* **restante** *poste restante*

poste *m* **vacant** *vacancy*

postproduction *f* *postproduction*

potentiel *m* **du marché** *market potential*

potentiel *m* **inutilisé** *idle capacity*

poterie *f* *pottery*

pouce *m* *inch; thumb*

poursuivre (en) justice *to prosecute*

préavis *m* **réglementaire** *required notice*

précédent *m* *precedent*

prélèvement *m* **automatique** *direct debit*

prélèvement *m* **obligatoire** *statutory deduction*

première classe *f* *first class*

première tranche *f* **d'imposition** *basic rate of tax*

prendre de la valeur *to appreciate*

preneur *m* **ferme** *underwriter*

préproduction *f* *preproduction*

préretraite *f* *early retirement*

présentation *f* *introduction; presentation; display*

présentation *f* **visuelle** *soft copy; visual display*

présentoir *m* **en vrac** *dump bin*

préservation *f* *preservation*

préserver *to conserve*

président(e) *m(f)* *chairman/woman; president*

(la) presse *f* *(the) press*

presse *f* **nationale** *national press*

presse *f* **professionnelle** *trade press*

pressing *m* *dry cleaner's; valet service*

prêt *m loan*
prêt *m* **bancaire** *bank loan*
prêter *to lend; to loan*
prêt-logement *m* **avec assurance mixte** (*pl* ~**s**-~) *endowment mortgage*
prêt *m* **non-garanti** *unsecured loan*
prêt *m* **personnel** *personal loan*
prêt *m* **relais** *bridging loan*
prévision *f forecast; projection; estimate*
prévision *f* **des besoins en main-d'œuvre** *manpower forecast*
prévision *f* **de ventes** *sales forecast*
prévisions *fpl* **de demande** *demand forecasting*
prévoir *to forecast; to anticipate*
prime *f premium; incentive; bonus; premium offer*
prime *f* **d'assurance** *insurance premium*
prime *f* **de départ** *golden handshake*
prime *f* **de sauvetage** *salvage*
prime *f* **en espèces** *cash bonus*
prise *f* **de courant** *power point*
prise *f* **de décision** *decision-making*
privatisation *f privatization*
privatiser *to privatize*
privé(e) *private; privately-owned*
priver d'un droit de représentation *to disenfranchise*
prix *m price; offer price; prize*
à prix réduit *cut-price*
prix *m* **à la reprise** *trade-in price*
prix *m* **à régie intéressée** *cost-plus pricing*
prix *m* **au comptant** *cash price*
prix *m* **concurrentiel** *competitive price*
prix *m* **conseillé** *recommended retail price (RRP)*
prix *m* **d'achat** *purchase price*
prix *m* **de catalogue** *list price*
prix *m* **de détail** *retail price*
prix *m* **dédouané** *duty-paid price*
prix *m* **de gros** *trade price*
prix *m* **de (la) location** *hire price*
prix *m* **de l'exemplaire** *cover price*
prix *m* **demandé** *asking price*

prix *m* **d'émission** *offer price*
prix *m* **de revient standard** *standard cost*
prix *m* **en entrepôt (de douane)** *in-bond price*
prix *m* **ferme** *firm price*
prix *m* **marchand** *market price*
prix *m* **sacrifié** *bargain price*
prix *m* **sur place** *spot price*
prix *m* **tout compris** *all-in price; delivered price*
prix *m* **unitaire** *unit price*
problème *m problem; issue*
problème *m* **de production** *production problem*
procédé *m process*
procédure *f procedure*
procédure *f* **conventionnelle** *agreed procedure*
procédure *f* **d'arbitrage** *grievance procedure*
procédures *fpl* **comptables** *accounting procedures*
procès *m lawsuit; action; trial*
processeur *m processor*
procès-verbal *m* (*pl* ~-**verbaux**) *minutes; report; ticket*
procuration *f* **(écrite)** *power of attorney*
procureur *m prosecuting counsel*
producteur *m production company*
producteur(-trice) *m(f) producer*
production *f production; output*
en production *on line; on stream*
production *f* **à la chaîne** *flow-line production*
production *f* **par lots** *batch production*
productivité *f productivity*
produire *to produce; to output*
produit *m product; commodity*
produit *m* **en tête du marché** *market leader*
produit *m* **fini** *end product; finished product*
produit *m* **intérieur brut (PIB** *m*) *gross domestic product (GDP)*
produit *m* **national brut (PNB** *m*) *gross national product (GNP)*
produits *mpl* **de base** *primary*

products
produits *mpl* **de consommation courante** *convenience goods*
produits *mpl* **finis** *finished goods*
produits *mpl* **manufacturés** *manufactured goods*
produits *mpl* **non-sollicités** *unsolicited goods*
profil *m* **de la clientèle** *customer profile*
profil *m* **du poste** *job description*
profit *m* *profit*
profit *m* **fictif** *paper profit*
progiciel *m* *(software) package*
progiciel *m* **d'application** *application package*
programmateur *m* *programming unit*
programmation *f* *programming*
programme *m* *programme; schedule; program*
programme *m* **de diagnostic** *diagnostic program*
programme *m* **de recherches** *research programme*
programmer *to program*
programmeur(-euse) *m(f)* *programmer*
progression *f* *progress*
projecteur *m* *projector*
projecteur *m* **de diapositives** *slide projector*
projet *m* *project; plan; blueprint*
projet *m* **collaboratif** *collaborative project*
projeté(e) *projected*
projeter *to project*
projeter (de faire) *to plan (to do)*
projet *m* **pilote** *pilot project*
promesse *f* *promise*
promesse *f* **d'achat à terme** *forward contract*
promesse *f* **de vente** *promise to sell*
promettre *to promise*
promoteur *m* **immobilier** *property developer*
promotion *f* *promotion*
promotion *f* **des ventes** *sales drive*

promotion *f* **immobilière** *property development*
promouvoir *to promote*
propriétaire *m/f* *owner; landlord; landlady*
propriété *f* *property; estate*
propriété *f* **collective** *collective ownership; collective property*
propriété *f* **de l'État** *public ownership; government property*
propriété *f* **foncière libre** *freehold property*
propriété *f* **industrielle** *patent rights; intellectual property*
propriété *f* **littéraire et artistique** *intellectual property*
propriété *f* **louée à bail** *leasehold (property)*
au prorata *pro rata*
prospecter *to canvass*
prospection *f* *canvassing*
prospectus *m* *prospectus; leaflet; brochure; circular*
protection *f* **du consommateur** *consumer protection*
protectionnisme *m* *protectionism*
protégé(e) **contre l'écriture** *write-protected*
protéger *to protect*
protocole *m* *protocol*
prototype *m* *prototype*
provision *f* *provision*
provisions *fpl* *allowance; provisions*
pub *f* *ad*
public *m* *public*
publication *f* *publication; publishing*
publication *f* **assistée par ordinateur (PAO** *f***)** *desktop publishing (DTP)*
publication *f* **d'ouvrages de référence** *reference publishing*
publications *fpl* **enfantines** *children's publications; children's publishing*
public *m* **cible** *target audience*
public *m* **d'adultes** *adult audience*
public *m* **de jeunes** *young audience*
publicité *f* *advertising; advertise-*

ment; publicity

faire de la publicité (pour) to advertise

publicité f **au point de vente** point-of-sale advertising

publicité f **directe par correspondance** direct-mail advertising

publicité f **en double page** double-page spread; centre spread

publicité f **institutionnelle** corporate advertising

publicité f **par courrier individuel** direct-mail advertising

publicité f **rédactionnelle** display advertising

publicité f **subliminale** subliminal advertising

publicité f **sur le lieu de vente** point-of-sale advertising

publier to publish

publier en feuilleton to serialize

publipostage m mailshot

pub f **paneuropéenne** euro-ad

puce f (micro)chip

quai m quay; platform; dock

à quai ex dock

quai m **de chargement** loading dock

qualité f quality; position

de qualité inférieure substandard

qualité f "courrier" letter quality

qualité f **d'entrée égale qualité** f **de sortie** GIGO (garbage in garbage out)

quantité f quantity

quartier m **résidentiel** residential area

quasi-monnaie f (pl ~-~s) near-money

question f question; issue

quotidien(ne) daily

quotidien m daily (newspaper)

quotidien m **populaire** tabloid

rabais m discount; allowance

au rabais cut-price

rachat m takeover; buyout; surrender

rachat m **de l'entreprise par ses salariés (RES** m**)** management buyout

racheter to buy back; to buy up; to buy out; to surrender

radiateur m radiator

radio f radio

radioactivité f radioactivity

radiodiffusion f (radio) broadcasting

raffinerie f refinery

rafraîchissements mpl refreshments

RAM f RAM (random access memory)

rapide m express train

rappel m reminder

rappel m **de salaire** back pay

rappel m **d'impôts** back duty

rappeler to call back, to remind

rapport m report; link; contact

rapport m **annuel** annual report; annual return

rapport m **d'activité** progress report

rapport m **de construction** structural report

rapport m **de ventes** sales report

rapport m **dividendes-résultat** dividend cover

rapport m **réglementaire** statutory report

rapport m **sur l'environnement** environmental statement

ratification f ratification

ratifier to ratify

rationalisation f rationalization

rationaliser to rationalize

réaction f reaction; feedback

réaffectation f redeployment; reallocation

réaffectation f **des ressources** reallocation of resources

réalisateur(-trice) m(f) producer; film director

réalisation f realization

réaliser to realize; to make; to produce

réaménagement m redevelopment

réaménager to redevelop

réamorcer to reboot

réassurance f reinsurance

réassurer to reinsure

réception f reception; receipt

réceptionniste m/f receptionist

récession f recession

recettes *fpl* revenue; takings
recevable admissible; actionable
recevoir to receive; to get; to receive visitors
à recevoir receivable
réchauffement *m* **de la planète** global warming
recherche(s) *f(pl)* research
faire des recherches (sur) to research (into)
recherche *f* **appliquée** applied research
recherche-développement *f* **(R-D** *f***)** research and development (R & D)
recherche *f* **documentaire** information retrieval; desk research
recherche *f* **et remplacement** *m* **(automatiques)** (global) search and replace
recherche *f* **pure** pure research
recherche *f* **sur le terrain** field research
récépissé *m* **de dépôt** deposit receipt
récépissé *m* **des douanes** customs receipt
réclame *f* advertisement; special offer
recommandation *f* recommendation; testimonial; endorsement
recomposer le numéro to re-dial
reconnaissance *f* **de la parole** speech recognition
reconnaissance *f* **officielle du syndicat** trade union recognition
reconstruire to rebuild
recouvrir to cover; to overwrite
recrutement *m* recruitment
recruter to recruit
rectification *f* rectification
reçu *m* receipt
récupérer to recover; to get back; to salvage
recyclable recyclable
recyclé(e) recycled
recycler to recycle
rédacteur(-trice) *m(f)* **publicitaire** copywriter
rédaction *f* **des actes de cession de**

propriété conveyancing
redevance *f* licence fee; dues
redevance *f* **foncière** ground rent
redevance *f* **sur les ventes** royalty on sales
réduction *f* reduction; discount; cutback
réduction *f* **des pertes** mitigation of loss
réduction *f* **d'impôt** tax cut
réductions *fpl* **de prix** price-cutting
réduire to reduce; to cut; to cut back
rééchelonnement *m* rescheduling
rééchelonner to reschedule
réévaluation *f* revaluation
réexporter to re-export
référence *f* reference
référence *f* **commerciale** trade reference
références *fpl* **bancaires** banker's reference
reformater to reformat
refus *m* refusal
refus *m* **d'honorer** repudiation
régime *m* **de retraite** pension scheme
régime *m* **de retraite professionnelle** occupational pension scheme
régime *m* **de retraite avec retenues sur le salaire** contributory pension scheme
régime *m* **de retraite sans retenues** non-contributory pension scheme
régisseur *m* estate manager; stage manager; assistant director
registre *m* register
registre *m* **des procès-verbaux** minute book
registre *m* **des salaires** payroll
règlement *m* payment; regulation; by(e-)law; adjustment; settlement
règlement *m* **à l'aimable** out-of-court settlement
réglementation *f* **douanière** customs regulation
régler to settle; to pay; to adjust
régler sa note to pay one's bill; to

check out

régulateur(-trice) *m(f) regulator*

réinitialiser *to reboot*

réintégration *f reinstatement*

réintégrer *to reinstate*

rejet *m repudiation; spoil; rejection*

relance *f follow-up; boost; revival*

relance *f* **économique** *reflation*

relancer *to follow up; to boost; to reflate*

relations *fpl* **du travail** *industrial relations*

relations *fpl* **humaines** *human relations*

relations *fpl* **publiques (RP** *fpl)* *public relations (PR); public relations department*

relevé *m* **de compte** *bank statement; statement (of account)*

remboursable *refundable; redeemable*

rembourser *to refund; to redeem; to pay off*

remise *f discount; allowance*

remis(e) à neuf *refurbished*

remise *f* **à neuf** *refurbishment*

remise *f* **au comptant** *cash discount*

remise *f* **professionnelle** *trade discount*

remise *f* **sur la quantité** *volume discount*

rendement *m output; outturn; yield; return*

rendement *m* **courant** *current yield*

rendement *m* **du capital** *return on capital*

rendement *m* **net** *output; outturn*

renouveler *to renew*

renouvellement *m renewal*

renseignements *mpl information (desk); directory enquiries*

rentabilité *f profitability; cost-effectiveness*

rentabilité *f* **des investissements** *return on investments (ROI)*

rentable *profitable; cost-effective*

rente *f annuity*

rente *f* **différée** *deferred annuity*

rentes *fpl* **consolidées** *consols*

rente *f* **viagère** *life annuity*

réparations *fpl* **de structure** *structural repairs*

répartiteur *m* **d'avaries** *adjuster*

repeint(e) *repainted; redecorated*

repère *m benchmark; indicator*

répertoire *m directory; address book*

répertoire *m* **de caractères** *character set*

répondant(e) *m(f) referee; guarantor*

répondeur *m* **automatique** *answering machine*

report *m postponement; transfer; contango*

reportage *m* **exclusif** *exclusive (story)*

reportage(s) *m(pl)* **des médias** *media coverage*

reprendre *to take back; to take over; to rally*

reprendre possession de *to repossess*

représentant(e) *m(f)* **de commerce** *sales representative*

représentation *f representation*

représenter *to represent*

reprise *f* **de possession** *repossession*

reprogrammer *to reschedule*

requérant(e) *m(f) claimant*

réseau *m network*

réseau *m* **de distribution** *distributor network*

réseau *m* **local d'entreprise (RLE** *m)* *local area network (LAN)*

réservation *f reservation*

réservation *f* **ferme** *firm booking*

réserve *f reserve; storeroom; reservation*

en réserve *in stock; in reserve*

faire des réserves *to stock up; to have reservations*

sous réserve de confirmation *subject to confirmation*

sous réserve d'un contrat *subject to contract*

réserver *to reserve*

réserves *fpl* **de trésorerie** *cash re-*

serves

réserves *fpl* **d'or** *gold reserves*

résiliation *f* **de contrat** *termination of contract*

résilier *to cancel*

résistant(e) aux chocs *shockproof*

responsabilité *f* *responsibility; liability*

responsabilité *f* **contractuelle** *contractual liability*

responsabilité *f* **illimitée** *unlimited liability*

responsabilité *f* **limitée** *limited liability*

responsabilité *f* **patronale** *employer's liability*

responsable *adj* *responsible; liable*

responsable *m/f* *person in charge*

responsable *m/f* **administratif(-ive)** *office manager*

responsable *m/f* **de clientèle** *account executive*

responsable *m/f* **de la comptabilité de gestion** *management accountant*

responsable *m/f* **de la comptabilité générale** *financial accountant*

responsable *m/f* **de la formation** *training officer*

responsable *m/f* **de la gestion des stocks** *stock controller*

responsable *m/f* **de la sûreté** *safety officer*

responsable *m/f* **de l'équipe de représentants** *field sales manager*

responsable *m/f* **des relations publiques** *public relations officer*

responsable *m/f* **du suivi** *progress chaser*

ressortissant(e) *m(f)* **de la CEE** *EEC national*

ressources *fpl* **humaines** *human resources*

ressources *fpl* **naturelles** *natural resources*

restauration *f* *catering (industry)*

restauré(e) *restored*

reste *m* *residue*

résumé *m* *summary; résumé; abstract*

résumé *m* **des objectifs publicitaires** *advertising brief*

rétablir *to reinstate*

retard *m* *delay; lateness*

retard *m* **de livraison** *late delivery*

retardé(e) *delayed*

réticence *f* *non-disclosure*

retirer *to withdraw*

retour *m* **(automatique) à la ligne** *wordwrap*

retrait *m* *withdrawal*

retraite *f* *retirement*

prendre sa retraite *to retire*

retraite *f* **anticipée** *early retirement*

retraite *f* **proportionnelle** *graduated pension*

rétrogradation *f* *demotion*

rétrograder *to demote*

rétroprojecteur *m* *overhead projector*

retrouver *to find; to retrieve*

réunion *f* *meeting*

réunion *f* **de vente** *sales meeting*

réunion *f* **du conseil d'administration** *board meeting*

réunion *f* **du service commercial** *sales conference*

réutilisable *reusable*

revenu *m* *income; earnings*

revenu *m* **de placement** *investment income*

revenu *m* **disponible** *disposable personal income*

revenu *m* **du travail** *earned income*

revenu *m* **financier** *unearned income*

revenu *m* **non-imposable** *non-taxable income*

révision *f* *review; servicing*

révision *f* **des salaires** *salary review*

révocation *f* *revocation*

révoquer *to revoke*

revue *f* *magazine*

revue *f* **de luxe** *glossy magazine*

revue *f* **mensuelle** *monthly (magazine)*

rez-de-chaussée *m* **(pl inv)** *ground floor*

du rez-de-chaussée *adj* *downstairs*

risque *m* risk

risque *m* **financier** *financial risk*

risque *m* **professionnel** *occupational hazard*

ristourne *f* **d'impôts** *tax rebate*

RLE *m* **(réseau** *m* **local d'entreprise)** *LAN (local area network)*

robot *m* robot

robotique *f* robotics

rôdage *m* soak test; running in

romain *m* roman

romain *m* **incliné** sloped roman

roman *m* novel

romans *mpl* **à sensation** pulp fiction

romans *mpl* **de qualité** quality fiction

rotation *f* **des stocks** stock turnover

RP *fpl* **(relations** *fpl* **publiques)** PR (public relations)

ruban *m* ribbon

ruban *m* **correcteur** correction ribbon/tape

rubrique *f* **affaires** business section

rupture *f* **de contrat** breach of contract

rupture *f* **de contrat par anticipation** anticipatory breach

en rupture de stock out of stock

saisie *f* attachment; seizure; foreclosure; repossession; capture

saisie *f* **(de données)** (data) capture

saisie *f* **(du bien hypothéqué)** foreclosure

saisir to seize; to foreclose; to capture

salaire *m* salary; pay; wage(s)

salaire *m* **au mérite** merit pay

salaire *m* **au rendement** performance-related pay

salaire *m* **de base** basic wage

salaire *m* **garanti** guaranteed wage

salaire *m* **majoré de moitié** time-and-a-half

salaire *m* **minimum** minimum wage

salaire *m* **minimum garanti** guaranteed minimum wage; threshold agreement

salaire *m* **net** net pay; take-home pay

salle *f* hall; room

salle *f* **à manger** dining room

salle *f* **d'attente** waiting room

salle *f* **d'eau** shower (room)

salle *f* **de bains** bathroom

salle *f* **de bains attenante** en suite bathroom

salle *f* **de bains particulière** private bathroom

salle *f* **de conférences** conference room; conference hall

salle *f* **d'embarquement** departure lounge

salle *f* **de réunion** meeting room

salle *f* **de transit** transit lounge

salle *f* **d'exposition** exhibition hall; showroom

salle *f* **du courrier** mailroom

salon *m* lounge

salon *f* **de première classe** first class lounge

salon *m* **de thé** teashop; coffee shop

sanctions *fpl* sanctions

satellite *m* satellite

satisfaction *f* **professionnelle** job satisfaction

sauvegarde *f* saving; backup

sauvegarder to save; to back up

sauver to save; to salvage

sauveteur *m* **d'entreprise** white knight

scolarité *f* education

SCSI *f* SCSI (small computer systems interface)

SE *m* **(système** *m* **expert)** expert system

séance *f* meeting; session

séance *f* **de l'après-midi** afternoon session

séance *f* **du matin** morning session

séance *f* **du soir** evening session

sec(sèche) dry; straight

sèche-cheveux *m inv* hairdryer

secrétaire *m/f* secretary

secrétaire *m/f* **général(e)** company secretary

secrétaire *m/f* **particulier(-ière)** personal assistant (PA)

secteur *m* **de croissance** *growth market*

secteur *m* **de la fabrication** *manufacturing sector*

secteur *m* **de la transformation** *processing industry*

secteur *m* **de l'énergie** *power industry*

secteur *m* **de l'information** *information industry*

secteur *m* **du tourisme** *travel industry*

secteur *m* **nucléaire** *nuclear industry*

secteur *m* **pétrolier** *oil industry; petroleum industry*

secteur *m* **privé** *private sector*

secteur *m* **public** *public sector*

secteur *m* **tertiaire** *tertiary sector*

sécurité *f* **de l'emploi** *job security*

sécurité *f* **des informations** *data security*

Sécurité *f* **sociale** *National Insurance*

SED *m* **(système** *m* **d'exploitation sur disques)** *DOS*

semaine *f* *week*

semaine *f* **de travail** *working week*

semestriel(le) *bi-annual; half-yearly*

semi-automatisé(e) *semi-automated*

semi-remorque *m* **(***pl* ~-~**s)** *articulated lorry*

semi-remorque *f* **(***pl* ~-~**s)** *trailer*

sens *m* **commercial** *salesmanship*

série *f* *series*

série *f* **dramatique** *drama series*

serveur *m* *system operator*

service *m* *department; service; service charge; favour*

du service *departmental*

en service *on line; on stream; in use*

service *m* **affaires** *business service centre*

service *m* **après-vente (SAV** *m***)** *after-sales service*

service *m* **clientèle** *customer ser-*

vices department

service *m* **colis postaux** *parcel post*

service *m* **de comptabilité** *accounts (department)*

service *m* **de création** *creative department; design department*

service *m* **d'entretien** *service department*

service *f* **de recherche** *research department*

service *m* **des archives** *records department*

service *m* **des chambres** *room service*

service *m* **des expéditions** *shipping department; dispatch department*

service *m* **des réclamations** *complaints department*

service *m* **des relations publiques** *public relations (department)*

service *m* **des sinistres** *claims department*

service *m* **des ventes** *sales department*

service *m* **d'exportations** *export department*

service *m* **d'informatique** *computing department*

service *m* **du contentieux** *legal department*

service *m* **du marketing** *marketing (department)*

service *m* **du personnel** *personnel department*

service *m* **international** *international division*

service-lecteurs *m* **(***pl* ~**s**-~**)** *Business Reply Service*

service *m* **public** *public utility*

services *mpl* **bancaires** *banking services; banking facilities*

services *mpl* **de secrétariat** *secretarial services*

services *mpl* **municipaux** *public utilities; local services*

serviette *f* *briefcase; towel*

seuil *m* **de rentabilité** *break-even point*

shareware *m* *shareware*

sidérurgie *f* *(iron and) steel industry*

siège *m* **social** *head office; registered office*

signataire *m/f signatory*

signature *f signature; completion*

simulation *f simulation*

sinistre *m* **total** *total loss*

site *m* **vierge** *greenfield site*

sit-in *m* (*pl inv*) *sit-in*

slogan *m slogan*

société *f company; corporation; society*

société *f* **affiliée** *associated company*

société *f* **à la tête du marché** *market leader*

société *f* **anonyme** *public (limited) company*

société *f* **bancaire anonyme par actions** *joint-stock bank*

société *f* **cotée en bourse** *listed company*

société *f* **de financement** *finance company*

société *f* **de placements** *investment trust*

société *f* **de services** *service industry*

société *f* **de services et de conseils en informatique (SSCI** *f*) *software house*

société *f* **de télévision** *television company*

société *f* **d'investissement à capital variable (SICAV** *f*) *unit trust*

société-écran *f* (*pl* ~-**s**-~**s**) *shell company*

Société *f* **financière internationale (SFI** *f*) *International Finance Corporation (IFC)*

société *f* **inscrite au registre du commerce** *registered company*

société *f* **mère** *parent company*

société *f* **non-cotée (en bourse)** *unlisted company*

société *f* **par actions** *joint-stock company*

société *f* **privée** *private (limited) company*

socio-économique *socioeconomic*

software *m software*

sol *m floor*

solde *m balance; sale*

solde *m* **créditeur** *credit balance*

solde *m* **débiteur** *debit balance*

solde *m* **disponible** *balance in hand*

solvabilité *f solvency; creditworthiness*

solvable *solvent*

somme *f* **exigible** *monies due*

sonal *m jingle*

sonnerie *f ringing tone; bell*

sortie *f way out; exit; output; publication; release*

sortie *f* **(d'imprimante)** *printout*

sortie *f* **de secours** *emergency exit; fire exit*

sorties *fpl outgoings*

sortir *to come out; to go out; to take out; to bring out; to print out; to output*

sortir (du système) *to log off/out*

soumission *f tender*

faire une soumission pour *to put in a tender for*

souris *f mouse*

sous-capitalisé(e) *undercapitalized*

souscripteur *m subscriber*

souscription *f subscription*

souscrire *to subscribe; to underwrite*

sous-directeur(-trice) *m(f)* (*pl* ~-~**s**) *assistant manager*

sous-emploi *m under-employment*

sous-louer *to sublet*

sous-main *m* (*pl inv*) *desk pad*

sous-produit *m* (*pl* ~-~**s**) *by-product*

soussigné(e) *m(f) undersigned*

sous-sol *m* (*pl* ~-~**s**) *basement*

sous-traiter *to subcontract*

soutien *m* **(financier)** *backing*

spacieux(-euse) *spacious*

spécialisation *f specialization*

spécialiste *m/f* **en valeurs de trésor (SVT** *m/f*) *Government Broker*

spécimen *m* **de signature** *specimen signature*

spéculateur(-trice) *m(f) speculator*

spéculation *f* **(immobilière)** *(prop-*

erty) speculation
spéculer *to speculate*
spirale *f* **prix-salaires** *wage-price spiral*
spot *m* **(publicitaire)** *commercial; commercial break; spot*
SSCI *f* **(société** *f* **de services et de conseils en informatique)** *software house*
stabilisation *f stabilization*
stabilité *f* **de l'emploi** *security of tenure*
stage *m course; (work) placement*
stage *m* **de formation** *training course*
stage *m* **de gestion** *management course*
stage *m* **préparatoire** *induction course*
stagflation *f stagflation*
stagiaire *m/f trainee*
stagnant(e) *sluggish; stagnant*
stagnation *f stagnation*
stand *m stand*
standard *m switchboard; operator service*
standardisation *f standardization*
standardiste *m/f switchboard operator*
stand-by *m inv stand-by ticket*
station *f* **de taxi** *taxi rank*
station-service *f* (*pl* ~**s-**~) *service station*
statut *m statute; status*
statutaire *statutory*
statut *m* **d'égalité** *single status*
statuts *mpl* **d'une société** *articles of association*
steward *m steward*
stimulant *m incentive*
stock *m stock*
en stock *in stock*
stocker *to stock; to file*
stocker en surabondance *to overstock*
stocks *mpl* **régulateurs** *buffer stocks*
stratégie *f strategy*
stratégie *f* **de l'entreprise** *corporate strategy*

stratégie *f* **publicitaire** *advertising strategy*
structure *f* **financière** *capital structure*
studio *m* **d'enregistrement** *recording studio*
style *m* **de vie** *lifestyle*
stylisme *m* **maison** *house style*
subrécargue *m supercargo*
substance *f* **toxique** *noxious substance*
substitut *m* **(de créancier)** *subrogation*
subvention *f subsidy*
subvention *f* **d'équipement** *investment grant*
subventionner *to subsidize*
subvention *f* **pour l'aménagement du territoire** *regional development grant*
succès *m success*
succès *m* **de librairie** *bestseller*
succursale *f branch*
suite *f result; continuation; suite; sequel*
supplément *m supplement*
supports *mpl* **audio-visuels** *audio-visual aids*
supports *mpl* **publicitaires** *advertising media*
suppressions *fpl* **d'emplois** *job losses*
sûr(e) *sure; certain; secure*
faire du surbooking *to overbook*
surcapacité *f overcapacity*
surcapitalisé(e) *overcapitalized*
surcapitaliser *to overcapitalize*
surchauffe *f* **de l'économie** *overheating of the economy*
surestarie *f demurrage*
suroffre *f excess supply*
surproduction *f overproduction*
surréservé(e) *overbooked*
sursouscrit(e) *oversubscribed*
surtaxe *f* **à l'importation** *import surcharge*
syndic *m property manager*
syndicat *m trade union*
syndic *m* **de faillite** *official receiver*
synopsis *m synopsis*

synthèse *f* **vocale** *speech synthesis*

synthétique *synthetic; man-made*

système *m* *system*

système *m* **comptable** *accounting system*

système *m* **d'alarme** *early warning system*

système *m* **de classement** *filing system*

système *m* **de contrôle** *control system*

système *m* **de données mobile** *mobile data system*

système *m* **de primes** *incentive scheme*

système *m* **de rémunération au rendement** *payment-by-results system*

système *m* **de sonorisation** *PA system*

système *m* **d'exploitation** *operating system*

système *m* **d'intéressement (aux bénéfices)** *profit-sharing scheme*

système *m* **expert (SE** *m***)** *expert system*

système *m* **hybride** *hybrid system*

système *m* **intégré de gestion (SIG** *m***)** *management information system (MIS)*

Système *m* **monétaire européen (SME** *m***)** *European Monetary System (EMS)*

tabac *m* *tobacco; tobacco industry; tobacconist*

tableau *m* *table; chart; spreadsheet; board*

tableau *m* **à feuilles mobiles** *flip-chart*

tableau *m* **blanc** *whiteboard*

tableau *m* **d'affichage** *bulletin board*

tableau *m* **des arrivées** *arrivals board*

tableau *m* **des départs** *departures board*

tableau *m* **noir** *blackboard*

table *f* **de mortalité** *actuarial tables*

tachygraphe *m* *tachograph*

taille *f* **de l'audience** *audience figures*

TAO *f* **(traduction** *f* **assistée par ordinateur)** *MAT (machine-assisted translation)*

taper (à la machine) *to type*

tarif *m* *tariff; rate; price list; offer price*

tarif *m* **à la pièce** *piece rate*

tarif *m* **des chambres** *room rates*

tarif *m* **douanier commun** *Common External Tariff (CET)*

tarif *m* **maximal** *peak rate*

tarif *m* **normal** *standard rate*

tarif *m* **postal** *postage rate*

tarif *m* **réduit** *cheap rate; second class post*

tarifs *mpl* **publicitaires** *advertising rates*

tarif *m* **tout compris** *all-in-rate*

taux *m* **de base** *base rate*

taux *m* **de change** *exchange rate*

taux *m* **de change à terme** *forward rate*

taux *m* **d'écoute** *audience figures*

taux *m* **de croissance** *growth rate*

taux *m* **de rendement** *rate of return*

taux *m* **d'escompte** *bank rate; lending rate*

taux *m* **de TVA nul** *zero-rating*

taux *m* **d'imposition ordinaire** *standard rate of tax*

taux *m* **d'intérêt** *interest rate*

taux *m* **effectif global (TEG** *m***)** *annual percentage rate (APR)*

taux *m* **uniforme de salaire** *flat rate of pay*

taxe *f* *tax; duty*

taxe *f* **douanière** *import levy*

taxe *f* **proportionnelle** *ad valorem tax*

taxer *to tax*

taxes *fpl* **d'aéroport** *airport tax*

taxe *f* **sur les produits de luxe** *luxury tax*

technicien(ne) *m(f)* **de laboratoire** *laboratory technician*

techniques *fpl* **non polluantes** *clean technology*

technologie *f* *technology*

technologique *technological*
TEG *m* (**taux** *m* **effectif global**) *APR (annual percentage rate)*
télécommunications *fpl telecommunications*
télécopie *f fax*
télécopieur *m fax machine*
téléfilm *m television film*
télémarketing *m telemarketing*
téléphone *m telephone*
téléphone *m* **à carte** *card phone*
téléphone *m* **cellulaire** *cellular telephone*
téléphone *m* **de secours** *emergency telephone*
téléphone *m* **de voiture** *car phone*
téléphone *m* **public** *payphone*
téléphoner *to telephone*
téléphone *m* **sans fil** *cordless telephone*
télétexte *m teletext*
télévision *f television; broadcasting*
télévision *f* **par câble** *cable TV*
télévision *f* **par satellite** *satellite TV*
télex *m telex; telex machine*
temps *m* **d'accès** *access time*
temps *m* **d'arrêt** *downtime*
temps *m* **de réponse** *response time*
temps *m* **d'immobilisation** *turnaround time*
temps *m* **mort** *idle time; downtime*
temps *m* **partagé** *time-sharing*
temps *m* **réel** *real time*
tendance *f trend*
tendance *f* **à la baisse** *downward trend*
tendance *f* **à la hausse** *upward trend*
tendances *fpl* **du marché** *market forces; market trends*
terme *m term; deadline; account*
termes *mpl* **de commerce international** *Incoterms*
terminal *m terminal; air terminal*
terminal *m* **intelligent** *intelligent terminal*
terminal *m* **passif** *dumb terminal*
terminus *m rail terminal; bus termi-*
nal
terrain *m land*
terrain *m* **à bâtir** *building land*
terrain *m* **agricole** *agricultural land*
terre *f earth; land*
par terre *on the ground or floor; to the ground or floor*
test *m* **d'aptitude** *aptitude test*
test *m* **de compétence** *proficiency test*
test *m* **d'évaluation de performance** *benchmark test*
test *m* **en aveugle** *blind test*
texte *m text; copy; body copy*
texte *m* **publicitaire** *advertising copy; blurb*
textile *m textile(s); textile industry*
ticket *m* **repas** *luncheon voucher*
tiers *m third party; third*
timbre *m stamp*
tirage *m circulation; drawing*
tiré *m drawee*
tireur(-euse) *m(f) drawer*
titre *m title; job title*
titre *m* **d'action** *share certificate*
titres *mpl stocks and shares; securities*
titres *mpl* **à court terme** *shorts*
titres *mpl* **convertibles** *convertible loan stock*
titres *mpl* **de propriété** *documents of title*
titres *mpl* **d'État** *government stock*
titulaire *m/f* **d'un passeport de la CEE** *EEC passport-holder*
titularisation *f security of tenure; permanent job*
toilettes *fpl toilet*
toit *m roof*
tolérance *f tolerance; allowance*
tonalité *f dialling tone*
tonalité *f* **continue** *continuous tone*
tonalité *f* **numéro hors service** *number unobtainable tone*
tonalité *f* **"occupé"** *engaged tone*
touche *f key*
touche *f* **de commande** *control key*
touche *f* **de fonction** *function key*
touche *f* **directe** *hot key*
toucher *to touch; to cash; to en-*

cash

tour *m* *tour; walk; ride; lathe*

tourisme *m* *tourism; tourist industry*

toxicité *f* *toxicity*

toxine *f* *toxin*

toxique *toxic*

traceur *m* *plotter*

train *m* *train*

train *m* **de marchandises** *goods train; freight train*

train-paquebot *m* (*pl* ~s-~) *boat train*

traite *f* **bancaire** *bank(er's) draft*

traitement *m* **avec jeu d'instructions réduit** *RISC (reduced instruction set computing)*

traitement *m* **de commandes** *order processing*

traitement *m* **de données** *data processing (DP)*

traitement *m* **de texte** *word processing; word processor*

traitement *m* **graphique** *graphics*

traitement *m* **multitâche** *multitasking*

traiter *to treat; to process; to deal with*

traiteur *m* *caterer*

tranche *f* *slice; section; bracket; tranche; block*

tranche *f* **d'imposition** *tax bracket*

transaction *f* *transaction; deal*

transbordement *m* *transhipment*

transborder *to tranship*

transférer *to transfer; to download; to relocate*

transfert *m* **d'actions** *transfer of shares*

transfert *m* **électronique de fonds** *electronic funds transfer (EFT)*

en transit *in transit*

transitaire *m* *forwarding agent; freight forwarder*

transparent *m* *transparency*

(faire) transporter *to transport; to freight*

transporteur *m* *carrier*

travail *m* *work; job; labour*

travail *m* **administratif** *paperwork*

travail *m* **au noir** *moonlighting*

travail *m* **d'équipe** *teamwork*

travail *m* **en retard** *backlog of work*

travailler *to work*

travailler à son compte *to be self-employed; to work freelance*

travailleur(-euse) *m(f)* **à domicile** *homeworker*

travailleur(-euse) *m(f)* **indépendant(e)** *freelance (worker)*

travailleur(-euse) *m(f)* **manuel(le)** *blue-collar worker*

travailleur(-euse) *m(f)* **posté(e)** *shiftworker*

travailleur(-euse) *m(f)* **temporaire** *casual worker*

travail *m* **posté** *shiftwork*

travaux *mpl* **en cours** *work in progress*

travaux *mpl* **publics** *public works*

traveller *m* *traveller's cheque*

trésorerie *f* **négative** *negative cash flow*

trésorerie *f* **positive** *positive cash flow*

tribunal *m* **administratif** *administrative tribunal*

trier *to sort*

trimestriel(le) *quarterly*

troc *m* *barter*

trombone *m* *paper clip*

trop dépenser *to overspend*

tutoyer quelqu'un *to address somebody as "tu"*

tuyauterie *f* *plumbing*

TVA *f* **(taxe** *f* **à la valeur ajoutée)** *VAT (value-added tax)*

union *f* **douanière** *customs union*

Union *f* **européenne** *European Union*

Union *f* **européenne de radiodiffusion (UER** *f*) *European Broadcasting Union (EBU)*

Union *f* **internationale des télécommunications (UIT** *f*) *International Telecommunications Union (ITU)*

union *f* **monétaire européenne** *European Monetary Union*

unité *f* *drive*

unité *f* **centrale** *mainframe*

unité *f* **centrale de traitement** *CPU (central processing unit)*

unité *f* **de commande** *control unit*

Unité *f* **de compte européenne (UCE** *f***)** *European Unit of Account (EUA)*

unité *f* **de microdisquette** *microdrive*

unité *f* **physique** *device*

usine *f* *factory; plant; works*

usine *f* **chimique** *chemical plant*

usine *f* **de mise en bouteilles** *bottling plant*

usine *f* **de montage** *assembly plant*

usine *f* **de traitement** *recycling plant*

usine *f* **de transformation** *processing plant*

usine *f* **pilote** *pilot plant*

usiner *to machine*

usure *f* *wear and tear; usury*

utilisateur(-trice) *m(f)* *user*

utilisateur(-trice) *m(f)* **final(e)** *end user*

vaccination *f* *vaccination*

valeur *f* *value; denomination; asset*

valeur *f* **comptable** *book value*

valeur *f* **de liquidation** *break-up value*

valeur *f* **de rachat** *cash surrender value*

valeur *f* **de remplacement** *replacement value*

valeur *f* **marchande** *market value*

valeur *f* **mobilière sans échéance** *undated stock*

valeur *f* **nominale** *par value*

valeur *f* **par défaut** *default*

valeurs *fpl* *securities*

valeurs *fpl* **(mobilières)** *stocks and shares*

valeurs *fpl* **sûres** *gilt-edged securities*

valider *to validate*

valise *f* *suitcase; toolkit*

à **valoir** *on account*

valorisation *f* *appreciation; development*

variation *f* *variation; fluctuation*

varier *to vary; to fluctuate*

vendable *saleable; marketable*

vendeur(-euse) *m(f)* *salesman/woman; seller*

vendeur(-euse) *m(f)* **à découvert** *short (seller)*

vendre *to sell*

à **vendre** *for sale*

vendre **à perte à l'extérieur** *to dump*

vendre **au rabais** *to discount*

vendre **en cession-bail** *to lease back*

vendre **moins cher que** *to undersell*

vente *f* *sale*

en **vente à bas prix** *underpriced*

vente *f* **agressive** *hard sell; commando selling*

vente *f* **au détail à prix imposé** *resale price maintenance (RPM)*

vente *f* **directe** *direct selling*

vente *f* **face à face** *face-to-face selling*

vente *f* **groupée** *banded pack*

vente *f* **porte-à-porte** *door-to-door selling*

ventes *fpl* **à l'étranger** *foreign sales*

ventes *fpl* **à terme** *forward sales*

ventes *fpl* **brutes** *gross sales*

ventes *fpl* **par téléphone** *telesales*

ventes *fpl* **sur le marché intérieur** *domestic sales; home sales*

ventilation *f* **des frais généraux** *allocation of overheads; overhead absorption*

vérificateur(-trice) *m(f)* **externe** *external auditor*

vérificateur(-trice) *m(f)* **interne** *internal auditor*

vérification *f* **annuelle** *(annual) general audit*

vérification *f* **de conformité** *compliance audit*

vérification *f* **des comptes** *audit*

vérification *f* **interne** *internal audit*

vérifier *to check; to verify; to audit*

versement *m* **à titre gracieux** *ex gratia payment*

versement *m* **partiel** *instalment*

verser *to pay out; to pay in; to pour (out)*

vert(e) *green*

vestibule *m entrance hall*

carte *f* **VGA** *VGA (video gate array) card*

vice *m* **caché** *latent defect*

vice-président(e) *m(f)* (*pl* ~-~(e)s) *vice-chairman/woman; vice-president*

vidage *m dump*

vidéo *f video*

vidéo(cassette) *f video (cassette)*

vidéodisque *m videodisc*

vidéotex *m Viewdata* ®

vider *to empty; to dump*

vigile *m security guard*

villa *f villa*

vin *m wine*

virement *m transfer*

virement *m* **automatique** *standing order*

virement *m* **bancaire** *bank giro credit; credit transfer*

virer *to transfer*

virus *m virus*

visa *m visa*

visioconférence *f video conference*

visiophone *m videophone*

visite *f* **de relance** *follow-up call*

visite *f* **impromptue** *cold call*

visiteur(-euse) *m(f) visitor*

vitesse *f* **en bauds** *baud rate*

viticulture *f winemaking*

vitre *f car window*

vocation *f* **résidentielle** *residential use*

voisin(e) *m(f) neighbour*

voiture *f car*

voiture *f* **de fonction** *company car*

voiture-lit *f* (*pl* ~s-~s) *sleeping car or compartment*

voiture-restaurant *f* (*pl* ~s-~s) *dining car; restaurant car*

voix *f* **prépondérante** *casting vote*

vol *m flight; theft*

vol *m* **charter** *charter flight*

vol *m* **intérieur** *domestic flight*

vol *m* **international** *international flight*

vol *m* **régulier** *scheduled flight*

vouvoyer quelqu'un *to address somebody as "vous"*

voyage *m* **d'affaires** *business trip*

voyageur *m* **de commerce** *travelling salesman*

zone *f* **d'aménagement** *development area*

zone *f* **d'aménagement prioritaire (ZAC** *f*) *special development area (SDA)*

zone *f* **dollar** *dollar area*

Zone *f* **européenne de libre échange** *European Free Trade Area*

zone *f* **exploitable** *development area*

zone *f* **industrielle** *industrial estate*